LIFE IN A CAVE IN PETRA WITH THE BDOUL

1981–1986

LIFE IN A CAVE IN PETRA WITH THE BDOUL

1981–1986

Judith S. McKenzie

منار الآثار

MANAR AL-ATHAR, University of Oxford

MANAR AL-ATHAR MONOGRAPH 6

Series Editor
Judith S. McKenzie

Volume Editor
Andres T. Reyes

Manar al-Athar, University of Oxford,
Ioannou Centre for Classical and Byzantine Studies,
66 St Giles', Oxford OX1 3LU, United Kingdom
www.manar-al-athar.ox.ac.uk

Front cover photograph: Judith McKenzie in front of the south doorway of the Khasneh, 1981/2 (A. Phippen).
Back cover photograph: Judith McKenzie with Umm Khaled, 1981/2 (A. Phippen).

A record of cataloging-in-publication data is available from the Library of Congress.
A catalogue record of this book is available from the BritishLibrary.
ISBN: 978-0-9954946-6-4 (hardcover)
eISBN: 978-0-9954946-9-5 (PDF)

This paper meets the requirements of ANSI/NISO Z39.48-1992 (Permanence of Paper).

CONTENTS

MAPS AND FIGURES

FOREWORD

Before her untimely death on 27 May 2019, at the age of 61, Judith McKenzie had largely readied for publication an account of the time she had spent in Jordan in 1981–82, 1984 and 1986 among the Bdoul tribe, then still living in caves within the ancient Nabataean site of Petra. She intended this publication as a record of a way of life that had started to vanish when, in 1985, the Bdoul began their move to the new village of Umm Sayhoun nearby, under the direction of the Jordanian government. Circumstances, however, now dictate that this book must also stand as a memorial to Judith herself.

Judith first travelled to Jordan in 1981 to do fieldwork for the doctoral thesis she was preparing for the Department of Archaeology at the University of Sydney under the direction of J.-P. Descoeudres and A. W. McNicoll. In her fourth year as an undergraduate there, she had studied the problem of how particular architectural features found in Petra came to appear in Second-Style Pompeian wall-painting of the first century BC, before such baroque elements were used in Roman architecture itself. To conclude that the architecture of ancient Alexandria was, in fact, the link between Petra and Pompeii, Judith realized that she had to establish rigorously the dates of the monuments at Petra – an archaeological problem of notorious intractability. She therefore developed a novel surveying method to record the architectural mouldings on buildings, intending to survey moulding-profiles on the monuments of Petra and use their minute stylistic changes to establish a chronological framework. The development of this survey-method alone would have been worth the awarding of a doctoral degree.

The talent for survey she had inherited from her maternal grandfather, James Dalzell Dewar. He had been a surveyor in the Australian army during the First World War, assigned to locate and plot the graves of Australians who had fallen in battle in Europe, so that families could find any remains once the war ended. Like her grandfather nearly 70 years earlier, Judith, armed with a theodolite lent by the University of Sydney, travelled overseas to begin her work. After three seasons at Petra, she submitted her dissertation to the University, one of the earliest to be completed successfully at the Department of Archaeology there. The Faculty awarded her the degree of Doctor of Philosophy in 1987, and in 1990, her book *The Architecture of Petra* appeared, presenting the results of her thesis.

Judith was, by then, a junior research fellow in Archaeology at St Hugh's College, Oxford. She later became Professor of the Archaeology of Late Antique Egypt and the Holy Land at the same university, where she founded, in 2012, Manar al-Athar, an online photo-archive for research on the Middle East. Her photographs of the buildings at Petra taken during her fieldwork may be viewed on the Manar al-Athar website: http://www.manar-al-athar.ox.ac.uk/. The editor of the present volume is grateful to Elizabeth Macaulay, Bryan Ward-Perkins, and Ine Jacobs, directors in succession to Judith, for the continued maintenance and curatorship of Judith's archaeological archive in the offices at Oxford.

Judith elaborated on the argument that the art and architecture of ancient Alexandria connected Petra with Second-Style Pompeian wall-painting when she published, in 2007, *The Architecture of Alexandria and Egypt: 300 BC–AD 700*. She continued to write articles on Nabataean archaeology throughout her career, and her last significant contributions to this subject in her lifetime were *The Nabataean Temple at Khirbet et-Tannur* (2013), in two volumes, and a review-article of L. Nehmé et al., *Atlas archéologique et épigraphique de Pétra, fascicule I, De Bāb as-Sīq au Wādi al-Farasah'* (McKenzie 2014), in which Judith reconsidered the chronology she had herself proposed decades earlier. Judith also registered additional thoughts on a few Jordanian sites in gazetteer-entries she wrote and edited as part of a book on "architectural conversion" that she was working on at the time of her death (e.g., Jerash; Khirbet edh-Dharih). That book is now being prepared for publication by Ross Burns, Miranda Williams, and the present editor.

Life in a Cave in Petra with the Bdoul: 1981–1986, therefore, is a pendant to Judith's original (in all senses) monograph on Petra. In editing it, Andres Reyes has been responsible for preparing this book for publication. For the plates, Judith, as ever, had left careful instructions for labelling and presentation. She had given fewer instructions for the revision of her text, but all who knew Judith will be aware of her direct style of expression, delivered, despite many years in England, with distinctively Australian vowels, locutions, and frames of reference. To maintain the distinctiveness of Judith's voice, therefore, the text has been emended only when there was an ambiguity to resolve or an inadvertent slip to correct. The bibliography stands as it was in early 2019, with no attempt made to add to it.

I am grateful to Angela Phippen, Judith's first fieldwork assistant, for reading through the text, as Judith had wished, and clarifying accounts of certain events. I would also like to thank Mohamed Kenawi, a former pupil and colleague of Judith, for looking over the glossary of Arabic terms, the transliterations for which follow generally agreed or familiar spellings (p. 241). In her preface, Judith thanks others who helped her write this book, for the publication of which the Classics Faculty at Oxford University, the Oxford Centre for Byzantine Research, and anonymous donors have kindly provided a subvention.

The maps are also Judith's, all originally prepared for her other publications, with the last three reproduced from *The Architecture of Petra*. There are slight discrepancies between Arabic transliterations in these maps and ones used for this book, but they are unlikely to cause confusion. In any event, Judith, who regarded archaeology as both art and science, would probably maintain that, since the maps from *The Architecture of Petra* had been prepared by hand, any digital revision of them would inevitably result in some loss of accuracy.

It will be tempting to see this book as a longing for a way of life no longer extant, or as wistfulness for a time of romantic archaeological exploration, or as an elegy for Judith herself, taken at the height of her intellectual powers. Judith would have been dismayed by any of that. She largely eschewed sentimentality and would have remonstrated against perspectives that privileged nostalgia over improvement through the years of infrastructure and amenities in Jordan. Instead, this book is simply a memoir of lifestyles now difficult to imagine and apt to be forgotten if not set down, as well as a call to continue the conservation of one of humanity's great achievements. It is a reminder too of Judith's clear-sightedness and her ferocious intelligence, with its insistence on precision that was relentless "as rain on a tin roof". (A Judith-ism: she expressed surprise that rainfall in England did not sound as it did in Canberra, where she grew up.) Above all, this book records her love and admiration for the many in Jordan who welcomed her warmly and alongside whom it was her privilege to live, in a cave at Petra, forty years ago.

Andres Reyes
Oxford
July 2020

PREFACE

I became aware that my experiences of living in a cave in Petra in Jordan were of interest to a new generation when, in summer 2017, I had a seventeen-year old volunteer, Layla McDermott, working in the Manar al-Athar open-access photo-archive office at Oxford University. She and her younger sisters were fascinated that, over thirty years before, I had lived in a cave without electricity or running water, let alone a phone or a vehicle. I was there during the last few years that the Petra Bedouin, the Bdoul tribe, lived in the caves, prior to moving to their new village of Umm Sayhoun in 1985. Layla's curiosity made me realise that these experiences were of interest to a new generation in the West. At the same time, many of the older adults we had known in Umm Sayhoun, who were the grandparents of the current generation of the Bdoul, had died, and their children had only childhood memories of growing up in Petra. Knowledge of the customs and experiences of the Bdoul when they had lived in the caves in Petra was fading.

The only first-hand detailed written record of life in Petra in the years before the move to the new village was Marguerite van Geldermalsen's autobiography, *Married to a Bedouin*, published in 2006. She had lived there since 1978, when she met and married Mohammad Abdallah Othman. Her account, written as a series of incidents, is very accurate in its details and covers virtually all Bdoul customs. It is thus an excellent and reliable record, of which more notice should be taken by anthropologists in the future. The few scholarly articles stimulated at the time by the move to the new village provide an academic record of some specific aspects of Bdoul life, or specific characteristics of the Bdoul, such as their use of space[1] and tribal names,[2] as well as observing how the Bdoul lifestyle could elucidate the interpretation of archaeological evidence of transitory occupation,[3] and the effects of tourism.[4] However, none of those studies provides the kind of information about Bdoul life contained in van Geldermalsen's book.

The account published here provides a further record of life in Petra in the early 1980s. Although my research concerned the monuments, because each of my assistants and I spent so much time socialising with the Bdoul, I came to observe many aspects of Bdoul life in a series of visits over three main field seasons in late 1981/early 1982, early 1984, and early 1986. As women, we had access to the world of young girls and women, which men from outside did not, while we were also sometimes treated as honorary men.

I kept notes about those experiences. The notes were generally written at the end of a week and included the highlights of it, but they were largely an *aide-mémoire* for weekly letters home to our parents. Many details which I remembered were missing from the notes, so this volume is a memoir. In addition, rather than following the strict chronological order of a diary, I have combined experiences into vignettes involving particular individuals and places to avoid confusing the reader by jumping backwards and forwards between people and locations. I have only combined descriptions within a field season, not between them (I have not moved experiences, for example, from 1981/2 to 1984 or 1986). I have, however, often used photographs of later years to adequately illustrate the narrative. I have kept the approximate overall chronology within each field season. I have had to check many details, in particular, names, with Marguerite van Geldermalsen, who has been enormously helpful. My aim has been to be as accurate as possible so that this can be a record of our experiences for the grandchildren of the Bdoul children we knew in Petra in 1981–86, and for their children to come.

In those days, as taking a photograph of someone felt potentially intrusive, we were often hesitant to do so. This is in sharp contrast to the era of camera-phones when photographs are taken of everyone and everything, without necessarily asking. We did not take photographs of many of the incidents described and very few of women whom we did not know well. That custom applied even if we took Polaroid photographs of them for them to keep. Just as at home in Sydney at the time, if having tea with a friend, it would have felt uncomfortable to interrupt it to take a photograph of the event, we did not do so with our Bdoul friends. We consequently took relatively few photographs of people. Almost all of those which I took are published here.

On seeing some of my photographs in late 2018, Marguerite van Geldermalsen observed, "I sometimes forget how really, really basic and hard life was. The people have forgotten too, I think."[5] With Umm Sayhoun visible on the hill overlooking the centre of Petra, so many large souvenir

1 Bienkowski and Chlebik 1991.

2 Ohannessian-Charpin 1986; Russell 1993.

3 In caves: Bienkowski and Chlebik 1991. In tents: Simms 1988; Banning and Köhler-Rolefson 1986.

4 Shoup 1985.

5 Marguerite van Geldermalsen, pers. comm. 30 September 2018.

stands, numerous public toilet blocks, an asphalt access road, and over half a million tourists a year, it is difficult for people who did not know it then to imagine how simple the lifestyle was, nor how cut-off and isolated from the world Petra felt, frozen in time.

In the 1980s, it was assumed that there was no evidence for the Bdoul being in Petra before World War I. This was used to argue that they had no historic right to live in Petra and to justify that they should be moved from the Petra caves to a newly-built village. However, when I reached London in May 1986 and examined the accounts in the British Library of travellers of the nineteenth and early twentieth centuries, it became apparent that there was considerable evidence for the Bdoul living in Petra at that time. I have presented some of these descriptions, as well as a brief history of the development of the site for tourism prior to when my account begins, in order to provide further context.

How I Came to Live in a Cave in Petra

Before I went to Sydney University, I had never heard of Petra. This was in the days before Petra had become a World Heritage Site (1985), or the film *Indiana Jones and the Last Crusade* (1989) had featured the Holy Grail in the Khasneh. I was first introduced to Petra in 1978 as a third-year Archaeology student in lectures on the 'Cities of the Silk Road' (Palmyra, Dura Europos, Jerash, Begram, and Petra) given by Anthony (Tony) McNicoll. He explained how the Khasneh at Petra related to examples of architecture also depicted on Roman wall-painting of the first century BC. Both had broken pediments and circular pavilions before such features were thought to have been built in free-standing architecture (figs. 90–91). In our lectures on Roman wall-painting, Jean-Paul Descoeudres made similar points. They each explained that, because one of them was a Near Eastern archaeologist and the other a Classical archaeologist, they did not have the knowledge of the other discipline in order to be able to pursue the mystery of the connection between the wall-paintings and the rock-cut architecture, noticed as early as 1862 by the French architect Jacques Ignace Hittorff.[6]

As their student, I decided to study the problem for my fourth-year honours thesis, which I did without going to Petra. The wall-paintings were well dated, but the monuments at Petra were not, and I developed a hypothesis for dating them. I also explored the possibility that the common source of influence for the new architectural forms in the wall-paintings and at Petra was the architecture of Ptolemaic (Hellenistic) Alexandria, the capital of Egypt founded by Alexander the Great in 331 BC.

After completing the fourth year of my Bachelor of Arts Honours degree, Tony McNicoll encouraged me to apply to be Annual Scholar of the British School of Archaeology in Jerusalem. The British School of Archaeology was the British base for archaeology in Jordan prior to the 1967 Six-Day War. However, after that, the British Institute at Amman for Archaeology and History was established to provide a new base for British archaeologists working in Jordan. My application was successful, influencing the course of my life for many years to come. The scholarship provided me with funds for an academic year to do fieldwork and a base at the British Institute in Amman from which to conduct it.[7] I was also awarded a Commonwealth Postgraduate Research Award to do my PhD on the topic, enrolled at the University of Sydney. The aim of my research was to test the theories I had suggested in my honours-year thesis. To do that, it was necessary to record the architectural details of the main monuments at Petra.

The Director of the Sydney University expedition to Pella in Jordan, Professor Basil Hennessy, had been director of the British School in Jerusalem before the Six-Day War and had worked at Pella for many years after he had become Edwin Cuthbert Hall Professor of Near Eastern Archaeology at the University of Sydney. Consequently, he had very good relations with the Director General of the Department of Antiquities of the Hashemite Kingdom of Jordan, Dr Adnan Hadidi, who gave me a letter of permission to work in Petra. Professor Hennessy also provided key logistical support by organising for the Pella foreman Abu Isa (Badri Hasan Maadi) to take us to Petra the first few times we went.

Because I had been bushwalking many times in the Snowy Mountains in Australia (going away for three days or so with friends, taking all our provisions and tents), the idea of living in a cave for two or three weeks at a time (with a week or two in Amman, in between each visit) did not seem as daunting as might be imagined. Extra considerations were involved, such as ascertaining what medical supplies to take and how and when to use them, but organising other supplies was much the same, only on a larger scale.

I had to find an assistant, who had to be female. A fellow student, Angela Phippen, had planned an open-ended overseas trip to the Middle East, Europe, and the UK. The opportunity to live in a cave in Petra and be my assistant fitted well with her plans, and I could not have wished for a better assistant in 1981/82. I subsequently returned to Petra two years later in early 1984 with Pamela Watson and again in early 1986 with, consecutively, Jane Lydon, Kathleen Boswell, and Torla Evans.

After this third field season, I moved to Oxford in 1986 where I completed my book on *The Architecture of Petra*, which included the results of the fieldwork, published in 1990. As I then moved on to work further on *The Architecture of Alexandria and Egypt 300 BC – AD 700* (The Pelican History of Art, 2007), which had arisen out of my work in Petra, I did

6 Hittorff 1862.

7 See McKenzie 1990: xv–xvii for more information regarding sources of funding for each trip, full acknowledgements, and other background information.

not return to Jordan for 15 years, until a brief visit to Petra in 2001, and longer visits, of a few days each, in 2003 and 2010.

By May 2018, when my young colleagues (Miranda Williams, Sean Leatherbury, Maria Lidova, and Steve Welsh) went there, the atmosphere of the site had changed so much that it no longer felt cut off from the world or "half as old as time". At the same time, they met some of the grown-up children of those whom I had known as children or adults in Petra, which I found most pleasing.

Acknowledgements

Full acknowledgements of those who helped at the time with the field seasons, and sources of funding can be found in *The Architecture of Petra* (1990), xvii. In the preparation of this volume, I offer my thanks to Marguerite van Geldermalsen for answering innumerable questions and in particular for help with the names of the Bdoul. Those who kindly answered other questions or otherwise provided assistance include: Piotr Bienkowski, Ian Carroll, Felicity Cobbing, EWA Digital London, Suleiman Farajat I, Bill Finlayson, Muna Hadad, Jessica Holland, Nina Joukowsky, Mohamed Kenawi, Muhammad Murshed Khadija, Aya Khairy, Sean Leatherbury, Alison McQuitty, Michael Mockford, Carol Palmer, Angela Phippen, William Phippen, Asma Rababeh, Simon Rickerby, Zeyad al-Salameen, Micaela Sinibaldi, Rachael Sparks, Amara Thornton, Ernie Wickens, and Miranda Williams.

For help with editing and typing, I would like to thank Miranda Williams and Andres Reyes, as well as Martha Buckley for reading and providing editorial comments on the manuscript.

For use of her photographs, I am especially grateful to Angela Phippen. For use of other photographs, I would like to thank Rebecca Banks (courtesy APAAME), Piotr Bienkowski, Phillip C. Edwards, Torla Evans, Sean Leatherbury, Maria Lidova, Otto Nieminen, Sarah Norodom, the Palestine Exploration Fund, Jane Taylor (for photographs in the American Center of Oriental Research, Amman [ACOR] archive), University College London Institute of Archaeology, Pamela Watson, Steve Welsh, Marlena Whiting, and Miranda Williams. Uncredited photographs are my own.

Map 1. The Mediterranean and Near East.

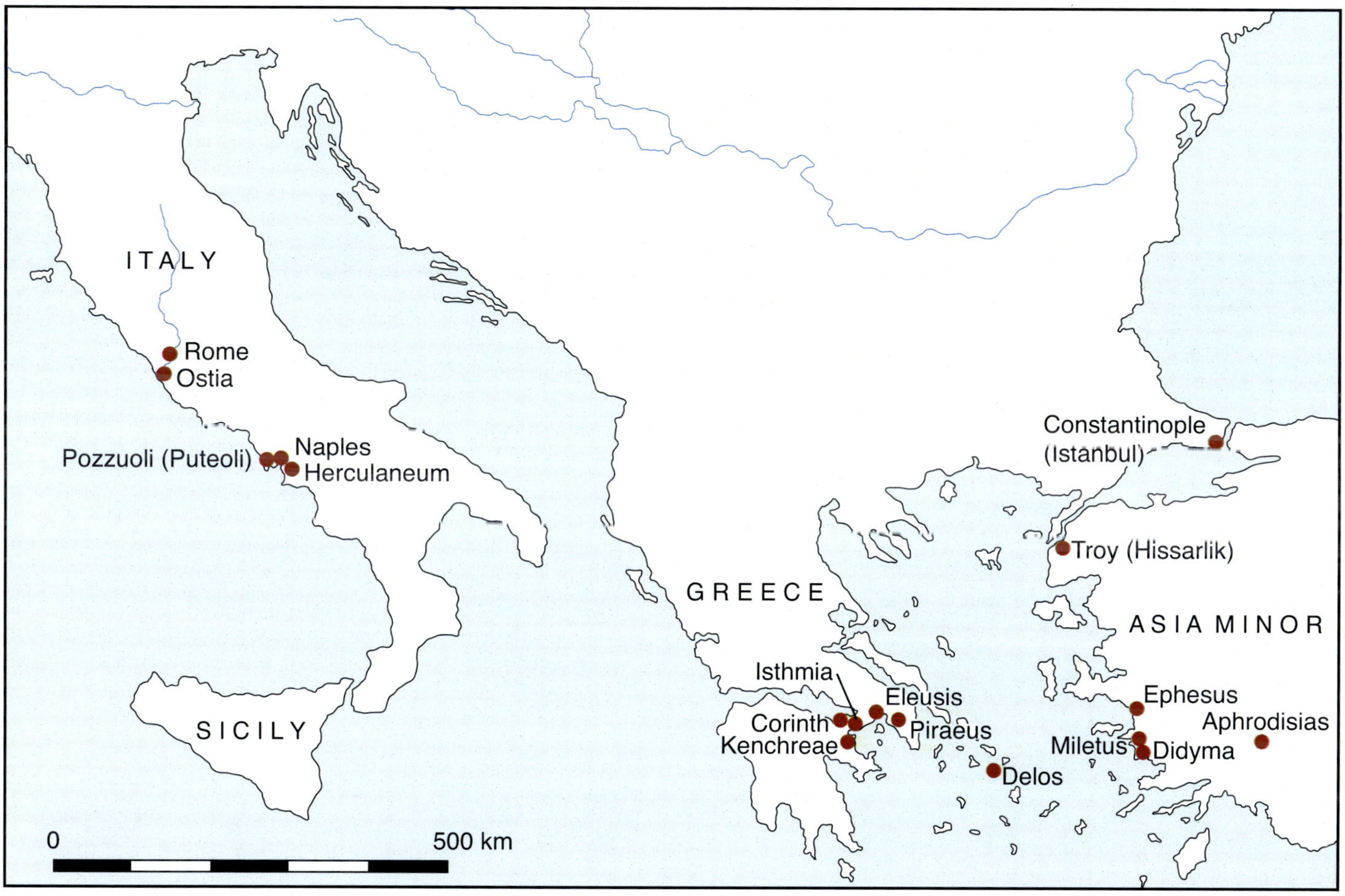

Map 2. The Mediterranean: Italy, Greece, and the western coast of Asia Minor (Turkey).

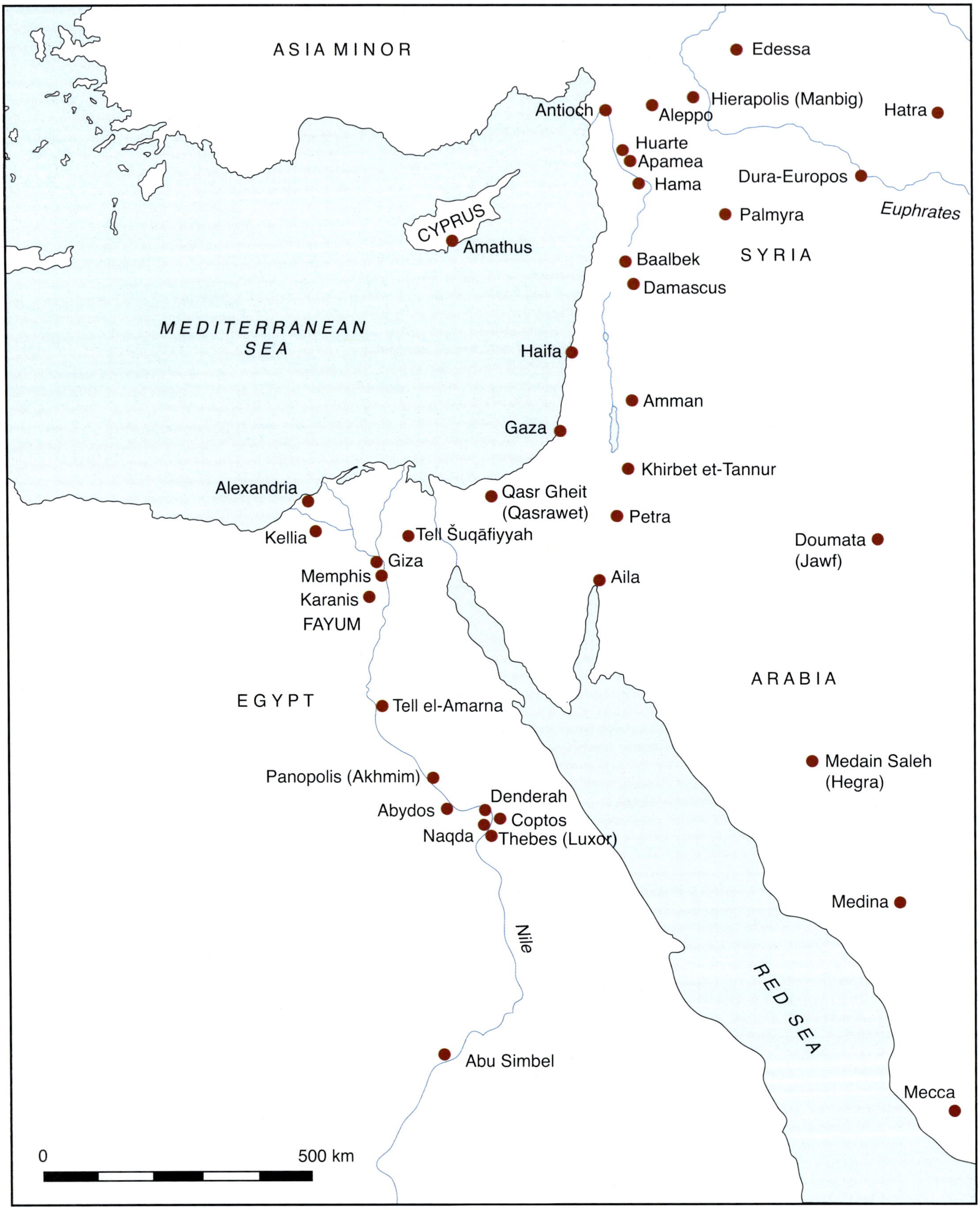

Map 3. The eastern Mediterranean and Red Sea area.

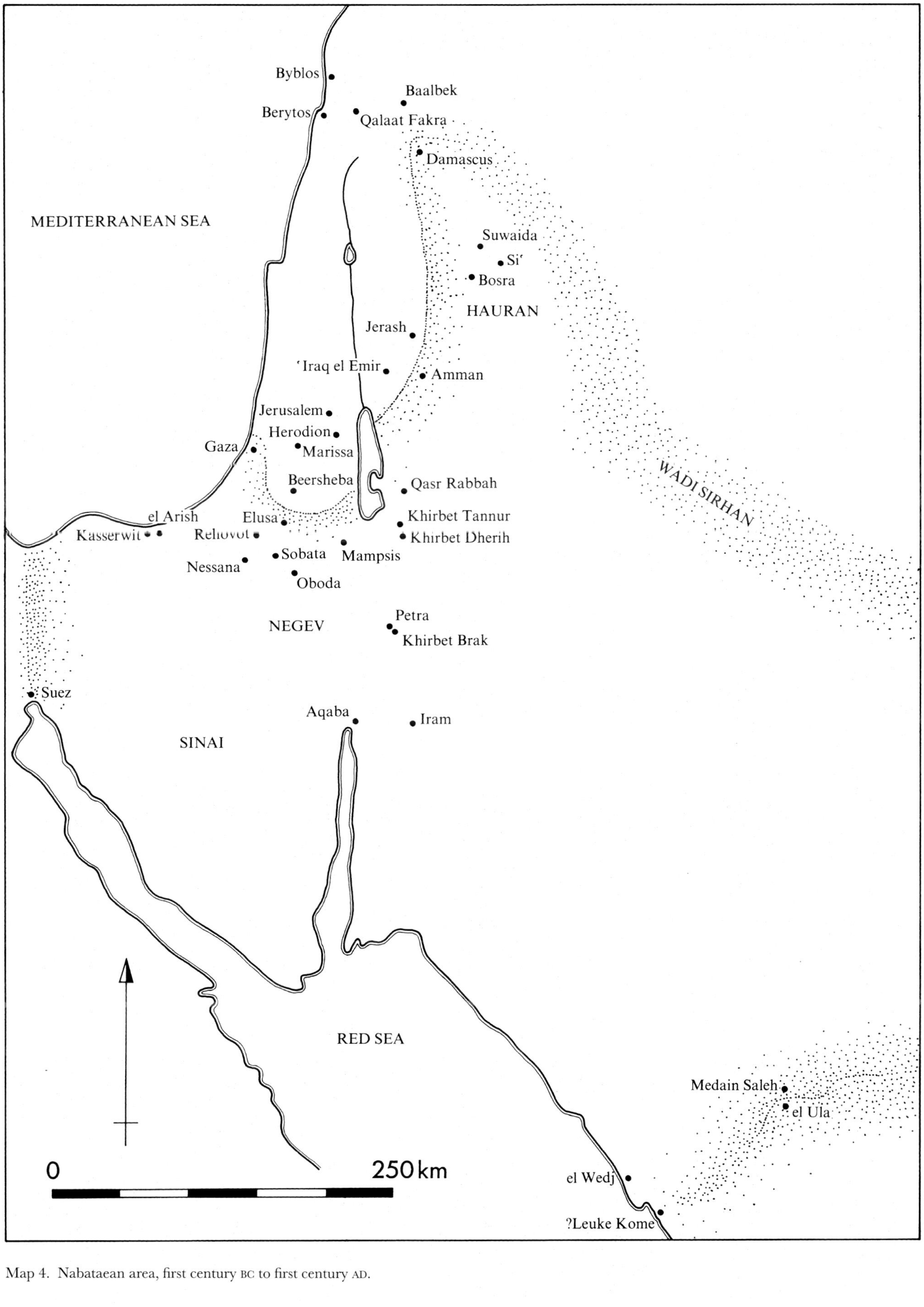

Map 4. Nabataean area, first century BC to first century AD.

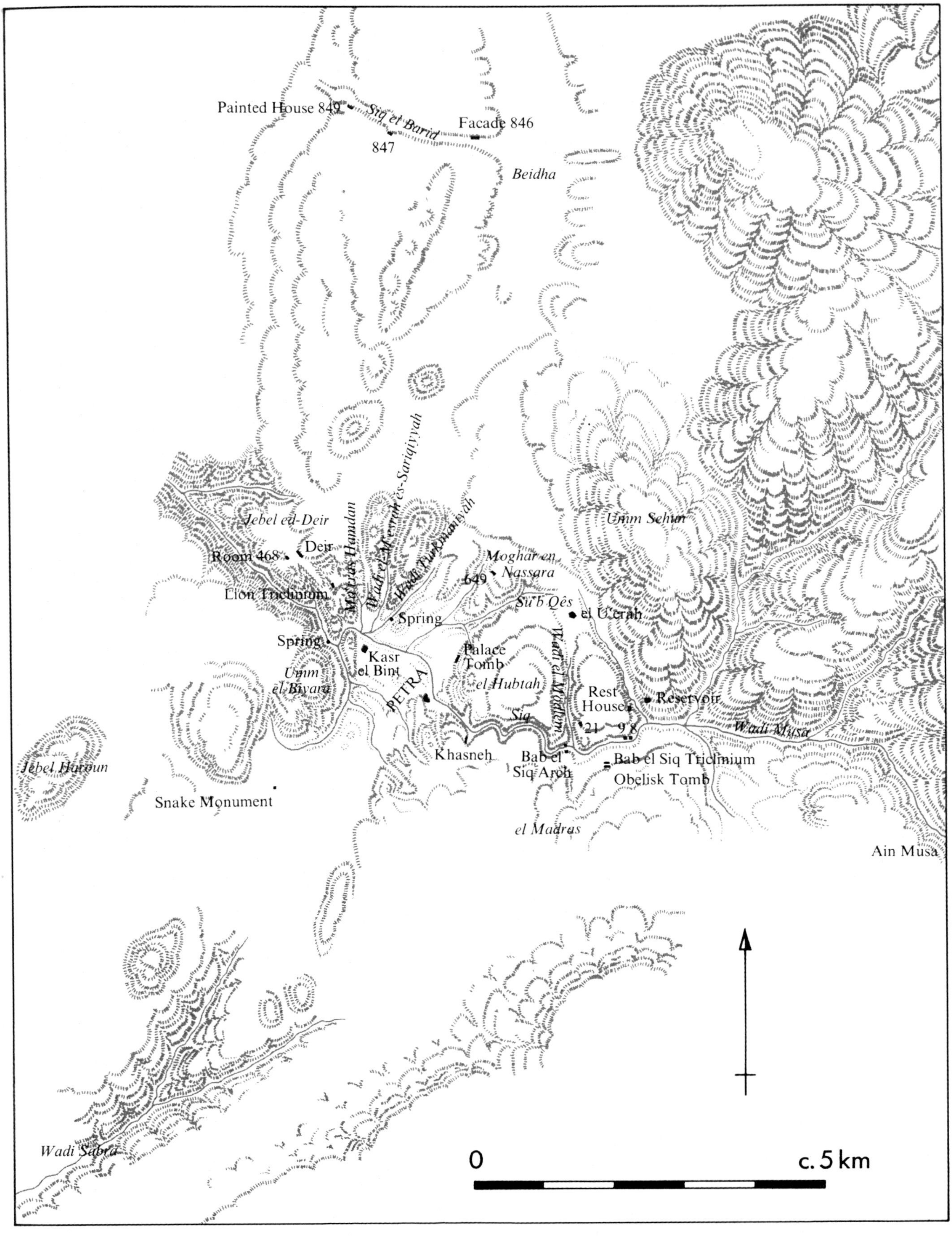

Map 5. Area around Petra.

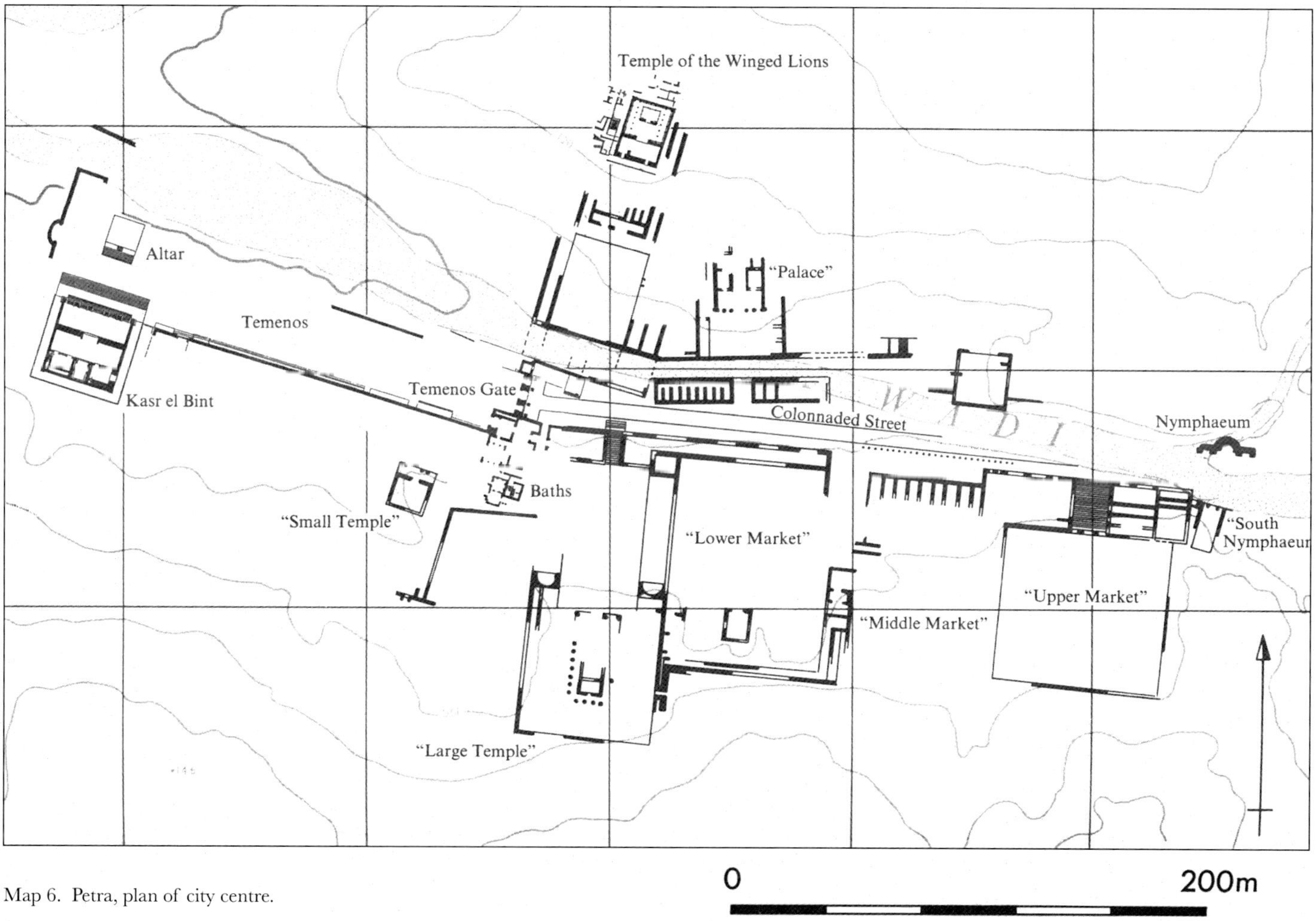

Map 6. Petra, plan of city centre.

CHAPTER 1

The Bdoul in Petra in the Nineteenth and Early Twentieth Centuries

Introduction

In the Jordanian desert, the craggy hills of Petra are an obvious place for human habitation, as the site has a perennial water supply, is easily defended, and has some arable land. In winter it is more protected than the surrounding limestone hills.

The Edomites are attested in Petra in the Iron Age, from the seventh to sixth centuries BC on the mountain of Umm el-Biyara.[1] There is evidence from the nearby Edomite site of Busayra to suggest, contrary to what had previously been assumed, that there was contemporaneity of overlap between Iron Age settlement there and the Nabataeans in Petra in the fourth century BC.[2] The historian Diodorus Siculus (19.94.2–95.2) described the Nabataeans by the fourth century BC as living in Petra with a nomadic lifestyle, like that of the Bedouin.

As they became increasingly wealthy from the trade in frankincense and myrrh, the Nabataeans built permanent structures such as houses and public buildings. In the sandstone mountainsides they carved at least 800 chambers for use as tombs and houses, and also cisterns, which enhanced the natural suitability of the site for human habitation. The Nabataeans were conquered by the Romans in AD 106, but Petra remained a city into the Byzantine period, until at least the sixth century AD, with an active Christian community. This and other archaeological evidence attest to the continuous occupation of the Petra valley and its caves during the period from the city's decline in the seventh century, until the arrival of the Crusaders.[3]

Chamfered ("arrow slit") windows were cut in some of the tombs so that light could still enter while the door was closed (without people being able to climb in). As the tooling on these windows is not Nabataean, this suggests that they were not part of the original tomb designs, but rather that some of the former tombs were converted for use by the living, the way the Urn Tomb became a church in the mid-fifth century AD. It is not completely clear when (after the Nabataeans) these arrow slit windows were carved. It might have been as late as the twelfth century, when the valley was occupied by the Crusaders and continued after that.

1 Bienkowski 2011; 2013: 31.
2 Bienkowski 2013: 29, 32.
3 Sinibaldi 2016, with more detailed bibliography.

The caves were inhabited by the Bedouin at the time of the Crusades. When Baldwin I entered Petra in 1100 with the Crusader army, Wadi Musa and Jabal Haroun were still inhabited. The Crusaders did not stay, but when they returned in 1107 Baldwin I retaliated against the Bedouin by smoking them out of the caves, in which they lived, and taking their flocks.[4] When the Crusaders returned again, in 1127, they fortified the valley with castles, including one near Wadi Musa (al-Wu'ayra) and a fort inside Petra (on el-Habis) which they held until 1188/9.[5] Excavations have also revealed Crusader period activity in some parts of the Petra valley, and that the Crusaders buried their dead near the Garden Temple in Wadi Farasa, where they left gravestones with crosses on them (burials were probably also made in the Tomb of the Broken Pediment, where they cut a western coffin-shaped grave[6]). Although the monastery on the plateau of Jabal Haroun was finally destroyed in the ninth or tenth century, monks continued to live on the summit until at least the early thirteenth century.[7] Archaeological evidence indicates that until the beginning of the nineteenth century AD the site of Petra had continuous human occupation.[8] Occupation after this is attested by written accounts.

A selection of the main accounts of nineteenth-century travellers who mention the Bdoul in Petra are presented here for the picture they give.[9] A couple of points about terminology need to be made which affect their accurate interpretation. Firstly, the common English name for the site has changed. What is now called Petra was usually referred to by its Arabic name of Wadi Musa. Wadi Musa ran all the way into the ancient site from the spring of 'Ain Musa, above the town of Eldji, the small town now called Wadi Musa. Thus, when the term "Wadi Musa" occurs in a quotation given

4 Runciman 1952: 98.
5 Fiema 2002: 241–42; 2016: 566. Crusader period sources in detail: Frösén and Miettunen 2008: 13–14, with references. History of Crusaders in Wadi Musa: Pringle 1998: 373–77.
6 McKenzie 1990: pl. 133.
7 The Christian pilgrim, Thetmar, who visited Sinai and Jabal Haroun in AD 1217, recorded that there was still a church on the "summit", with two Greek Christian [Orthodox] monks living there, Thetmar, *Iter ad Terram Sanctam* cap. 14 (ed. and Italian trans. de Sandoli 1983: 270–73). Frösén and Miettunen 2008: 14.
8 Sinibaldi 2016, with more detailed bibliography.
9 A list of nineteenth-century visitors is given in Brünnow and von Domaszewski 1904: vol. 1, 192–94, 480–510. It is augmented by Lewis 2003. See also Kennedy 2018 on the larger numbers of travellers from 1835 to 1867 than previously known from fascinating unpublished archival records.

here from one of these sources it generally refers to Petra, the site of the archaeological ruins and rock-cut chambers. Secondly, although the term *fellahin* usually refers to settled "peasants", it is also sometimes used in the descriptions for semi-nomadic Bedouin.

The present-day visitor enters Petra through the town of Wadi Musa (Eldji). Many of the visitors in the nineteenth century approached Petra from Aqaba along the Wadi Araba and entered it by the route from the south, past Jabal Haroun. They often left by this route to avoid meeting the inhabitants of Wadi Musa (Eldji), the Liathneh. The other main way they approached Petra was from Kerak which meant they either went through Wadi Musa (Eldji) or skirted around it, using the routes from the north.

Johann Ludwig Burckhardt

The first western visitor to Petra since the Crusaders, Johann Ludwig Burckhardt visited in the heat of the summer in August 1812.[10] To reach Petra he hired a guide in Eldji (now Wadi Musa), which the Liathneh lived in and around.[11] He describes Eldji:

> Ain Mousa is a copious spring, rushing under a rock at the eastern extremity of Wady Mousa … a little lower down the valley is a mill … Eldjy, the principal village of Wady Mousa … contains between two and three hundred houses,[12] and is enclosed by a stone wall with three regular gates. It is most picturesquely situated, and is inhabited by the Lyathene … a part of whom encamp during the whole year in the neighbouring mountains. The slopes of the mountains near the town are formed into artificial terraces, covered with corn fields and plantations of fruit trees. They are irrigated by the waters of the two rivulets and of many smaller springs which descend into the valley below Eldjy, there the soil is also well cultivated.[13]

He further explains:

> The town is surrounded with fruit-trees of all kinds, the produce of which is of the finest quality. Great quantities of the grapes are sold at Ghaza, and to the Bedouins. The Lyathene cultivate the valley as far as the first sepulchres of the ancient city [of Petra]; in their town-houses they work at the loom. They pay tribute to the Howeytat [tribe] and carry provisions to the Syrian pilgrims at Maan, and to the Egyptian pilgrims at Akaba. They have three encampments of about eighty tents each.[14]

Passing himself off as a Muslim travelling alone, Burckhardt used the excuse of wanting to sacrifice a goat to Aaron on Jabal Haroun to gain access to Petra, where he spent a day. When he approached the Khasneh, the Siq still would have been full of oleanders and other plants. The oleanders growing in front of the Khasneh, with their pink flowers, would have provided a green contrast to the colour of the sandstone (fig. 1). Burckhardt describes how

> … an excavated mausoleum came into view, the situation and beauty of which are calculated to make an extraordinary impression on the traveller, after having traversed for nearly half an hour such a gloomy and almost subterraneous passage as I have described. It is one of the most elegant remains of antiquity existing in Syria; its state of preservation resembles that of a building recently finished, and on a closer examination I found it to be a work of immense labour.[15]

Burckhardt's guide sacrificed the goat quickly at the foot of Jabal Haroun,[16] suggesting that the guide was fearful of being seen. Even though it was the heat of summer, the guide apparently expected there to be some human presence in the ancient site and that it was not within the control of his own tribe, the Liathneh.

Although Burckhardt did not see the Bdoul in Petra, he later met some of them in their tents nearby. After he had left Eldji, he met the Jdeylet ("Djaylat"), a clan of the Bdoul, camped in their tents. He describes heading south-south-east from Eldji:

> At the end of three hours, after having turned a little more southward, we arrived at a small encampment of Djaylat, where we stopped to breakfast. The Bedouin tents which composed a great part of this encampment were the smallest I had ever seen; they were about four feet high, and ten in length. The inhabitants were very poor, and could not afford to give us coffee; our breakfast or dinner therefore consisted of dry barley cakes which we dipped in melted goat's grease.[17]

10 On the Ottoman control, or not, of the area from ca. 1700 and intertribal conflicts, see Russell 1993: 23–28.

11 Burckhardt 1822: 421.

12 Irby and Mangles (1823: 404) give the number of houses as forty or fifty, but Robinson in 1838 (1841: 513 n. 2) thought Burckhardt's figure more accurate.

13 Burckhardt 1822: 420–21.

14 Burckhardt 1822: 433.

15 Burckhardt 1822: 424.

16 Burckhardt 1822: 430.

17 Burckhardt 1822: 434; see also Russell 1993: 20–21.

Irby, Mangles, Laborde, and Linant de Bellefonds

The next western visitors to Petra were the royal naval officers, Charles Irby and James Mangles, who were in Petra in late May 1818 and give a very detailed description of the site's monuments. They visited with Abu Rashid, who was the principal Sheikh of the northern Huweitat.[18] As the ancient site was under the control of "Abu Zatoun", the "Sheikh of Wady Mousa [Petra]", they nearly caused a war between the tribes over their visit (fig. 2).[19] In 1838 Robinson mentions the "Sheikh of the Bedûn".[20] According to Thomas Leigh, who travelled with them, the tents of the tribe of Abu Zatoun were erected on the ridges above Eldji.[21]

Irby and Mangles describe the site of Petra "at present... without a single human being living near it".[22] As Irby and Mangles, like Burckhardt, visited Petra in the heat of the summer, when the Bdoul were living in tents on the surrounding ridges, rather than the caves, they would not have necessarily seen anyone in Petra at the time. It would be easy for a visitor to see few, if any, of them, particularly if they did not wish to be seen.[23]

Léon de la Laborde and L. M. A. Linant de Bellefonds spent eight days in Petra making drawings in March 1828. They visited the site with the "Alaouins".[24] While they were there, the five hundred inhabitants of "Wadý Musa" [Petra] stayed in their tents because of the fear of the plague.[25] They did meet some "peasants" on the rock-cut path down from the Deir.[26] Laborde mentions that the triclinium opposite the Tomb of the Roman Soldier was used as a stable for their herds.[27] They also observed agriculture on the terraces of Jabal Haroun.[28]

Fig. 1. Khasneh, oleander with pink flowers in front, 1898–1946. [American Colony, G. Eric and Edith Matson Photograph Collection, Library of Congress, Prints and Photographs Division, LC-DIG-matpc-04475].

Mid-Nineteenth-Century Travellers

When Edward Robinson visited Petra with the "Jehâlîn" in late May 1838,[29] he mentioned "the Sheikh of the Bedûn, a clan of the Haweitât who pasture in and around Wady Mûsa [Petra], had arrived in the night with several armed men in order to claim from us a Ghufr, that is, a tax, tribute".[30] This was old "Mukeibil Abu Zeitûn" "the Sheikh of Wadi Mûsa [Petra]".[31] Robinson mentions that the "peasants, it was said, had sometimes come around, and asked for bakshîsh", but that other visitors since Irby and Mangles had not met Abu Zeitun probably because of the shortness of their visits.[32]

The ʿAmmârîn and a brother of Sheikh Hussein the "ʿAlawy" also accosted Robinson. He notes that, based on the Bedouin rights of thoroughfare, Wadi Musa [Petra] was not strictly speaking in the territory of either of the tribes, the "Jehâlîn" and "ʿAlawîn": "they endeavour to avoid the notice of the neighbouring Arabs, and make their visits as short as possible, feeling that they are doing that for which they may, perhaps, be called into question".[33]

18 Irby and Mangles 1823: 432; Russell 1993: 21.
19 Irby and Mangles 1823: 383–84, 391; Laborde 1836: 144–46; Stephens 1839; reprint. 1862: vol. 2, 52, 63–64; Russell 1993: 21.
20 Robinson 1841: 535.
21 Leigh in MacMichael 1819: 223, 226.
22 Irby and Mangles 1823: 439.
23 E.g., Kinnear 1841: 161–62.
24 Laborde 1836: 159. Stephens (1839: reprint. 1862, vol. 2, 63–64) gives an account of the negotiations that Laborde undertook for permission to stay in Petra.
25 Laborde 1836: 147, 174.
26 Laborde 1836: 147, 184.
27 Laborde 1836: 188.
28 Laborde 1836: 194–95.
29 Robinson 1841: 535–56, 544.
30 Robinson 1841: 535–36. Musil, who visited Petra a number of times at the turn of the century and recorded Bedouin tribes in detail, lists "el-Bdûl, el-Beden" as a clan of "Ḥwêṭât ibn Ǧâd, also known as el-ʿAlâwîn" (Musil 1908: vol. 3, 54). Musil gives the watering places of "el-Bdûl" as Wadi Mûsa and el-Ḥeǧna (Musil 1908: vol. 3, 54). He also gives Wadi Musa as the watering place of the "el-Mašâʿele, Mašʿali" a family of the "ʿObêdyje, ʿObêdi" clan of the Liathneh (Musil 1908: vol. 3, 58).
31 Robinson 1841: 540.
32 Robinson 1841: 546. On those travellers who did meet Abu Zeitun, Russell 1993: 21.
33 Robinson 1841: 543 n. 1.

Fig. 2. Abu Zatoun al-Faqara of the Bdoul, Sheikh of Wadi Musa [Petra], 1840 [Formby 1843: title page].

Fig. 3. Bdoul man, with cloak, 1843 [Wilson 1847: 287].

Robinson observed the cultivation of a scanty wheat crop at Beidha.[34] The cultivation of cereal crops around Petra is also noted by other travellers. Lord Lindsay and John Kinnear mention "corn" (grain) being grown in Petra.[35] Travelling into Petra in early 1853, Arthur Stanley observed "corn" growing in the area between Jabal Haroun and Petra, and in Petra itself.[36] Russell reports that, according to Bdoul informants in the 1980s, the al-Faqara clan traditionally had agricultural land near the Qasr el-Bint temple in the city centre of the ancient site.[37] Cereals are still cultivated by the Bedouin, including the Bdoul, near Beidha (where they are also grown by the ʿAmmarin), and near Jabal Haroun (at Stouh an-Nabi Haroun). Within the ancient site, cultivation of crops was allowed until 1965.

In what appears to be Wadi Siyyagh, Irby and Mangles observed that "the carob, fig, mulberry, vine, and pomegranate line the river-side; a very beautiful species of aloe also grows in this valley".[38] Similar plants are cultivated by the Bdoul near the modern spring in Wadi Siyyagh in Petra.

David Roberts visited Petra in March 1839. Like Austin Henry Layard the following year, he visited Petra in the colder months, when the Bdoul were living in the caves. Roberts had to pay Abu Zeitun for the right to draw the facades, but the "Fellaheen" Arabs who lived in Petra also demanded their share of his tribute.[39] Roberts observed: "The Fellaheen, or Arabs, who haunt its cliffs and chasms, amount to several hundreds. It is not wholly destitute of quadrupeds; the camel is everywhere in Arabia, and the wild goat browses among its recesses."[40] He also mentions that the "Alloeens" had occupied one of the larger caves as rain was expected.[41] He noticed caravan traffic passing through Petra.[42]

In January 1840, Layard, who is best-known for his later discoveries of Assyrian reliefs at Nineveh in Iraq, visited Petra. Travelling without another European, he had the protection of Sheikh Abu-Dhaouk of the Jehalin,[43] "a chief of the Howitat which were encamped in the neighbourhood of the ruins".[44] However, he was asked for money by the "Sheikh of Wadi Musa" "in whose territory the ruins were situated",[45] so that Layard takes up most of his account on these negotiations. Having selected a site to erect his small tent, Layard observed the occupants of Petra:

34 Robinson 1841: 511.
35 Lindsay 1838: vol. 2, 39; Kinnear 1841: 168–69. Other travellers who also recorded crops: Russell 1993: 22–23.
36 Stanley 1856: 88.
37 Russell 1993: 21.
38 Irby and Mangles 1823: 427.
39 Roberts 1855: text to pl. 101.
40 Roberts 1855: text to pl. 100.
41 Roberts 1855: text to pl. 106 (quoting Kinnear 1841: 163).
42 Roberts 1855: text to pl. 95.
43 Layard 1887: 4–7.
44 Layard 1887: 3.
45 Layard 1887: 15, 17.

Fig. 4. Bdoul man, rear view, without cloak to show long hair [Wilson 1847: 337].

> I dismounted and spread my carpet. I had scarcely done so when a swarm of half-clad Arabs, with dishevelled locks and savage looks, issued from the excavated tombs and chambers and gathered around me. I asked for some bread and milk, which was brought to me ... many of the tombs [are] sculptured in the precipitous cliffs forming the sides of the valley. These tombs, some of which were elaborately ornamented with pediments, friezes, and columns, were mostly used as habitations by Arab families, and their spacious chambers were filled with smoke and dirt.[46]

Three years later John Wilson depicted one of the Bdoul fully armed and also with long hair-locks (figs. 3–4).

Harriette Martineau stayed in Petra in March 1847 with a party of fifteen. She was surprised how many inhabitants of the caves there were, revealed by the number of fires at night. There was heavy rain, resulting in water rushing down the Siq and a flash flood, causing her to look out of her tent in the evening:

> I was startled to see how many were looking at it with me. All along the opposite ridge, and on every point of the descent, were dim figures of Arabs; and in the precipices, there was quite an illumination. Row beyond row of the caves gave out yellow gleams; and in the moonlight rose little pillars and wreaths of white smoke. The Arabs had come up from the whole country round, at the sound of the waters; and I had seen Petra populous once more.[47]

She went out the following night and again observed the fires.[48]

> A series of strange wild heads popped up from below the platform, showing that the ragged regiment of the Sheikh of Petra was upon us. Suleiman, Sheikh of Wadee Mousa [Petra], and of the tribe Aulad Benee Israel, was here in person. His followers were a dark and wild-looking set of fellows, with their ready match-locks, daggers and spears, as could be seen: but they never did us any harm, nor offered any.[49]

The rain brought down Facade 66, with the Greek inscription, near the Khasneh.[50] As a result, her visit was remembered by the Bdoul nearly a century later.[51]

Martineau noticed that the Urn Tomb "contains nothing but the little partition walls which the modern Arabs have built up of loose stones".[52] These would have been built especially for protecting the baby goats in the winter/early spring, as in the herds she observed passing along the Siq:

> I saw to-day a group of goats and their herdsmen, entering into the deepest shadow from a reach of sunshine; and a child standing with two kids on a point of rock above my head; and a wild troup of shaggy Arabs, clattering their arms as I passed; and here and there a solitary figure, with his matchlock, brown tunic, and white teeth, perched on a pinnacle or striding over a distant slope.[53]

Photography

Five years after Harriette Martineau's visit, John Shaw Smith was in Petra, in 1852, photographing the site and some of the monuments, such as the Theatre (fig. 5). He was followed by Frank Mason Good in 1866–7, who photographed the still standing arch over the Siq (fig. 39). His photograph of the Palace Tomb also shows details at the top of the ashlar

46 Layard 1887: 15–16, 18.

47 Martineau 1848: vol. 3, 28.
48 Martineau 1848: vol. 3, 32.
49 Martineau 1848: vol. 3, 10.
50 Martineau 1848: vol. 3, 32.
51 Canaan 1930: 8–9.
52 Martineau 1848: vol. 3, 9. The caves were sometimes used as tombs, as Martineau comments that "no dead body (except of a modern Arab or two) has ever been found in them" (Martineau 1848: vol. 3, 4, 21).
53 Martineau 1848: vol. 3, 13.

Fig. 5. Theatre, photographed by John Shaw Smith in 1852 [J. S. Smith, Palestine Exploration Fund photograph P/2557].

Fig. 6. Palace Tomb, photographed by Frank Mason Good, 1866–67 [F. Mason Good, Palestine Exploration Fund photograph P/2037].

masonry part, which have since fallen down (fig. 6). At that time, and until the end of the nineteenth century, there was considerable ground cover, as in the 1895 photograph of the Deir taken by Charles Alexander Hornstein (fig. 7).

Late Nineteenth-Century Travellers

The Cambridge Orientalist Edward Henry Palmer visited Petra in early 1870 during the rainy season, when it snowed.[54] He entered the ancient city by the route past Jabal Haroun, but once in Petra was challenged by the Liathneh.[55] The camp of the Liathneh, and their Sheikh Silmán, which was on the hills above Eldji, "consisted of about a hundred tents arranged in a great square, with a double row forming a street on either of the two sides".[56] Palmer was told by Selámeh ibn ʿAwwad, the Sheikh of the ʿAmmarin, that "Wády Músa [Petra] belonged to him and to his ancestors, but that the Liyátheneh a few years back had taken it from the ʿAmmarín by force of arms, and were confirmed in their possession of it, conjointly with the Haweitát, by Turkish officials".[57] However, Beidha was in the territory of the ʿAmmarin not the Liathneh.[58] Palmer describes Eldji as consisting of "only a few rude stone houses".[59]

Palmer met "fellahin" in Petra (who also wanted their share of money from his visit), and noted the occupation of the caves:

> At the northern turn of the wády, as you leave the western acclivities, are three large tombs with perfect fronts, the first and largest of them is called Magháret en Nasára, or the Christian's Cave, and was at that time of our entry occupied by several of the fellahín. Every tomb has its owner, who dwells there with his wives and family during the cold or wet weather.[60]

When Charles Doughty was in Petra in early 1875, he also observed the Bedouin using the caves: "Near the head of the valley, we found a Beduin and his wife and their flock, and sat down by the poor man, who went and milked his goats for us bountifully." He describes the tombs: "now they are the night stalls of the nomads' flocks and blackened with the herdsmen's fires."[61]

In his book on his visits to Petra made around the turn of the twentieth century, Rev. A. Forder, who was a medical missionary in Kerak, observed:

> but for a few beggarly nomads the once populous city is deserted. For a few months during the cold rainy season of the year a few families of Bedouin, with their goats' hair tents and their few goats, find a home and shelter in the val-

54 Palmer 1871: 53, 55.

55 Palmer 1871: 51.
56 Palmer 1871: 52.
57 Palmer 1871: 57.
58 Palmer 1871: 56.
59 Palmer 1871: 53.
60 Palmer 1871: 55.
61 Doughty 1888: vol. 1, 40–41.

leys and excavations, but as soon as the weather permits they go to the highlands, and Petra is left to its loneliness ... Other inhabitants of or near Petra are a small tribe of Arabs known as the Layathaney.[62]

Early Twentieth Century

At the end of the nineteenth century, the Bdoul became so impoverished that a number of visitors comment on their condition.[63] They were dominated by the Liathneh and the Ottoman authorities in a situation which continued through World War I,[64] with Turkish patrols taking their livestock and grain supplies (as Peake Pasha found in 1919).[65]

After World War I, the area of Jordan south of Shoubak was included in the Kingdom of Hijaz, and after it fell in 1925, the region was annexed to Transjordan.[66] This led to Petra again becoming more accessible for sustained visits.

Peake Pasha was involved in the early administration of Transjordan and in his study of the tribes in 1919 mentions:

> Al Bdul.—A very small tribe living in the hills around Petra and Jebel Harun ... At the present time these people are very poor, as they own but few sheep, and their land scarcely repays the effort required to plough it. Until 1926 they owned no tents, but lived in the caves around Petra; some of them were at that time clothed only in skins. They number 150 persons at the most.[67]

Peake Pasha also found that Turkish patrols continued to take the livestock and grain supplies of the Petra Bedouin.

In an article which includes photographs of Bdoul families, Ditlef Nielsen, who studied the ancient mountain sanctuaries of Petra as part of the Mond Expedition to Petra in 1929, describes the Bdoul:

> This poor tribe, – to all appearances a dying one numbering only about ten families—deserves more attention. The members of the Bdūl have neither camels nor horses, nor tents nor houses, but live in the caves of the Petra mountains, tending their small flocks of black goats, their sole property ... The Liāthneh possess the oasis of Elgī, east of Petra. As they act as guides to Petra they are described in the Petra literature as Petra beduin. Yet the real beduin of Petra, the Bdūl, who live in the Petra mountains, and know every stone there, do not pretend to be Moslems and know practically nothing of the religion ... the Bdūls are the sole people who have now their home at Petra.[68]

Fig. 7. Deir, photographed by Charles Alexander Hornstein in 1895 [C. A. Hornstein, Palestine Exploration Fund photograph P/2450].

Fig. 8. Wadi Musa, with Jabal Haroun on far left, ca. 1898–1946 [American Colony, G. Eric and Edith Matson Photograph Collection, Library of Congress, Prints and Photographs Division, LC-DIG-matpc-22002].

Taufiq (Tewfik) Canaan had considerable daily contact with the Bdoul in 1929 when he made a detailed study of the topographical names of the features of Petra, as part of the Mond expedition. His study includes descriptions of the customs of the Bdoul and Liathneh. He describes the Bdoul:

62 Forder 1923: 12–14.
63 Russell 1993: 27–28.
64 Canaan 1930: 64–65.
65 Russell 1993: 28.
66 Canaan 1930: 64–65; Russell 1993: 28–29.
67 Peake 1958: 203.
68 Nielsen 1933: 207, pls. 9.2, 14.2.

Fig. 9. Terraces of Wadi Musa (Eldji), looking west, with tents on far right, ca. 1900–1920 [American Colony, G. Eric and Edith Matson Photograph Collection, Library of Congress, Prints and Photographs Division, LC-DIG-matpc-00105].

Fig. 10. Wadi Musa, looking west, ca. 1940–1946 [American Colony, G. Eric and Edith Matson Photograph Collection, Library of Congress, Prints and Photographs Division, LC-DIG-matpc-04491].

> The Bdūl, a small tribe living mostly in Petra proper, require special mention... The Bdūl rarely leave their district. In the winter season they spend between two and three months in the caves of Petra; in the spring they encamp around the wâdîs, while the summer is spent at the tops of the high mountains of Petra or on one of the surrounding ridges. A few of them live in el-Bêḍâ. They are the poorest of all the Bedouin tribes of this district of the Transjordan. Their children mostly run about quite naked.[69] The adults wear ragged, dirty shirts. I found only one Bdūl who lived in Bêḍâ and had a gun. No agricultural work is done by them, but they keep some goats. Their šêh is Salâmeh bin Djumʿah. This tribe is related to the Bdūl Ḥasmâ who live near ʿAqabah.[70] These last are more respected, better to do and more numerous than the Bdūl of Petra. The Bdūl are not reckoned among the Liâṯneh but are affiliated to them.[71]

Although Canaan had the impression in 1929 that the Bdoul did not do agricultural work,[72] Peake's comment that the Bdoul land (in ca. 1927) "scarcely repays the effort required to plough it" implies that they did so.[73] Canaan also mentions that the insufficient rainfall of the previous three years resulted in a poor harvest in Eldji.[74] Agriculture in Eldji, which has a perennial water supply from ʿAin Musa, was less marginal than the cultivation of the land in and around Petra, where the yield is totally dependent on a good rainfall. Thus, it is probable that the Bdoul, having probably had no harvest for one or two years, did not sow any grain when Canaan was there.

Living Memories

Canaan noted that the Liathneh lived at Eldji, while the Bdoul lived in and around Petra and had a much more detailed knowledge of it. Like Musil,[75] Canaan noted some topographical names at Petra with "Bdūl" in them: Ḫallet el-Bdūl, Wadi Farʿet el-Bdūl'.[76] He observed:

69 Neilson, who was in Petra at the same time as Canaan, and Forder, who was there at the end of the nineteenth and early twentieth century, include photographs which have young naked boys in them, but the women, girls, babies, and older men are clothed (Forder 1923: top pl. on p. 15; Nielsen 1933: pl. 14.2 = fig. 18 here). The boys' stomachs are distended from malnutrition.

70 In his summary of the Bedouin tribes, Burckhardt (1831: vol. 2, 10) mentions the "Bedoul" tribe who reside in the vicinity of ʿAqaba and are in alliance with the "Omran and Howeytát". On the branch of the Bdoul near Humayma, who moved to join the Petra Bdoul in the summer, and with whom those in Petra intermarried, which John Wilson reports in 1843, see Russell 1993: 17, 19. Some of the Bdoul clans (e.g., al-Faqara) also have links with the Bedouin at Medain Saleh (Russell 1993: 19–20).

71 Canaan 1930: 80. Canaan noted the Bdoul "are not subdivided into subtribes, but, owing to their small number, into families which are: ḥamûlet Salâmeh Djumʿah el-Muassah, ḥamûlet Muṭlaq Itaiyym, ḥamûlet Sâlim Salmân, ḥamûlet Štaiyân Abû Djḏêl and ḥamûlet Salîm Abû Sâlim." (Canaan 1930: 80 n. 2).

72 Canaan 1930: 80.

73 Peake 1958: 203.

74 Canaan 1930: 63.

75 Musil 1908: vol. 2, part 2, map.

76 Canaan 1930: 41, 57.

> It is further of great importance to note that the Bdûl know and use many more place names in Petra than the Liâṯneh who live at Eldjî. Nearly every small valley and every mountain has a name according to the Bdûl. Such a name may not be old and fixed, but a changing one, based upon an important incident in the tribe's history. ... These Bedouins know more names than others because nearly all of them spend the whole of their lives, from the cradle to the grave, year in and year out in Petra.[77]

The continuity of the Bdoul's presence at the ancient site is seen in their living memory of the visit of Harriette Martineau in 1847, because it coincided with the heavy rains which dislodged Facade 66, causing it to fall to the ground. About eighty years later, in 1929, the Bdoul related this event to Canaan. They considered it had been caused by her presence, and the tale had been embellished by crediting her with the powers of a sorceress:

> A European lady who is said to have come to Petra a long time ago, lived in the ... Triclinium [opposite Facade 66]. One evening she sat on a stone at the door and turning her face to the monument [Facade 66] ... began to read aloud while incense was burnt beside her. Slowly she became more and more excited, the tempo of her reading was accelerated and greater quantities of incense were thrown on the fire. As soon as it grew dark she ordered her guides to leave the place, and scarcely had they moved away, when a thunder-like noise was heard and a large rock in the mountain wall opposite the Triclinium fell down.[78]

Continued Bedouin occupation of Petra and Wadi Musa since the Crusaders is also suggested by living memory in a tale, recorded by Canaan, associated with the site of the Crusader castle of al-Wuʿayra, behind the modern Crowne Plaza Hotel (former Forum Hotel) in Wadi Musa. It was built on a rock out-crop, so that it could only be accessed via a drawbridge across the gorge on its eastern side.

Fig. 11. Camels in Wadi Musa, looking west towards Jabal Haroun, ca. 1940–1946 [American Colony, G. Eric and Edith Matson Photograph Collection, Library of Congress, Prints and Photographs Division, LC-DIG-matpc-21175].

Fig. 12. Wadi Musa (Eldji), 1900–1930 [G. L. Robinson 1930: pl. opposite p. 32].

> Uʿêrah is said to have been inhabited by a very powerful nation, which did not respect anybody, not even the Almighty. They used to open the gates of the city in the morning and close them in the evening. Nobody could enter this fortified place without their knowledge and permission, until once when the inhabitants were returning from work, a stranger, not knowing this custom, entered unobserved with them, just before the gates were closed. As usual the supper, which was prepared in a common kitchen, was distributed to the inhabitants, and behold one remained without a share. ... [When the chief detected the stranger's presence,] the stranger stepped forward and said that as he was a guest he begged for the rights of hospitality. The tyrannical chief ordered his persecution and death. Immediately on the same day God punished the people of this nation for their pride, brutality, and inhospitality by destroying their city. Since that moment the mighty, fortified, and beautiful city sank into oblivion.[79]

77 Canaan 1930: 2.

78 Canaan 1929: 8.

79 Canaan 1930: 11.

Fig. 13. A street in Wadi Musa (Eldji), ca. 1896–1911 [B. Moritz, Library of Congress, Prints and Photographs Division, LC-DIG-ppmsca-38129].

Fig. 14. A street in Wadi Musa, with soldiers (no date) [Horsfield Archive, University College London, © UCL, Institute of Archaeology] (the same street as fig. 13).

Fig. 15. Liathneh in Wadi Musa, ca. 1896–1911 [B. Moritz, Library of Congress, Prints and Photographs Division, LC-DIG-ppmsca-38130].

In the late eighteenth century, there were still some Greek Christians living in Badabde, a village near the spring of ʿAin Musa, according to Burckhardt.[80] The presence of Christians in Petra (or knowledge of them) since the Crusades is also suggested by the names of the Deir (the Monastery) and Moghar an-Nasara (the Christian cave), where the name is applied to the Tomb with the Armour (No. 649).

Origin of the Bdoul and their Name

As far back as the mid-nineteenth century,[81] all recorded versions of the origin of the Bdoul have in common that they claim to be descended from the region's ancient inhabitants described then as "Children of Israel".[82] However, the explanation for the origin of the name of the Bdoul evolved during the twentieth century, influenced by political and other considerations.[83] According to Taufiq (Tewfik) Canaan, who was in Petra in 1929, the Liathneh explained that the inhabitants of Petra, when trapped by Moses and the Israelites on Umm el-Biyara, had changed their religion to that of Moses, while the Bdoul themselves "pretend" to be a branch of the Howeitat.[84] The Bdoul explained to Margaret Murray in 1934 that they had changed their religion from Judaism to Islam.[85] By the 1980s, accounts omitted any mention of Judaism but included the Nabataeans as part of their ancestry.

Wadi Musa (Eldji)

The tribes with areas adjoining the Bdoul include the ʿAmmarin who live around Beidha. The ʿAmmarin, like the Bdoul, practise some agriculture, as well as herding goats. The Saʿidiyyine lived in the historic village of Dlagha (Delaghah), but their territory, aside from the area around it, is at Wadi Sabra and in Wadi Araba. They cultivate cereals and herd goats, sheep, and camels.[86]

Taybeh and Wadi Musa as far as the entrance to the Siq were occupied by the Liathneh. In Wadi Musa they had irrigated agriculture, growing wheat and barley crops, as well as fruit and vegetables. Wadi Musa (Eldji) had "houses" which were used as houses and storerooms.

Fig. 16. Wadi Musa, with police post (top left), early 1960s [Kaiser 1971: top pl. opposite p. 22].

Fig. 17. A Bdoul man and three women, ca. 1900–1920 [American Colony, G. Eric and Edith Matson Photograph Collection, Library of Congress, Prints and Photographs Division, LC-DIG-matpc-05278].

80 Burckhardt 1823: 420.
81 Wilson 1847: vol. 1, 330–31; Russell 1993: 16–17.
82 Russell 1993: 17.
83 Russell (1993: 16–18) gives the most detailed summary of the different accounts. See also Shoup 1985: 289.
84 Canaan 1930: 81.
85 Murray 1939: 20–21; Russell 1993: 18.
86 Farajat 2012: 147–49.

Fig. 18. Bdoul family, ca. 1929 [Nielsen 1933: pl. 14.2].

Fig. 19. Bdoul, 1929 [Nielsen 1933: pl. 9.2].

Descriptions by nineteenth-century travellers, such as Burckhardt's,[87] and photographs taken in the first half of the twentieth century indicate that Wadi Musa was an agricultural centre.[88] It had extensive terraces on either side of it, where barley and wheat were grown (figs. 8–9).[89] Below the terraces, down in the wadi, fruit trees (apricots, pears, peaches, grapes, and figs) and, by 1929, vegetables (tomatoes, cucumbers, marrows, aubergines) were cultivated.[90] Retaining walls had been built to catch the run-off of the seasonal rain, to augment water from the perennial spring for watering crops (fig. 10). In order to attend to their crops, the Liathneh did not move far from Wadi Musa (some of their tents are visible in the top right of fig. 9). In 1929, Canaan noted how they numbered nearly 220 tents, with each sub-tribe having clearly defined areas and springs.[91] Their herds consisted of goats and a few sheep, with camels only used for transport (fig. 11).[92] Because Wadi Musa was so cold in winter, some of the Liathneh spent three months of the year in the caves near the entrance to the Siq, while others moved to more protected places, such as Beidha.[93] In the warmer months they pitched their tents around Wadi Musa.

The traditional single-room houses in Wadi Musa were made of rough stone (figs. 12–14). Each consisted of a nearly square rectangular space with a single door and ventilation holes high up in the walls but no windows. By 1929, a few of the newer houses in Wadi Musa had windows.[94] A study of the houses surviving in the area of Wadi Musa (Bani ʿAta village, Khirbet Raidan) found that they were a combination of single-room houses and courtyard houses,[95] whereas those of the small villages of the ʿAmmarin at Beidha and of the Saʿidiyyine at Dlagha (Delaghah) were single-room houses configured in rows, like the compartments of a Bedouin tent.[96]

By 1929, the Liathneh were already benefitting from tourism and guiding, with their horses and mules carrying tourists and their baggage into Petra.[97] With increased employment from tourism, including taking tourists down the Siq on horseback from the mid-1960s, the Liathneh rapidly became more settled (fig. 103). By the early 1980s, they only had a few flocks of sheep and goats[98] but still practised extensive agriculture (figs. 34, 105, 203). The "houses" in the village were largely used for storage.[99] By 1927 they included a school room.[100] B. Moritz photographed some of the "houses" and some of the Liathneh ca. 1896–1911 (figs. 13, 15). In the early 1960s, Wadi Musa (Eldji) still looked much as it had earlier in the century (fig. 16).

87 Burckhardt 1822: 420–21, 433.
88 Also described by Murray 1939: 3–4.
89 Canaan 1930: 61.
90 Canaan 1930: 61.
91 Canaan 1930: 61–62. At that time the Liathneh were noticeably poorer than the other Bedouin (Canaan 1930: 64).
92 Canaan 1930: 63.
93 Canaan 1930: 61.
94 Canaan 1930: 61.
95 Twaissi et al. 2016: 340, fig. 7.
96 Twaissi et al. 2016: 342, figs. 9–10. Other examples of houses in Jordan: Khammash 1986. For houses in Palestine: Amiry and Tamari 1989.
97 Canaan 1930: 63.
98 Shoup 1985: 290.
99 Canaan 1930: 60. The number of "houses" mentioned in the nineteenth century varied from 40–50 (Irby and Mangles 1823: 404) to 200–300 (Burckhardt 1822: 420; Robinson 1841: 513).
100 Canaan 1930: 61.

Summary

The examples given of accounts of nineteenth-century travellers indicate that the caves of Petra were occupied by the Bedouin in the colder months, and that they lived in the ridges around Petra and nearby during the rest of the year. They left evidence of their fires in the caves they had occupied, leaving ash on the floors and smoke-blackened ceilings and walls. They also used the caves as animal stables and fitted them out with small walls as pens for their flocks. Examples of this can be seen in the larger monuments, such as the Urn Tomb and Triclinium 235 opposite the Tomb of the Roman Soldier. They cultivated cereal crops at Beidha, near Jabal Haroun, and (until 1965) within Petra itself.

In a desert environment, the warm caves, cisterns, and springs mean that the continuous occupation of the valley of ancient Petra might well be expected from the time of the Nabataeans. Although the Bdoul clearly occupied Petra, there were some fluctuations in their fortunes. In the early to mid-nineteenth century, they numbered several hundred members. However, following years of attacks on them at the end of the nineteenth century, and in the period after World War I, they became an impoverished tribe of about 150 members – a situation which changed little until after the late 1950s (figs. 17–19).

CHAPTER 2

The Development of Petra for Tourism, 1925–1981

Before introducing the reader to Petra and what it was like when I worked there with Angela in 1981/2, some background should be provided on the development of the site for tourism before then.

In the nineteenth and early twentieth centuries visitors to Petra travelled there on camels or horseback. They had a choice of routes,[1] most of which tried to avoid the Liathneh in Wadi Musa by approaching from a different direction. They carried their own tents and food.[2] The first major change in the ease of access to the site came with the opening of the Hejaz railway in 1908. It could be taken to Maʿan, with only the final stage of the journey to be made on horse or camel-back.[3]

Around this time, the first scientific recording of the site's monuments was begun. In 1897 and 1898 Rudolf-Ernst Brünnow and Alfred von Domaszewski made a detailed record of all facades and established the numbering system for them, which they published in 1904.[4] They were followed by Alois Musil,[5] while Gustaf Dalman focused on rock-cut sanctuaries from 1904 to 1910,[6] and Heinrich Kohl published on the Qasr el-Bint.[7] During World War I, Theodor Wiegand, Carl Watzinger, and Walter Bachmann recorded the main free-standing buildings.[8] Alexander Kennedy's volume, published in 1925, attracted Anglophone interest in the site.[9]

Cook's Camp

In contrast to the decades before World War I under Ottoman rule, unrest in the area in the first few years after the war meant that it became very difficult for individual travellers to visit Petra.[10] Following the annexation of the Petra region to Transjordan in 1925, travel became much easier due to better security. The situation later improved so that from ca. 1925, Thomas Cook and Son, the British travel company, ran

Fig. 20. Thomas Cook's tent camp near el-Habis, 1927 [Horsfield Archive, University College London, © UCL, Institute of Archaeology].

tours to Petra where they established a seasonal tent camp at the foot of el-Habis, beside the Qasr el-Bint (figs. 20–22, 23).[11] The possibility of staying in the camp meant that visitors could travel as "tourists" in a group without needing to organise transportation of their own accommodation or assorted supplies.

By 1937, the tent camp had been bought by the Nazzals, a Palestinian family who owned a number of hotels in the region, including the Philadelphia Hotel in Amman.[12] Facilities in Nazzal's Camp included tents for accommodation and a large tent for formal dining (fig. 24).[13]

By the early 1930s, modern forms of transport made the journey to Petra much less physically arduous, while it was only possible to benefit from these improvements because

1 Baedeker (1912: 175–78) gives examples of routes from Jerusalem.
2 Vivid description of arrangements to make with a dragoman: Baedeker 1912: xvii–xx.
3 Baedeker 1912: 175.
4 Brünnow and von Domaszewski 1904: vol. 1, 125–532.
5 Musil 1907: vol. 2, part 1, 41–150.
6 Dalman 1908; 1911.
7 Kohl 1910.
8 Bachmann et al. 1921.
9 Kennedy 1925.
10 Forder 1923: 7–8.
11 Shoup 1985: 280–81; Russell 1993: 29.
12 Russell (1993: 29) provides references for the date, *contra* Shoup 1985: 281 (in the 1940s).
13 Most of the staff were brought from Egypt, although some locals were also employed (Shoup 1985: 281). Marguerite van Geldermalsen (2006: 45) mentions how, in the 1970s, the Bdoul knew some of the staff of the Philadelphia Hotel in Amman from working at Nazzal's Camp.

Fig. 21. Thomas Cook's camp kitchen in a cave, 1927 [Horsfield Archive, University College London, © UCL, Institute of Archaeology].

Fig. 22. Thomas Cook's seasonal tent camp, at the foot of el-Habis, looking south-east towards the Qasr el-Bint, with oleanders in flower, ca. 1925–1933 [American Colony, G. Eric and Edith Matson Photograph Collection, Library of Congress, Prints and Photographs Division, LC-DIG-matpc-12055].

Fig. 23. Thomas Cook's camp with tents, looking south-east from el-Habis, with crops growing on the terraces on top of the Temenos of the Qasr el-Bint, ?1936 [American Colony, G. Eric and Edith Matson Photograph Collection, Library of Congress, Prints and Photographs Division, LC-DIG-matpc-03103].

Fig. 24. Nazzal's Camp, dining tent set for dinner, 1940–46 [American Colony, G. Eric and Edith Matson Photograph Collection, Library of Congress, Prints and Photographs Division, LC-DIG-matpc-04502].

of the very firm, but careful hand kept on the region by the British Mandate government of Transjordan through the Arab Legion (Desert Patrol) and the police (fig. 25).[14] The Hejaz railway could be taken to Maʿan (fig. 26), which could also be reached by flying in a private plane from Jerusalem or Cairo.[15] The journey from Maʿan to Petra was then made by car. The journey could also be undertaken along other routes,[16] such as by taxi from Aqaba (fig. 27). Safety of car journeys was ensured by reporting in at the police stations along the route, which would wire ahead to the next police station.[17] This routine resulted in Petra being approached via the police station of Wadi Musa (Eldji).[18]

Fig. 25. Desert Patrol, 1934–35 [John D. Whiting, American Colony, Library of Congress, Prints and Photographs Division, LC-DIG-ppmsca-18429-00113].

14 Canaan 1930: 65; Murray 1939: 185–86. She mentions the "Three Englishmen, Colonel Cox, Colonel Peake, and Major Glubb, who, with the firm backing of the Emir [Abdallah] rule Transjordan" (Murray 1939: 185).

15 Murray 1939: 1.

16 Murray 1939: 1–2.

17 Murray 1939: 181–82.

18 Murray 1939: 184–85.

Fig. 26. Ma'an, Hejaz railway station, ca. 1908–1920 [American Colony, G. Eric and Edith Matson Photograph Collection, Library of Congress, Prints and Photographs Division, LC-DIG-matpc-01625].

Fig. 27. Lunch on a taxi ride from Aqaba to Petra, 1934–35 [John D. Whiting, American Colony, Library of Congress, Prints and Photographs Division, LC-DIG-ppmsca-17414-00074].

Fig. 28. Tourists having dinner in a cave in Petra, 1898–1946 [American Colony, G. Eric and Edith Matson Photograph Colletion, Library of Congress, Prints and Photographs Division, LC-DIG-matpc-09429].

First Excavations

The provision of a seasonal camp in Petra and its increased accessibility as a result of the improved safety of the area enabled the first two archaeological excavations at the site. Work was also undertaken to improve the site's presentation to tourists. The first excavations were done in 1929, when George Horsfield (Chief Inspector of Antiquities for Transjordan) and Agnes Conway (later Horsfield) dug a trench in al-Katuteh rubbish dump and excavated some rock-cut houses.[19] They also cleared the floors of the main tombs, making them more presentable to visitors. This involved removing the dung and ash floors down to bedrock and dismantling small walls built in them by the Bedouin for their use as goat pens, such as those in the Urn Tomb.[20] In 1934, Margaret Murray, assisted by J. C. Ellis and J. A. Saunders, excavated further rock-cut houses and tombs.[21]

The Bdoul

While nineteenth-century travellers mention the Bdoul in Petra, and they appear in early twentieth century photographs (fig. 17), it was only once it became possible to stay in Petra for longer that more detailed records of them were made, in particular by the Palestinian doctor and ethnographer Taufiq (Tewfik) Canaan, who accompanied the archaeologists on the Mond Expedition in 1929.

By 1934, when Margaret Murray worked in Petra, the Bdoul tribe consisted of 35 families and a total of 150 members.[22] The Bdoul tribe is still divided, into five "clans" or

19 G. and A. Horsfield 1938: 1–42; 1939: 87–115; 1942: 105–204.

20 Forder 1923: lower photograph on p. 11.

21 Murray and Ellis 1940. On how she came to excavate at Petra: Murray 1939: 180.

22 Murray 1939: 21. This gives an average of 2.3 children per family.

Fig. 29. Bdoul men and young women making coffee in the triclinium north of the Tomb of Sextius Florentinus, with young women and a man in a turban from Upper Egypt, 1934–35 [John D. Whiting, American Colony, Library of Congress, Prints and Photographs Division, LC-DIG-ppmsca-18429-00108].

Fig. 30. Bdoul sheikh (on far right in fig. 29) showing plaits under his *keffiyeh*, 1934–35 [John D. Whiting, American Colony, Library of Congress, Prints and Photographs Division, LC-DIG-ppmsca-18429-00109].

sub-tribes: al-Faqara (which is the largest – over half the tribe), al-Jamadah, al-Muwasa, as-Samahin, and al-Jdeilat.[23] When they lived in Petra, each clan largely occupied a particular part of it[24] and had a sheikh.[25]

In 1934, due to their poverty, the Bdoul were so badly nourished and in such poor health that some had tuberculosis. Consequently, the government provided them with a winter bread dole and medical attention.[26] They had some seasonal income from tourism (selling souvenirs and guiding), and from archaeological and government work.[27]

Visitors in the first half of the twentieth century included photographers from the American Colony in Jerusalem, in 1934–35. A photograph of tourists dining formally on a white tablecloth in a sandy cave (fig. 28) provides a contrast to their photographs of the Bdoul at around the time that Murray was working in Petra. In one photograph, the men are making coffee in the afternoon sun in the triclinium north of the Tomb of Sextius Florentinus, with women or girls and a man from Upper Egypt present (fig. 29). Some of the Bdoul men had donned waistcoats (figs. 29–30), and the young sheikh a fob watch (the chain is visible in fig. 30), plaiting his hair under his *keffiyeh* like other Bedouin young men.[28] The young women in these photographs wore headscarves with the ends tied at the back of their necks (fig. 29), and sometimes protecting the lower part of their faces with them (fig. 144). One young woman even had a veil decorated with coins and cowrie shells (fig. 31). In ca. 1940–46 the American Colony photographers recorded a mother and child in Wadi Deir (fig. 32).

Restoration and Archaeological Work from the 1950s

Following World War II, development of Petra for tourism and associated archaeological restoration projects did not commence until the mid-1950s. Accommodation for tourists inside Petra was improved with the construction of the Nazzal's Camp hotel building in the mid-1950s, tucked between the Qasr el-Bint and el-Habis (fig. 59).[29] It had a staircase to the main floor, with a large room along the front of it for a lounge and dining space, and a kitchen at the back. On the floor above, there were bedrooms and shared bathrooms. Electric light was provided by a generator and the water pumped from the spring. It also had a telephone.[30] Concrete bases were provided over which tents could be pitched, and two of the caves on el-Habis were converted for use as bedrooms. Nazzal's Camp remained in use as a hotel until 1978[31] but continued as a base for archaeologi-

23 Shoup 1985: 289; Ohannessian-Charpin 1986: 392; Russell 1993: 18–19 (gives Arabic spellings of names).

24 Ohannessian-Charpin 1986: 392, map 3.

25 Shoup 1985: 289 n. 2. Names of sheikhs ca. late 1980s: Russell 1993: table 1.

26 Murray 1939: 22, 27.

27 Murray 1939: 21.

28 Canaan 1930: 63; Murray 1939: 26. They were also worn by the Liathneh.

29 Records of the precise date of construction of Nazzal's Camp vary. Muhammad Khadija, pers. comm. 29 November 2018 (1954); Ohannessian-Charpin 1985: 387 (1958); Russell 1993: 30 (1956/7).

30 Muhammad Khadija, pers. comm. September 2018.

31 Marguerite van Geldermalsen (2006: 6) stayed at Nazzal's Camp in 1978, a few months before it closed.

cal teams. It was the first and only modern building within the site of Petra until 1981, when the Basin Restaurant was constructed (fig. 106). Other constructions continued to be prohibited in the Petra valley. In 1964, the amount of tourist accommodation for visitors to Petra was further increased with the opening of the Rest House in Wadi Musa.[32] Petra remained difficult to reach unless on an organised tour until 1980, when the JETT bus company began a daily return service from Amman to Wadi Musa, along with the chance to ride a horse down the Siq and have lunch.[33]

In 1961/2, facilities were created in the caves at the side of el-Habis (fig. 49) for the Department of Antiquities inspector, staff, and stonemason, who were brought from Amman to carry out restoration work as part of a tourism project.[34] This project included converting a large cave on el-Habis to a museum and, in 1966, the addition of public toilets.[35]

The construction of the Nazzal's Camp hotel building, followed by the Rest House in Wadi Musa, coincided with archaeological and restoration work in the city centre.[36] From 1955, the Colonnaded Street was cleared, and excavations undertaken beside it and nearby at the Temenos Gate, and the Qasr el-Bint.[37] During the following twenty-five years, reconstruction or consolidation work was done on key monuments. The fallen column in the front of the Khasneh was repaired and re-erected in 1959/60 by G. R. H. Wright,[38] and the heavy weathering of the lowest parts of the facade repaired. Parts of the Temenos Gate were reconstructed,[39] and missing sections of the outer walls of the Qasr el-Bint were rebuilt to increase its stability.[40] The orchestra of the Theatre was excavated in 1961–62, and the lowest parts of its stage building reconstructed.[41] Other restoration work, directed by Muhammad Khadija[42] from 1977 to 1981, included rebuilding the arched structures below the Urn Tomb podium to provide easy access to it.[43]

The restoration work and associated excavations did little damage to the appearance of the centre of the site, which had remained largely unchanged since the early twentieth century. The main differences were the newly uncovered Temenos and

Fig. 31. Bdoul girls, 1934–35 [John D. Whiting, American Colony, Library of Congress, Prints and Photographs Division, LC-DIG-ppmsca-18429-00110].

Fig. 32. Bdoul mother and child in Wadi Deir, ca. 1940–46 [American Colony, G. Eric and Edith Matson Photograph Collection, Library of Congress, Prints and Photographs Division, LC-DIG-matpc-12381].

32 Date: Muhammad Khadija, pers. comm. 27 September 2014. Russell 1993: 30.
33 Shoup 1985: 282.
34 Muhammad Khadija, pers. comm. 11 November 2004.
35 Date: Muhammed Khadija, pers. comm. 27 September 2018.
36 Summary, McKenzie 1990: 1–2.
37 Kirkbride 1960; Parr 1957; 1960; 1965; 1967–68; 1970.
38 Date: Muhammad Khadija, pers. comm. 29 November 2018. The rock for this column was faulty when the Khasneh was carved in antiquity, so it had originally been built free-standing. In the late nineteenth century, the capital was embedded, in the sand at the modern ground level, which meant that it had fallen down relatively recently.
39 Temenos Gate before and after restoration: McKenzie 1990: pls. 55–56.
40 Qasr el-Bint in 1898 (before repairs): McKenzie 1990: pls. 67–68a.
41 Hammond 1965.
42 For Muhammad Murshed Khadija; the spelling of Muhammad is followed here in references to him.The short form of his name is Muhammad Khadija, as used in the US.
43 Date: Muhammad Khadija, pers. comm. 27 September 2018; 30 December 2018.

Colonnaded Street paving and the re-erected columns, which provided an axis leading to the Temenos Gate (figs. 47–48). The excavation of the Temple of the Winged Lions, which began in 1974 on the north side of the street, was the first to uncover a substantial area of the hills in the city centre. Thus, when we arrived in Petra in 1981 to work there, the site still felt like a lost city "half as old as time",[44] largely undisturbed and cut off from the outside world.

From 1965 the Bdoul were no longer allowed to live in the main carved tombs or to cultivate crops in the city centre.[45] Despite this, the amount of time they spent living in the other caves of Petra or camping in the valley gradually increased because of the income from tourism and associated archaeological work. Sources of waged income included seasonal work on excavations and in Nazzal's Camp and the Rest House, steady jobs with the Department of Antiquities as guards or drivers, and working on restoration projects. Income generating initiatives of the Bdoul's own included providing horses and donkeys for tourist trips down the Siq and, further afield, acting as guides, and the sale of soft drinks and souvenirs.

The increased income made the Bdoul much better off, so that they were not as a rule malnourished by the beginning of the 1980s. Improved nutrition, combined with vaccinations, the use of antibiotics and free modern healthcare from 1979, greatly reduced the infant mortality rate, but none of these was, at that stage, accompanied by the advocacy of birth control. With six to eight children surviving in a family, the population exploded from the fairly static number of ca. 150 in the middle decades of the twentieth century, to a tribe of about 1000 members in 1981/2. At that time, work was proceeding on building the settlement for the Bdoul at Umm Sayhoun, on the cream-coloured hill north-east of Petra and north-west of Wadi Musa.

Background to the Construction of Umm Sayhoun

In the early 1930s, the government of Transjordan tried to alleviate the poverty of the Bdoul by providing additional medical aid to improve their health, but by the late 1950s, there was little change. Tuberculosis was an enduring problem in the 1960s, when the government organised an attempt to treat it.[46] Moving the Bdoul out of the caves and settling them in houses was seen as a possible way to improve their standard of living and health.

However, when the first formal suggestion to move the Bdoul out of Petra was made in 1968 by the United States National Parks service plan (funded by USAID), it advocated moving them out of the archaeological site on the grounds of the damage which their presence was causing.[47] Attempts to implement this policy in the early 1970s did not result in their departure from the site.[48]

By the 1970s, government-led settlement of nomadic and semi-nomadic peoples in Jordan was part of a wider process across the Middle East and North Africa.[49] Following a comprehensive social study by the Jordanian Department of Housing, the relocation of the Bdoul was recommended by a Jordanian government committee which had been formed by the Prime Minister in 1975 to consider the matter.[50] Umm Sayhoun was chosen as the site for the new village after various other locations in the area had been considered and rejected.[51] UNESCO also recommended the relocation of Petra's inhabitants outside the proposed World Heritage Site.[52]

A study in 1978 by UNESCO consultant Sherif al-Hakim stressed the need for the new housing to be functionally compatible with the Bdoul lifestyle and aesthetically compatible with the archaeological site.[53] In 1979, proposed plans for the designs of the houses were presented to the Bdoul. These plans included domed rooms, adjoining pens for their sheep and goats, stables for their donkeys and horses, and related storage areas.[54] However, the test house was built to a different plan, which the Bdoul rejected as too small and inadequate for their needs.[55] Despite this, the government proceeded to build a settlement of 100 of these houses. The houses were funded by the World Bank as part of the Petra tourism project, which included a restaurant in Petra (the Basin Restaurant near el-Habis) and an international standard hotel in Wadi Musa (the Petra Forum Hotel, now the Crowne Plaza).[56]

After they were finished, the small size of the housing units led to lengthy negotiations with the Bdoul over the agreed maximum number of family members per unit. At the time, the average number of individuals in a Bdoul family was seven.[57] The initial figure suggested per unit seems to have been ten. Eventually, an allocation of six people per unit was agreed.[58] Families with more would receive the adjoining unit to form a pair. This decision revealed that not enough units had been built to house the whole tribe, and consequently the Bdoul continued to refuse to move until 1985.

44 John William Burgon, "Petra" (1845).
45 Ohannessian-Charpin 1986: 389.
46 Van Geldermalsen 2006: 105. The injections were administered by Qublan (Gublan), Dakhilallah's father.
47 Farajat 2012: 150.
48 According to Shoup (1985: 283) the Bdoul threatened armed rebellion to resist moving. According to Farajat (2012: 151) an order of 1970 to achieve the move was not acted upon.
49 Angel 2012: 106.
50 Farajat 2012: 151. The committee included ministers of Interior, Finance, Tourism, and Housing.
51 Shoup 1985: 283; Farajat 2012: 151.
52 Angel 2012: 105.
53 Akrawi 2012: 34.
54 Van Geldermalsen 2006: 266; Farajat 2012: 151.
55 Shoup 1985: 283.
56 Farajat 2012: 152. The hotel is owned by Jordan's Public Social Security Corporation. It is managed by the Intercontinental Hotel Group (IHG) (*World Heritage State of Conservation Report* 2017).
57 Farajat 2012: 151, which accords with my impression. Shoup (1985: 283) suggests it was ten.
58 Shoup 1985: 283; van Geldermalsen 2006: 251–52; Farajat 2012: 151, 152; Mufleh, pers. comm. 1986.

Chapter 3

1981–1982

The Trip to Petra

At the beginning of October 1981, Angela and I set off from Amman on our first field trip to Petra in the Volkswagen combivan of the Sydney University expedition to Pella, driven by its foreman, Abu Isa (Badri Maadi) (Maps 3, 4).[1]

There are two roads from Amman to Petra. The King's Highway follows the route used for millennia, which winds from the plateau down and up the three deep canyons or valleys (called wadis) which run down to the Dead Sea. The Desert Highway, which runs further east across the flat desert from Amman to Aqaba, follows the Hajj pilgrimage route (from Damascus to Mecca), established by Suleiman the Magnificent (1520–66).[2] As the Desert Highway was much faster, it had become the main modern route to Petra. We took it rather than the scenic King's Highway which would have taken most of the day but would have conveyed a sense of the arduous journey in Nabataean and Roman times.

The Desert Highway from Amman ran beside the Hejaz Railway, which had been completed in 1908 and followed the line of the road. Although sections of the railway were blown up by Lawrence of Arabia during World War I, the line from Damascus to Amman and Maʿan was repaired, and a new branch line to Aqaba was added for shipments from the phosphate mines.

In 1981, the Desert Highway was a single carriage road, with one lane in each direction, like the old road from Canberra to Sydney. Most of the vehicles were heavy lorries bringing loads from the port of Aqaba to Amman or continuing on to Iraq. The road was badly pot-holed, so the custom was to drive on the wrong side of the road if necessary in order to avoid the potholes, then quickly move to the correct side of the road in order to pass the oncoming traffic.[3] The split-second timing of this move made the journey very nerve wracking. In addition, oncoming vehicles overtaking frequently occupied the wrong side of the road until the moment when they pulled back in. Headlights were flashed to signal the need for priority when a driver could not pull back in time. The dangers were evident from lorries lying beside the road, which had crashed in the previous few hours, and these scenes were repeated on our subsequent

Fig. 33. The Desert Highway, heading north, 1981 [Angela Phippen].

trips.[4] To reduce the risk, we later tried to travel on Fridays to avoid the lorry traffic.

The desert is flat and treeless, with little or no vegetation (fig. 33), and, further south, the cream soil is covered in nearly black basalt chips. In addition to the Hejaz railway stations, the only historic buildings along the route were the Ottoman Hajj fort of Qatrana, a rectangular building with arrow slits, and the police stations, which have crenellations like small fortresses. The road also passed three potteries, with rows and rows of very large pale cream pots, including those used to hold drinking water.

The only other buildings along the road were restaurants, which were called "rest houses", intended not for tourists, but for the lorry drivers, who were their main customers. They were fairly basic, with linoleum floors and chrome-legged tables with laminex tops, on which they served basic meals, as well as tea or coffee. The main halt for lorry drivers was Qatrana, where the JETT bus also stopped and, like us, tourists would have their first introduction to squat toilets. These consisted of a porcelain panel in the floor with a hole, with a ribbed surface on either side for standing on. It was flushed with water from a plastic jug, with a narrow spout for directing the flow of the minimum amount of water possible. Toilet paper was not supplied.

Eventually, we reached the turnoff for Petra and crossed the desert, devoid of buildings. The landscape gradually

1 Badri Maadi's given name: Alan Walmsley, pers. comm. 17 December 2018.

2 Shoup 1985: 279.

3 Marguerite van Geldermalsen (2006: 129) also comments on this.

4 Marguerite van Geldermalsen (2006: 128) also notes how people she knew had been killed or injured on it.

Fig. 34. Wadi Musa, looking west with the hills of Petra in the background. The highest mountain is Jabal Haroun, 1982.

Fig. 35. Notice at the entrance gate to Petra, in Wadi Musa, 1981/2.

became hilly as the road reached the limestone Shara mountains. Above these cream hills, the dark reddish-brown sandstone mountains of Petra became visible, with the white shrine of Aaron's Tomb glinting on the highest mountain, Jabal Haroun (Mount Aaron). In the foreground, there was the green oasis of the small town of Wadi Musa (Moses' Valley) (fig. 34). At the foot of the cream mountain, between Wadi Musa and Petra, the straight lines of the new Petra Forum Hotel stood out, then under construction.

The road wound down into Wadi Musa past the perennial spring of 'Ain Musa (Moses' Spring), where, according to legend, Moses struck the rock, and water gushed forth. We continued down the main street, which was lined with peppercorn trees and single storey shops, closed with roller blinds. Further down the hill, immediately before the site entrance, there was the only hotel, the Rest House. A sign at the site entrance gate warned against buying antiquities, while also noting that most of them were not authentic (fig. 35).

Entering Petra

The only route into Petra (from Wadi Musa) was via the narrow chasm, the Siq, which tourists had to walk or ride down. We were allowed to drive in the whole way with Abu Isa in the van. The Siq was just wide enough for a jeep or a pickup truck, but not a bus, to drive down it. Before reaching the Siq, passing through the entrance gate, the first monuments came into view on our right. These were a series of monolithic rock-cut tombs ("djinn blocks"), cut free from the rock on four sides (sometimes the burials were in the top) (fig. 36). The first large rock-cut monument appeared on our left. The Bab el-Siq Triclinium had a tomb with four obelisks above it, the Obelisk Tomb (fig. 37).

The entrance to the Siq is marked on either side by the rock-cut sides of an arch, which

Fig. 36. Monolithic tombs near the entrance to Petra, 2018 [Sean Leatherbury].

Fig. 37. Obelisk Tomb and Bab el-Siq Triclinium, 1984.

Fig. 38. The entrance to the Siq which was marked by an arch across it with rock-cut supports, 1986.

Fig. 39. Arch at the entrance of the Siq before it fell down in 1895, photographed by Frank Mason Good in 1866–67 [F. Mason Good, Palestine Exploration Fund P/2036].

had survived until it fell down in 1895 (figs. 38, 39).[5] Before the entrance to the Siq, there is a dam formed by the raised roadway, designed by the Nabataeans to stop flash floods from seasonal rains rushing down the Siq, instead diverting them to Wadi Mudhlim through a tunnel which they had carved from the rock. In 1963, over twenty French tourists and their guide drowned in a flash flood in the Siq before this dam was rebuilt.[6]

The floor of the Siq, which slopes downwards, was covered with worn limestone river pebbles, many of which were quite large (fig. 40). The sides of the Siq are very steep, creating an atmospheric canyon glowing with pink light. We wound along it in the combivan, weaving past the tourists on horses. For them, the only noise was the sound of their horses' hooves on the pebbles echoing off the rock-cut sides of the chasm, adding to the atmospheric approach.

Eventually, we glimpsed the Khasneh between the steep rock faces on either side (fig. 41). It gradually came into view and the chasm opened up in front of it (fig. 42). Like everyone on seeing it for the first time, we found the Khasneh was not only awe-inspiring for its size, but breathtaking for the beauty of its glowing pink colour and fine delicate carving (fig. 43).

Beyond the Khasneh, the chasm narrowed again to form the so-called Outer Siq. As the valley opened up, on our right were large tombs crowned by pairs of staircases, such as Hegr Tomb 813 (fig. 44). On our left, there were small tombs with one or two rows of crowsteps, in the so-called Street of Facades before the Theatre (figs. 45–46). Further along, on our right, there were more large tombs, before the so-called Royal Tombs (the Urn Tomb, Corinthian Tomb, and Palace Tomb) came into view, and the road turned left into the ancient city centre of Petra. Remains of a paved street, beside which some of the columns had been re-erected (fig. 47), led to the Temenos Gate (fig. 48). It was a triple arch which was the entrance to the Temenos (sacred enclosure) of the large temple, the Qasr el-Bint, the only other ancient building which had survived largely still standing (fig. 59). Immediately beyond them, there was the camel-shaped outline of el-Habis, with the taller, flat-topped mountain of Umm el-Biyara beside it, on its south (to the left).

5 McKenzie 1990: 131.

6 Marguerite van Geldermalsen (2006: 139) gives a description of this flood based on the accounts of eye-witnesses, such as her husband, Mohammad Abdallah.

Fig. 40. The Siq, 1981/2.

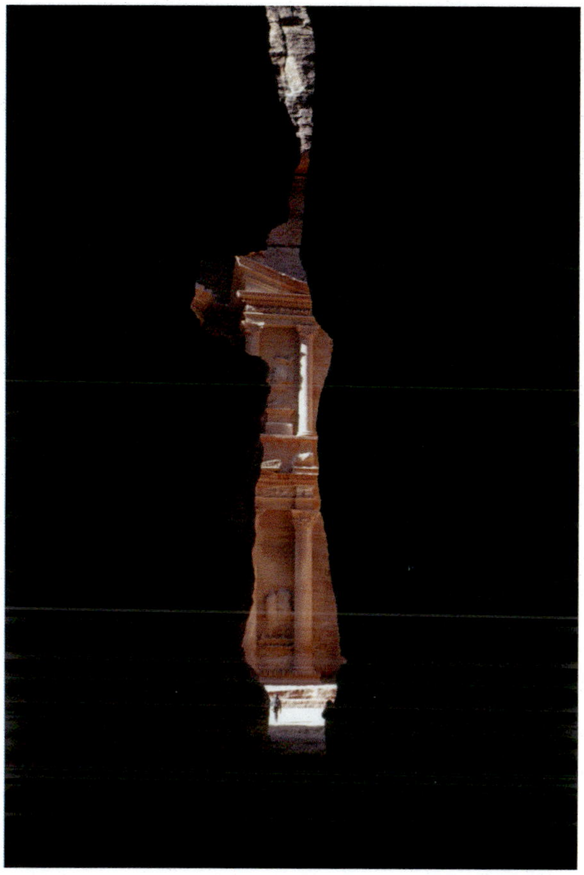

Fig. 41. The Khasneh, when it first comes into view from the Siq, 1981/2.

Fig. 42. The Khasneh, viewed from the exit of the Siq, 1981/2.

Fig. 43. The Khasneh, 1981/2.

Fig. 44. Tomb 813, beyond the Outer Siq, 2015 [Sarah Norodom].

Fig. 45. Pylon Tombs with one or two rows of Assyrian crowsteps in the Street of Facades before reaching the Theatre, 2010.

Fig. 46. The Theatre, on the left, when it first comes into view, 2015 [Otto Nieminen].

Fig. 47. The "Royal Tombs" along the base of el-Khubthah, viewed from the Colonnaded Street, looking east, 2015 [Otto Nieminen].

Fig. 48. The Temenos Gate and the west end of the Colonnaded Street, looking towards el-Habis. The kitchen and Museum are to the right of the trees, 2001.

Arrival at Our Cave

We pulled up in the area in front of el-Habis, unloading our luggage and equipment, which included the theodolite head and its wooden legs, pieces of a metal levelling staff, sleeping bags, and our supplies of tinned and other food.[7]

Beside the Qasr el-Bint, there was the former hotel building known as Nazzal's Camp. It was still used by archaeological teams, but we were going to stay in one of the caves on the side of el-Habis. These caves were rock-cut chambers which had been carved in Nabataean times. The front walls of two of them had not survived and had been replaced, and access to the cave was provided by new stairs and verandahs (fig. 49).

A wide staircase led up to a flat area in front of the first cave, used by Muhammad Murshed Khadija, the director of the tourism project, and his successor, Musa al-Smadi. Narrow steps provided access from that area to a verandah in front of two caves. The one on the left was to be our cave. The cave beside it was a Department of Antiquities office. Winding rock-cut steps continued up to the kitchen cave, which had porthole windows in its new front wall. Further stairs led up to the verandah in front of the Museum, which was in a huge rock-cut room with a high ceiling and very large windows. Off to one side, there were steps down to the toilets.

Like all of these caves, our cave had straight walls and ceilings carved by the Nabataeans, to which a smooth polished concrete floor and an iron frame door had been added in 1961–62 by the Department of Antiquities.[8] The cave was furnished with iron frame beds, foam rubber mattresses, a table, and a couple of chairs, while there were old Museum display cases running along one side wall (figs. 50–51). The window above the door and the one in the door itself were covered with cardboard for privacy and warmth (fig. 52). The cave door looked directly out to Wadi Abu ʿOlleqa (fig. 53).

Next to the door of our cave, there was a large water pot with a rounded bottom in a wooden stand, with a container below it (fig. 52). The water was kept cool by evaporation through the porous clay. (We didn't use it as it was not boiled.) It made me realise that it was possible that similar stands were used for round bottomed amphorae in antiquity,

7 I had carried the theodolite head from Australia. The legs had travelled with the equipment shipped for the Australian expedition to Pella.

8 Muhammad Khadija began working in Petra in 1961. Although el-Habis did have Nabataean houses on its east face, Muhammad Khadija (pers. comm. 11 January 2004) saw graves in the floors of the Museum cave and the caves used as offices by the Department of Antiquities before their floors were cemented over.

Fig. 49. The caves on the east side of el-Habis, with the balcony in front of our cave, the kitchen (with port-hole windows), and the Museum (top right), 1981.

Fig. 50. Museum cabinets in our cave, 1981/2 [Angela Phippen].

Fig. 51. Angela on her bed in our cave, 1981/2.

Fig. 52. The water pot near our cave door, 1981 [Angela Phippen].

rather than standing them up by burying their bases in the ground.

The toilets were below the stairs up to the Museum. They had no wall on one side (fig. 49), leaving an amazing view of the valley across to the "Royal Tombs", with a sheer drop below (fig. 54).[9]

9 The septic tank, like that of Nazzal's Camp, was emptied by a tanker which squeezed down the Siq and through the Temenos Gate. Until the Basin Restaurant opened, these were the only public toilets in the site.

Fig. 53. View from our cave to Wadi Abu 'Olleqa, 1981/2.

Fig. 54. View from the el-Habis toilets across to el-Khubthah, 1981/2.

Muhammad Murshed Khadija

Muhammad Murshed A. Khadija was in charge of the restoration of the monuments for the tourism project when we first arrived,[10] and the Department of Antiquities inspector was Nabil al-Qadi.

On our first evening, we sat outside Muhammad Khadija's cave, and he invited us to Wadi Musa for a drink at the Rest House. This was a test, because if women drank alcohol, they were considered available for other things, and an agreement to have an alcoholic drink was seen as tantamount to agreeing to go the whole way. In order not to be unfriendly, we agreed to accompany him to Wadi Musa, but only if Abu Isa came too.

We all hopped into Muhammad's Department of Antiquities Toyota land cruiser. He drove up the Siq in the dark at very high speed like a maniac. This was clearly another test, but of our nerves, to see if we broke down. He knew the split-second timing of every bend in its narrow winding route, as the vehicle sped over the road of loose pebbles, some quite large. It was unbelievably dangerous.

The Rest House in Wadi Musa was the only hotel there. It was built in 1964,[11] with its ground floor enclosing one of the tombs (Tomb 4). The tomb and its rock-cut colonnaded forecourt were used as its restaurant and bar, with parts of the colonnades extending into the foyer. The restaurant was lit by Damascene lanterns hanging from the ceiling, the light from their pierced brass and coloured glass creating an atmosphere which brought to mind Aladdin's cave.[12] The choice of soft drinks, from which we made a selection, was basically limited to Fanta, Pepsi, or 7Up, as in Petra.

The next morning, before Abu Isa left, we had breakfast with Muhammad Khadija and Musa al-Smadi at the table on the concrete patio in front of their cave (fig. 55). Breakfast was laid out in a series of small bowls, containing *labaneh* (thick yoghurt), *hummus* garnished with lemon juice and olive oil, diced tomato and cucumber salad, *zaʿata* (mixed herbs), and olive oil. Each of these was eaten by scooping it up in a small piece of Arab bread ("pita bread"). The *zaʿata*

10 Muhammad Khadija retired by the end of 1981, when he was succeeded by his assistant Musa al-Smadi.

11 Muhammad Khadija, pers. comm. 27 September 2018. He worked on excavating a sounding in front of it with Philip Hammond in 1961. Shoup (1985: 281) gives the date as the 1950s. According to Russell (1993: 30, citing USAID 1988: 40, 41), it was constructed in the early 1960s, paid for by USAID.

12 The Rest House was subsequently pulled down in 1991, so that the tomb, its facade, and courtyard in front were revealed again (fig. 283).

Fig. 55. Muhammed Khadija's cave, 1981.

Fig. 56. The garden in front of Muhammed Khadija's cave, left-hand (north) side of the wall of capitals, 1981.

Fig. 57. The garden in front of Muhammed Khadija's cave, right-hand (south) side of the wall of capitals, 1981.

was eaten by dipping a piece of bread in olive oil, then in the *za'ata*, and any piece of bread was only dipped into the bowls a single time. It was bad manners to bite from a piece of bread and then dip it in again. Customs such as this maintained hygiene. They had Arab bread made with white flour and yeast from the bakery in Wadi Musa where their driver went for it each day.[13] Breakfast was served with sweet black tea.

As with the amphora in our cave, local customs provided us with further understanding of Nabataean ones. Nabataean bowls are about ca. 18 cm (7 inches) in diameter and shallow with either a very small base, or none at all. They are made of fine pottery which is 1/8 of an inch (2 mm) thick and would break if any pressure were applied with a knife and fork. In Sydney, I had not been able to work out how these bowls were used. It was immediately obvious when seeing a Jordanian meal served with a variety of dishes, as at breakfast, lunch, or a *mezza*, how Nabataean bowls would have been perfect for this purpose.

In front of Muhammad Khadija's patio, there was a garden with canna lilies, geraniums, bougainvillea, and other flowering plants, creating a green haven. This garden was protected from goats and children by a stone wall with a wooden gate. From the outside, the stone wall looked as if it was made of plain re-used Nabataean stone blocks (fig. 55). Sitting at the table, once my eyes adjusted to the glare, I noticed that the wall was made of the top blocks of limestone capitals decorated with exquisitely cut flowers and leaves (figs. 56–57), which included poppies and even grape vines. Each block would have had a lower block decorated with a ring of acanthus leaves (fig. 58).

Muhammad Khadija was the king of Petra. Every year, he ensured that the rock-cut paths to monuments, such as the Deir and the High Place, were repaired after the winter rains. The rock-cut steps were worn so that they had to be built up in some places with extra blocks of stone held in place by cement. Despite this, the sudden run-off from the winter rains each year would dislodge or wash away some of these blocks.

Starting Work at the Qasr el-Bint

We began work by making trial readings on the theodolite on the Qasr el-Bint, the large roofless temple near our cave (fig. 59). In my earlier research in Sydney, I had noticed from photographs that the cornices on the tomb facades at Medain Saleh in Saudi Arabia seemed to become plainer and flatter with time. Medain Saleh was the southernmost Nabataean outpost and had tombs related to those at Petra. Unlike the

13 As late as 1978, Wadi Musa did not have a bakery (van Geldermalsen 2006: 74).

Fig. 58. One of the capitals in fig. 57, later reconstructed with the lower drum of acanthus leaves, 1986.

Petra tombs, however, some of the tombs at Medain Saleh had inscriptions on them giving their dates. Attempting to show scientifically the differences of the cornice mouldings at Petra required cross-section drawings of them. Because the mouldings were so high up, I developed a method of doing this from the ground using trigonometry, with a theodolite to measure angles, and a tape measure to measure distance. I devised the method from that used to measure the distance between two points which could not be reached on the other side of a river, but I rotated the plane of the measurements by 90 degrees.[14]

The interior of the Qasr el-Bint was filled with timber scaffolding for a French architect, François Larché, who was measuring and drawing the whole building in detail, including all of the stucco (fig. 59).[15] Timber was in such short supply that the scaffolding of the Department of Antiquities had been brought down to Petra from Jerash.

A Wedding Procession

While we were measuring the Qasr el-Bint, a noisy procession appeared, coming down Jabal Mʿaysrah to the north, and crossed the wadi in front of us heading south. It was a wedding party on their way to collect the bride from the other side of Petra. They were chanting, with the leader firing his gun in the air. They returned with the bride on a camel. The bride was wrapped in a beige cloth, with a man dressed in white on the camel in front of her to steer it (fig. 60). When the bride reached the groom's house on Jabal Mʿaysrah, they hoisted a large white flag.[16]

The Bdoul wedding custom was not to court until they were fifteen. The boys generally married when they were about twenty. When they went to ask for the bride, they signed the marriage papers, and then the groom came to collect the bride when he was ready. In this case, it was about one year later. About one week before collecting the bride, the Bdoul would start celebrating with dancing and chanting at night and shooting guns into the sky. On the last day, they would go in a procession to collect the bride from her house and bring her to the groom's house.

The Night Sky after Dinner

At the end of the day, we had to be back in time to cook dinner in daylight. Our cave and the kitchen did have electric light, but it only worked when the generator at Nazzal's

14 McKenzie 1985; 1990: 128–29 (summary), diagrams 4–6.

15 Zayadine et al. 2003.

16 Marguerite van Geldermalsen (2006: 22–28, 35) describes the festivities and formalities of a Bdoul wedding in 1978.

Fig. 59. The Qasr el-Bint (left) and Nazzal's Camp (right) from our cave, 1981/2.

Fig. 60. Wedding party, near the Qasr el-Bint, taking the bride to the groom's house, 1981 [Angela Phippen].

Fig. 61. Water tank for the kitchen, 1981/2.

Camp was running, if someone else was paying for the fuel to run it, and it was kept in working order. Tilley lamps were also used. They were pressurised kerosene lamps with fragile silk mantles and potentially dangerous. Although they provided a good light, they were very temperamental so that the evening was often used repairing one by the light of another. For us it was simplest to get up very early, cook by daylight, and use candles once it was dark.

We had to be careful to optimise our use of water. We would warm a bucket of water once a week for a sponge bath and to wash our hair. There was a sink with a tap with running water in the kitchen, supplied from a tank above it (fig. 61). This tank was filled by a youth who brought jerry cans of water from the spring in Wadi Siyyagh, around the back of el-Habis (fig. 62). He had two donkeys which each carried four 20-litre (4.4 Imperial gallons) plastic jerry cans, so that in one trip he could add 160 litres to the tank. The Bdoul women also obtained their water from the spring. They each loaded two or four jerry cans of water on their donkeys, depending on whether or not they were riding. Each evening we boiled all our drinking water for the next day for 20 minutes in a large saucepan, leaving it to cool overnight.

The kitchen had a gas ring, run from a gas canister, for cooking. There was no refrigeration, but I ensured our supplies were designed so that our dinners included one helping each of protein, carbohydrate, and vegetables. The fish or meat was tinned, consisting of tuna, salmon, or corned beef.

Fig. 62. Delivering water in jerry cans to the tank above the kitchen, 1981/2 [Angela Phippen].

We avoided bully beef and tinned mackerel, as we found their taste totally obscured any other flavours and could not be disguised. We also discovered that tinned frankfurters made without pork bore no relationship to the real thing. The meat or fish was accompanied by fried tomatoes and onion, along with potatoes, pasta, or rice. Our fresh vegetables (potatoes, onions, capsicums, tomatoes, and cucumbers) had to be purchased in Wadi Musa, either by asking the driver of the Department of Antiquities to buy them, or by getting a weekly lift there. Sometimes as a treat, I made pancakes using al-Ghazal vegetable ghee, flour, and eggs, served with Polish sour cherry jam and *labaneh* (thick yoghurt). Angela's signature recipe was tinned salmon and potato fishcakes, a traditional family recipe she called salmon rissoles.

We ate dinner sitting on the verandah looking out across the valley (as also at breakfast time, fig. 63), with the Qasr el-Bint in the foreground and el-Khubthah with the "Royal Tombs" in the distance. For hygiene, we washed the dishes in running water. As we had used the ledge of the verandah as our table, we stacked the plates in pairs facing inwards, so that the bottom surface of each (which had been on the verandah ledge) did not touch the inside of the plate below. One advantage of preparing dinner by daylight was that, afterwards, we sat on the verandah of the cave looking out east across the site towards the hills as the sun set behind us. When the full sun was on them, the colours were not as red as when they were in the shade (fig. 64). As the sun set, its light dispersed across the valley, which changed colour, as the cream hills north of the outcrops of pink sandstone of el-Khubthah gradually turned pink. They would then return to their original colour before the sun set.

Fig. 63. Angela at breakfast time on our balcony, 1981/2.

Fig. 64. View looking east to el-Khubthah, 1981/2.

After sunset, we watched the night sky. On about the third evening, Angela called me to watch the moon rise (fig. 65). We noticed how it rose further north and later each night, as its size gradually changed. Without the glow from city lights bleaching the sky, the stars were much more visible. Before the moon came out, the powdery part of the Milky Way could be seen, which I had thought required a telescope, as I had only seen it in books. Different types of stars could also be distinguished. We saw a falling star – we had not realised they actually existed. One star, which rose sometime after sunset, twinkled red and blue when we looked at it through the small hand-held telescope we had brought for examining details on the tombs.

Sitting watching the hills and the night sky as they changed became a new pleasure, and it was one which would also have been part of life in Nabataean Petra.

Measuring the Khasneh

In order to maximise the hours of daylight we had for the theodolite readings, we would get up at 5 am. Angela, whose last name was Phippen, dealt with this early rise by changing her watch to "Phippen Petra Time", so that she felt she was getting up at 7 am.

By first light, we ate breakfast on the verandah. Breakfast consisted of Arab bread and jam, with "La vache qui rit" (Laughing Cow) processed cheese as a butter substitute, as it did not require refrigeration. We also had tea or coffee, without milk. Nescafé was so expensive that we were limited to one cup per day as a luxury. If the Arab bread was becoming stale, as it did when it was two or three days old, we would freshen it over the gas ring.[17] Corn flakes were not on our menu, as they were very expensive and needed water for reconstituted powdered milk.

We packed our supplies for lunch – Arab bread, a box of "La vache qui rit" cheese wedges, two cucumbers, and a tin of sardines (or sometimes tuna) – and filled our water bottles with the water boiled the night before. Sometimes instead of Arab bread we had *shraak*, the unleavened Bedouin bread made with coarsely ground flour, cooked like a large stretchy pancake on a large domed iron plate (*sāj*). However, as the leavened Arab bread from Wadi Musa was made with more finely ground white flour, it provided us with more energy, and we asked the Department of Antiquities driver to bring some from Wadi Musa every few days. Sometimes when we visited the Bdoul, they offered us a piece of *taboun* bread, which was about an inch or so thick and baked in a specially made oven which used dung as fuel.[18]

Fig. 65. The moon rising over el-Khubthah in the east as the sun sets in the west, 1981/2.

As we headed off, the sun would be rising over el-Khubthah. The paving of the Colonnaded Street became visible before the other buildings, as its crystalline structure caught the light (fig. 66). If there had been a full moon, when we looked back towards el-Habis in the dawn light, we would see the moon setting (fig. 67).

We walked around to the Khasneh (fig. 68). I carried the theodolite head in my red backpack, which I had used for bushwalking, and we arrived by about 6:30 am. The old guard, Abu Ali al-Tweissi from Wadi Musa, swept the inside of the Khasneh and picked up any litter in front of it.[19] He then collected twigs to make a small fire in an old tin set sideways, to boil the teapot (fig. 69), and invited us to drink *shay* with him. It was amazing how small a fire was needed to boil a kettle of tea compared with the fires I made in Australia for the purpose when I went bushwalking. We also noticed how dried donkey or camel droppings made good fuel.

We began to set up our first theodolite station, marking it with a rock too large to be kicked by a tourist. However, Abu Ali came and cleaned the rock away. The vendors came at 8:00 am and opened their tables, which contained the souve-

17 The social taboo on throwing bread out was also a reminder to try to use it all; otherwise we had to lose it somewhere the animals could help themselves. Marguerite van Geldermalsen (2006: 145) describes her first experience of this custom.

18 Marguerite van Geldermalsen (2006: 75) provides more detail about *taboun* bread.

19 Abu Ali means father of Ali, who would have been his eldest son.

Fig. 66. Sunrise over el-Khubthah, with the paving of the Colonnaded Street glowing in the first light, 1981/2.

Fig. 67. The moon setting over el-Habis, 1981/2.

Fig. 68. The Khasneh, 2003.

Fig. 69. The guard of the Khasneh, Abu Ali al-Tweissi, 1982 [Angela Phippen].

nirs (fig. 70).[20] The metal tables had lids, so that the souvenirs could be locked in them overnight. Abu Ali lay on the ledge of the Khasneh and went to sleep.

In the quiet time before the tourists would arrive, we talked to Mohammad Abdallah Othman (Marguerite's husband), who was one of the vendors, about how much they charged the tourists.[21] Besides postcards and packets of slides, they sold other souvenirs. For a double-edged Bedouin knife (*shabriya*) with a hammered metal sheath, Mohammad charged three to twelve dinars. If it had a gazelle horn handle, it was five to fifteen dinars. These knives were locally made, not imported.[22] Mohammad carved primitive sculptures out of fine grain limestone.[23] With great pride, he showed us the lamps he had baked.

20 Marguerite van Geldermalsen (2006: 184) describes how her husband, Mohammad Abdallah Othman, made a metal table for himself (presumably, his was the first of these tables), so that he did not need to carry his stock home each day.

21 Marguerite van Geldermalsen (2006: 117–18) also describes the variety of items they sold and the differences between the tourists depending on their nationality.

22 Marguerite van Geldermalsen (2006: 204) describes an itinerant artist, Riyadh Hoshaan, who made these knives with ornate sheaths. They were also stocked by the shop in Amman where Mohammad bought many of the souvenirs he sold to the other vendors. Examples in fig. 232.

23 Marguerite van Geldermalsen (2006: 261) describes how Mohammad would find the best pieces of fine limestone to carve them. The Nabataeans had used this limestone for finer details, such as floral capitals, as well as column bases. Margaret Murray (1939: 31), who was in Petra in 1934, describes the Bdoul sheikh making such limestone figures and staining the stone.

Fig. 70. The vendors and camel in front of the Khasneh waiting for tourists, 1981.

Fig. 71. South doorway of the Khasneh vestibule with the theodolite, 1981/2 [Angela Phippen].

Fig. 72. Khasneh, badly damaged sculpture of a Tyche in front of the circular pavilion, 1986.

The other main souvenirs were not made in Jordan. The cast bronze imitation dagger paper knives were made in Syria, as were the small bronze vases. The vendors put the bronzes in the ground for two weeks, so that they turned green, and then they told the tourists that they were "ancient". The silver jewellery with scarabs set into it was made in Egypt. One vendor had a bronze cross with broad arms with German writing on the back in capital letters with the words joined together, which he sold as Byzantine. He even told Germans that it had a Nabataean inscription on the back. They also sold fake coins, which were a greenish colour and easily distinguishable from real Nabataean ones by their size alone. They were about 2 cm in diameter (or about the size of an American quarter, a British 10 pence piece or a 1-euro coin), whereas real Nabataean ones are about 1.2–1.5 cm or less in diameter. One of the vendors had a silver tin full of genuine Nabataean coins which he showed us, assuming that we knew the others were blatant fakes.

As it was a quiet day with not many tourists, they sold very little. The solitary camel there was well treated, even pampered, by its owner Juma Samaheen. He gave it rounds of Arab bread for lunch, and it ate half of one in one mouthful. It could also drink Pepsi from a bottle. Then it became bored, and decided to nibble the souvenirs, beginning with a brass pot. Finally, it laid its long neck flat along the ground and went to sleep, while the vendors relaxed too (fig. 70).

We began making the theodolite readings, running the telescope from the top of the mouldings downwards, with me dictating the readings to Angela, who wrote them in a school exercise book (fig. 71). With the magnification of the telescope, we could see details of the very ornate decoration on the Khasneh which are not normally noticed by the naked eye, even if the theodolite image was upside down.

The top storey of the Khasneh had a circular pavilion (tholos) between the two half-pediments. The circular structure had a badly damaged figure of a Tyche, goddess of good fortune, draped and holding a patera (dish) in her right hand, with a horn of plenty (cornucopia) resting on her left arm (fig. 72). Through the theodolite, we could see the detail on the acroterion on top of the pediment below this figure, a motif which I recognised as the horns of the Egyptian goddess Isis (fig. 73). Besides some flowers, this Isis crown motif had ears of wheat on either side. Isis was attested elsewhere in Petra, and the ears of wheat alluded to the identification of Isis with Demeter, the Greek goddess of corn who was also associated with mourning.[24] Years later, research revealed that Nabataean queens, the wives of the Nabataean king Aretas IV (9 BC – AD 40) were represented on coins as Isis, with the Isis crown on their head, indicating that they had become goddesses.[25] The function of the Khasneh had been a mystery, but these associations suggest that it almost certainly was a royal tomb. Its probable role as a tomb was further indicated by the discovery of a tomb directly below it in 2003 (pp. 203–204).

The most surprising discovery which the theodolite telescope revealed was that the facade of the Khasneh had painted details on it. The sandstone was so fine that these details were painted directly onto it, without even needing a layer of plaster to smooth it first. On the lower frieze, the small rectangular teeth-like blocks, known as dentils, had reddish-brown paint between them, accentuating their shape (fig. 74). Even more amazing were the fine painted details on the frieze below them, with lines marking the ribs, or carinations, visible on a vase. The quality of the fine carving and the creativity and variations in the flowers on the columns' beautifully preserved capitals were stunning (fig. 75). We would come back on another day to photograph the details with a strong telephoto lens and a tripod.

Details on the Khasneh, such as the capitals, were in pristine condition because the structure was in a chasm, so that it was not as badly exposed to being worn by the sand blowing against it as the other monuments were. The amount of loose sand in front of the Khasneh had further been reduced by the oleanders filling the area in front of it for much of the past millennium and a half. However, there was man-made iconoclastic damage to its figures and animals, whose heads had been knocked off, and their arms and legs attacked (figs. 68, 72).[26] In addition, musket balls and bullets had left holes pockmarking the figure of Isis and the rock-cut urn following attempts to dislodge the urn at the top. According to legend, this held gold treasure – hence the monument's Arabic name, the Khasneh (the Treasury).[27]

Fig. 73. Symbol of the Egyptian goddess Isis at the top of the pediment of the Khasneh (below the statue in fig. 72), 1986.

Fig. 74. Khasneh, vase with painted carinations on entablature of the lower order, 1986.

Fig. 75. Khasneh, southmost floral capital on lower order, 1986.

24 McKenzie et al. 2013: vol. 1, 203–204.

25 Haldu and her successor Shaqilat, the wives of Aretas IV (9 BC–AD 40): McKenzie et al. 2013: vol. 1, 203, figs. 352–53. Ptolemaic queens were also deified (before 30 BC).

26 For a detailed analysis of iconoclasm in Petra, see McKenzie et al. 2013: vol. 1, 269–90.

27 The Bdoul call it *edj-Djarrah* (The Urn): Canaan 1930: 8, 41; van Geldermalsen 2006: 106.

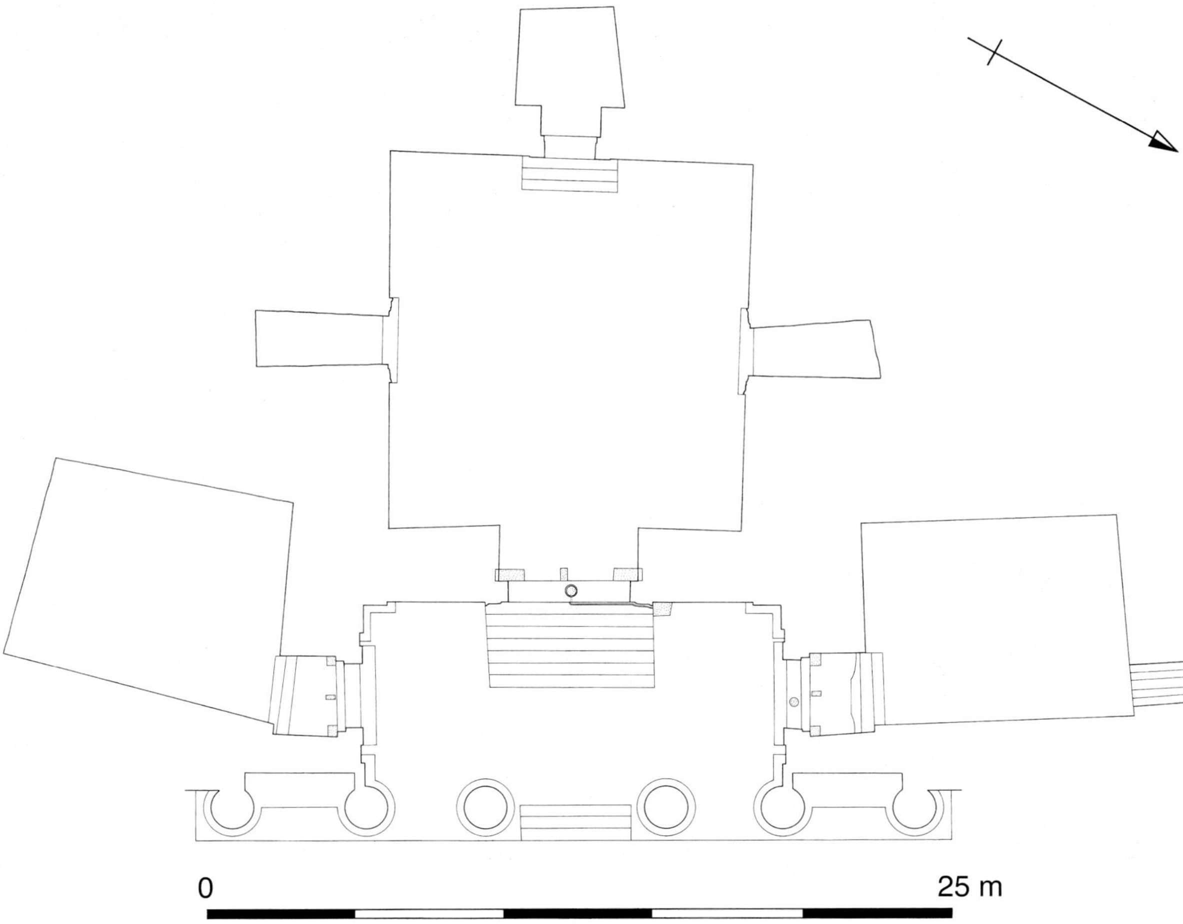

Fig. 76. Khasneh, plan.

Nearly all the rock-cut tombs at Petra have only a single chamber behind the facade. By contrast, the Khasneh has a side chamber on either side of the portico, and the main chamber has a further inner chamber in its back wall (fig. 76). The main chamber had a large *loculus* in the left-hand and right-hand side walls. *Loculi* are cuttings for holding the sarcophagi and coffins in which bodies are buried, and the *loculi* in the Khasneh are larger than those in other tombs. The details on the frames of these *loculi* in the main chamber, and those in the doorway leading to the inner chamber, were eroded by moisture which came down inside the chamber (fig. 77).[28]

Opposite the Khasneh, the top part of a two-sided tomb with small pilasters on the top of it (Tomb 64.1) protruded from the ground. The fact that the top of the tomb was visible above the current ground level indicated that in Nabataean times the ground level in front of the Khasneh would have been much lower (fig. 78).

At the end of the day, we headed back to our cave, with the theodolite legs and level being given a lift on a horse (fig. 79). On the way, in the Outer Siq, we passed a Hegr Tomb (No. 69) which we had visited earlier in the day. Inside, it was littered with lots of little piles of toilet paper. The dung beetles and nature had dealt with the rest. After that, whenever we used a cave, as we did when out in the day time, we burnt our toilet paper afterwards. We always carried a box of matches on us, which we also used for offering to light cigarettes, the fires for tea, and our gas stove.[29]

Dakhilallah's Shop

In the late afternoon, we would come back and sit outside the little store below our cave and have a Fanta or *shay*. The store was run by Dakhilallah, when he wasn't working as a stonemason on the monuments (fig. 80). When we arrived, Dakhilallah was saying his prayers to Allah, as he did each day after the sun went down, standing up and kneeling a few times, facing south-east. We were often joined by the black and white cat, Keenya (fig. 63), which was named after the eucalyptus trees near Nazzal's Camp. Its fur was slightly pink, saturated with Petra sand.

28 For later observations on this erosion, see pp. 233–40. When I later stayed in Abu Shaher's cave, on a subsequent visit, the roof leaked when it rained.

29 Angela Phippen notes: "It is important to remember that in 1981/82, in the entirety of Petra, there was only one location where there were public toilets, and that was below the Museum, near our 'sleeping' cave, which could be as much as an hour away from where we were working during the day." (pers. comm. to A. T. Reyes, 22 September 2019)

Fig. 77. Khasneh, main chamber, looking south-west, 1986.

Fig. 78. Angela on top of Tomb 64.1, opposite the Khasneh. The rest of it was below the present ground level, indicating a lower ground level when it was carved.

Fig. 79. Returning from work, with the theodolite head in my backpack and the levelling staff on horseback, 1981 [Angela Phippen].

Fig. 80. Dakhilallah and Angela outside his shop, 1981/2.

Fig. 81. Dakhilallah and Mohammad al-Jamadeh inside Dakhilallah's shop, 1981/2.

The Fanta came in small glass bottles which were carefully kept after drinking and counted for sending back to the bottling plant for the next batch (fig. 80, far left). They were quite worn on the outside from all those trips. They had crown seals on top, which required a bottle opener, or a substitute, such as a souvenir bronze lion, to open them. *Shay* is sweet tea. It was made with one small Duralex tumbler of sugar per pot, and about a teaspoon of tea. The teapot was heated on a fire, and brought to the boil three times, ensuring that the water was well boiled. Everyone served the *shay* in small Duralex tumblers (to the right of the tea chest, fig. 81). The tea had a very smoky flavour, like Australian billy tea when made over a fire in the bush.

Inside, Dakhilallah's shop looked like an old Australian country store, with the shelves made from stacked wooden boxes which were tipped sideways (fig. 81). In a glass-fronted cabinet in the corner, there was a photograph of King Hussein of Jordan, whom Dakhilallah greatly admired. The ceiling was smoke blackened from fires, when it would have been inhabited by the Bdoul in the past.

The shop was a gathering point, especially in the late afternoon. It was not primarily for tourists, but rather for most of the basic supplies needed in Petra. In those days, there was just one brand for many items in much of Jordan. The essential items in Dakhilallah's shop included boxes of locally-made matches, and tea leaves in a large tea chest, as well as tins of al-Ghazal vegetable ghee, small and large boxes of locally-made plain biscuits, "La vache qui rit" processed cheese, tinned tomato paste, tinned sardines, tall cans of Unium lunch meat, and Polish jam. The sardine tins had to be opened with a metal "key", which was not always attached to the tin. The key had a slit in it which hooked onto the strip of metal that was wound around the side of the tin as it opened. If the key was lost, it was very difficult to open the tin easily. Dakhilallah also stocked a few other items, such as enamel bowls, biro pens, and batteries for torches.

Dakhilallah also sold Polish-made blue enamel teapots and boxes of small Duralex tumblers, which were ubiquitous in Petra, as people drink *shay* all day. We bought these as they were the most evocative souvenir of Bdoul life in Petra. The few souvenirs he stocked for tourists included some brass ashtrays and small jugs. He also sold imitation Nabataean lamps he had made of plaster of Paris and then painted. Dakhilallah told us that Diana Kirkbride, the archaeologist, had taught him the technique for making the moulds for them. As she had excavated in Petra and Beidha in the late 1950s and early 1960s, he must have been quite young when she showed him. He could make ten of the lamps in one day. Like Mohammad Abdallah, Dakhilallah also made pottery lamps by pressing the clay into two moulds and joining the two halves of the lamp, as the Nabataeans had done.

Dakhilallah, a Modern Nabataean Stonemason

I showed Muhammad Khadija my honours year thesis, in which I had proposed the theory that the classical decoration on the monuments at Petra, such as the cornice mouldings, became simpler with time. The aim of our fieldwork was to record the classical details on the main monuments in order to test that theory, which involved dividing the monuments into groups based on their decorative details. Because some of the monuments had been dated by excavated evidence or inscriptions, it was possible to place some of the groups in a sequence. I used the photographs in my thesis to explain the theory to Muhammad.

One of the key dated monuments was the Temenos Gate. The relevant details on it included a bust of a figure with a spear which was carved in a simple style. It was *in situ* on the gate. Muhammad Khadija insisted that Dakhilallah had carved it. We asked Dakhilallah to come with us to the gate, and he confirmed, with great pride, that the bust was his work (fig. 82).[30] This was a big shock to me, because it could no longer be used as evidence. In subsequent work I did identify an authentic bust from the gate, which also had a simple style in its drapery. However, the basic point remained, which was that care should be taken when using restored monuments as evidence, as it was essential to be certain which parts of them were original and which were not in order to avoid unwittingly using those as evidence.

A related problem arose when ancient pieces from another building were used to reconstruct a monument which they did not originally come from. An example of this was the two columns in front of the Temenos Gate which had initially been rebuilt with small drums supporting elephant-head capitals, now known to have come from the Great Temple.[31] The columns and capitals had subsequently been taken down, when the mistake was realised. Blocks were also sometimes restored on their original monument but in the wrong position. This occurred on the Theatre, where an upside down lower drum of a Nabataean capital was used as a base for one of the columns.[32]

Mufleh

One of the people around el-Habis was Mufleh, whose home was at the back of the mountain (fig. 83). He had married a Swiss woman, whose Arabic name was Nawal, and they had a small daughter. They were there at the beginning of our visit, until their daughter became very ill with diarrhea, and Nawal took her to Switzerland for treatment to save her.

Mufleh brought three pale yellow scorpions to show us. They were about 2–3 inches (5–8 cm) long. At the front, they had pincers like a lobster. At the end of their tail they had a very fine thorn, which was about one eighth of an inch (2 mm) long, with a bag of poison behind it, which was one eighth of an inch (2 mm) in diameter. Mufleh put the scorpions on the sand, then would taunt them by stroking them with a stick, to try to make them to curl back on themselves and poison themselves with the poisonous thorn at the end of their tail.

Scorpion stings are very poisonous and can be fatal. A scorpion sting can kill babies and children, while most adults have a bad reaction, but do not die from it.[33] We needed to shake out our shoes in the morning to be sure scorpions were not lurking in them, although we did not have trouble with them in our cave.[34] The risk of a scorpion sting was the main reason that it was essential to wear closed shoes, not sandals, when walking around the sandy site.[35] Because Australians

Fig. 82. Dakhilallah below the panel with a bust with two arrows, which he carved for it when it was being restored, 1981.

30 The blocks with vegetal decoration above and below it were ancient ones put back up in the restoration.

31 Parr 1980: 145, fig. 4.

32 McKenzie 1990: 144.

33 Marguerite van Geldermalsen (2006: 111) gives examples of how scorpion stings could be fatal to small children.

34 Marguerite van Geldermalsen (2006: 230–31) notes how she and Mohammad had considerable problems with them in their cave some years and not other years.

35 One of our English colleagues was stung when wearing sandals, and another one by a scorpion in a shoe.

Fig. 83. Mufleh, 1986.

are used to native spiders, such as red-backs, if they pick up a rock to look underneath it, they automatically turn it over and drop it as they glance at it quickly, before picking it up again. This method was essential in Petra too because of the scorpions. By contrast, the English people on site would pick up a rock and hold it, risking a direct encounter with a scorpion.

On another occasion Mufleh brought three Nabataean coins he had found at al-Katuteh. He cleaned them overnight in lemon juice. Each time it rained, the sand would move to reveal small Nabataean coins. After a while, we began to notice them as our eyes became used to recognising them in the freshly moved sand. With practice, this became easy.

Mufleh would often keep us company on our balcony chatting in the early evening, usually while he mended a Tilley lamp. We never invited him or any of the other men into our cave, nor did they ask to come into it.[36] Before we left Amman, Penny Vickers, the secretary who was running the British Institute while the Director, Crystal-M. Bennett, was on leave in England, advised me to draw a clear line at the door and to enforce it for both western and Arab men. It was essential to have the same rule for both to avoid misunderstandings and to protect our reputations.

36 The only exception was the Jordanian archaeologist Dr Fawzi Zayadine, who simply walked in one day uninvited.

Fig. 84. View, looking west, with Umm el-Biyara on the left, 1982.

Fig. 85. Zibb Farʿoun, 1982.

Fig. 86. Al-Katuteh, Nabataean city rubbish dump, 1981 [Angela Phippen].

Umm el-Biyara

One afternoon, Mufleh offered to take us up Umm el-Biyara, the tall flat-topped mountain to the south of our cave (fig. 84). It was a source of fascination as it was so steep and apparently inaccessible. As it was so difficult to find the route up and down, it was essential to go with a guide to show the way between the fallen rocks and carved steps. In a subsequent year when I was in Petra, some young archaeologists from the Sydney University expedition to Pella insisted on going up without a guide, and one of them had to be rescued by helicopter from the rock ledge on which they had become stuck.

The path up Umm el-Biyara had not been repaired, unlike the paths up to the Deir and the High Place. The path up Umm el-Biyara is so difficult that at times we had to go on our hands and knees over loose rocks, and the ascent is so steep that it felt like something to be done only once in a lifetime. Part of the way, there is a rock-cut "ceremonial" ramp. At the top, there is a 900 foot (ca. 300 m) sheer drop down to Petra, and a fantastic view. As Umm el-Biyara is higher than the mountains of Petra (such as el-Khubthah in which the "Royal Tombs" are carved), the monuments appear smaller when seen from the top of Umm el-Biyara. When they are viewed from the valley within Petra, they appear to be very high (fig. 64).

The top of Umm el-Biyara, which is surprisingly flat, has the remains of 7th- to 6th-century BC dwellings built of a slate-like rock by the Edomites, who were the predecessors of the Nabataeans mentioned in the Old Testament.[37] These dwellings were excavated by Crystal-M. Bennett in 1960–1965.[38] There are also bell-shaped rock-cut cisterns, lined with plaster – hence, the mountain's Arabic name Umm el-Biyara, "Mother of the Cisterns". We noticed a Nabataean column base, which suggested that there had also been monumental Nabataean buildings there.[39] It was amazing to imagine anyone living there when access was so difficult, although for the Edomites this would have provided some protection. As Mufleh was not always as sensible as might be hoped, we had started our climb up Umm el-Biyara with

37 On whether there was any continuity between the Edomites and Nabataeans: Bienkowski 2013.

38 Bienkowski 2011.

39 Nabataean structures on Umm el-Biyara were explored in more detail from 2010, revealing that they included a bathhouse (Schmid et al. 2012: 75–85).

him relatively late in the day. Consequently, our descent was made in a tremendous hurry in the fading dusk light.

While the earliest buildings in Petra were on Umm el-Biyara, the latest construction was on el-Habis, where there were remains of a small Crusader fortress built in the 12th century (ca. 1127–1188/9).[40] Although the Edomite occupation was on Umm el-Biyara, when Petra began to be settled by the Nabataeans in the fourth century BC, it was in the city centre near the later sites of the Qasr el-Bint temple and the Colonnaded Street. In the late first century BC and the first century AD, the monumental buildings constructed by the Nabataeans in the city centre included the Qasr el-Bint and the Temple of the Winged Lions. After Petra and the Nabataean kingdom became part of the Roman Empire in AD 106, structures continued to be erected in the city centre, contrary to what had been assumed when we were working there. The subsequent discovery of the Petra Church revealed the continuity of occupation at the site through to the 6th or 7th century AD.

The Crusader presence in the region was most obvious from the Crusader castle at Shoubak, which we visited on a day trip with Marguerite, Mohammad Abdallah, and Mufleh. It was very well preserved, with the castle alone occupying the whole hilltop. It was striking because it stands on a hill, looking directly across the desert. Its construction is similar to the castle at Kerak, which is larger. The one at Shoubak has a tunnel with 350 steps down to the wadi below for a secret water supply. It was still possible to go down the steps, but Mufleh mentioned that the air there was very stale. There were also remains of a Crusader castle at Wuʿayra, in Wadi Musa, which was not on high ground, but on a rock outcrop (behind the new Forum Hotel, which was under construction), that could be defended with a drawbridge. Much less of its walls have survived than of the castles at Shoubak and Kerak.

Tomb of the Broken Pediment in Wadi Farasa

Petra was bounded to the east and west by mountains – to the west by el-Habis and Umm el-Biyara, and to the east by el-Khubthah (in which the "Royal Tombs" were carved). To the north and south, the city had been protected by city walls in the Nabataean and Roman periods. From the area of al-Katuteh, the rubbish of the Nabataean city was thrown over the south city wall, forming an enormous rubbish dump, riddled with potsherds.

Tombs had been carved on the sides of the mountains and wadis beyond both city walls to the south and north. The main wadi with tombs in it to the south-east of the central area of Petra was Wadi Farasa, with the Tomb of the Broken Pediment, the Renaissance Tomb, and the Tomb of the Roman Soldier. The first of the tombs we needed to examine was the Tomb of the Broken Pediment.

To reach Wadi Farasa we headed up a path behind the Qasr el-Bint and past the Zibb Farʿoun column, nick-named after a certain part of the Pharaoh's anatomy (fig. 85), and then past al-Katuteh rubbish dump (fig. 86). From there, the difficulty arose of choosing a path in the sand which would lead to the tombs. As it was hilly, this was surprisingly difficult (fig. 87). We had discovered that only paths with evidence of goats having passed by recently (their hoof prints and droppings) would lead anywhere reliably. If the paths had footprints of shoes on them, this was an even more reliable indicator that they would lead in the right direction. We became very good at recognizing the different footprints and droppings of animals (goats, donkeys, horses, and camels). We also started to recognise the soles of distinctive shoes. Just as mine were the only "Dunlop Volley" sandshoes, so too Mufleh's shoes had unique soles. From these, we could tell when he was following to keep an eye on us when we worked so as to make sure we were safe, even if we did not see him.

When we arrived at the Tomb of the Broken Pediment (fig. 88), there were two black goats standing on the steps. The cave next to it was inhabited, and the woman in it invited us in for *shay*. This was the first time we were invited into a cave for tea. Inside the cave was a smooth, clean, concrete floor, with a brightly coloured woven plastic mat on it. Stuck on one wall was a group of postcards, including an old one of the Khasneh, with oleander in flower in front of it, from a time when there were still oleander bushes growing there. The woman made *shay* on a kerosene primus pressure stove, which only burnt about half of its vapour. Two of her neighbours also came in to drink *shay*, bringing their children with them. She wore a black dress (a *mudraga*) with embroidery around the yoke and hemline.[41] It had long pointed cap sleeves folded back on themselves at the shoulders. Her arms were covered by the long sleeves of her colourful underdress. She had a black scarf (*misfah*) wound round her face with its ends tucked into the yoke of her dress. This scarf was held in place by another black scarf (an *asaba*), which was folded into a band and tied across her forehead. The women wore moulded black plastic shoes and sometimes had a gold cap on their right-hand eye tooth. One of her friends was wearing very large square gold earrings.

The Tomb of the Broken Pediment was of particular interest to us because it has two half-pediments on it as on the Khasneh, but it is only a single storey high (fig. 88). The Khasneh has a circular pavilion (tholos) carved between the half-pediments (fig. 68). When we examined the facade of the Tomb of the Broken Pediment, we could see an allusion to the circular pavilion in low relief. The mouldings on the facade were much simpler than those on the Khasneh.

40 On Crusader presence in Petra, Wadi Musa, and Jabal Haroun: Fiema 2002: 241–42; 2016: 566; Sinibaldi 2016.

41 For a detailed description of Bdoul women's clothes, see van Geldermalsen 2006: 61–62.

Fig. 87. Looking from ez-Zantur, south-east across to Wadi Farasa, 2003.

Fig. 88. Tomb of the Broken Pediment, 1982.

Fig. 89. Angela having tea in the Tomb of the Broken Pediment, 1981.

A few weeks later, while walking past the Tomb of the Broken Pediment, we were invited for *shay* in the tomb itself, rather than the cave next door where they had previously invited us. With great pride, they showed us the inside, which had a row of flat, tapering pilasters around the wall, surmounted by another smaller set with cut-out holes for inset capitals (fig. 89). This was significant because the tomb was in effect carved as a three-dimensional version of the arrangement of a tholos between half-pediments in front of a colonnaded court on the upper part of the Khasneh (fig. 90), like that depicted in the Roman or Pompeian wall-paintings, such as the House of the Labyrinth in Pompeii in the first century BC (fig. 91). This was important because it meant that this architectural scheme was being carved in three dimensions before it was being built in Roman architecture.

We realised we would need to photograph this interior. A few days later, we returned with a large box of biscuits, in the hope of asking if we could photograph the inside of the tomb which was their home. They put the kettle on to serve us *shay*, making a fire which produced a great deal of smoke. While Angela drank tea, I tried to photograph the walls through the smoke (fig. 89).[42]

Their smaller cave, the one in which we had *shay* the first time, was used as their "main cave", as it would have been warmer to sleep in at night (it was smaller and fitted with a wooden door). The cave with pilasters was much larger and was their "kitchen cave". A rough wooden bench had some kitchen equipment stacked on it, which primarily consisted of a flat metal circular tray for making bread, a domed sheet for baking bread on, a large pot for making stew, and the deep circular dish for washing clothes (*ligan*).[43] They used some of the *loculi* in the tomb for storage. One *loculus* contained a 44-gallon water drum, which would have been filled with water from the spring brought in jerry cans on their donkey. There was brushwood for the fire in one corner.

Marguerite and Mohammad Abdallah

We had first met Marguerite (or Fatima, her Bdoul name) beside the Qasr el-Bint, with her small daughter Salwa. She was dressed similarly to the other younger Bedouin women, in a long sleeveless dress with embroidered yoke over a long-sleeved shirt and cotton trousers. The cloth for dresses was plain, but while the older women wore black, the younger ones chose bright colours, such as dark green, dark turquoise, or purple. Marguerite was distinguished from them by her blonde fringe poking out from under her headscarf, which was tied behind her head rather than under her chin. She explained that she avoided engaging with tourists by pretending not to speak English.[44]

She had come to Petra a tourist in 1978 when she was 22 years old, met Mohammad Abdallah, stayed, and married him. She gradually learnt the old-fashioned Arabic dialect of the Bdoul, on which people further afield would sometimes comment.[45] As she was a qualified nurse, she ran the clinic in Petra which provided most of the Bdoul's day-to-day medical needs and vaccinations, in association with the hospital in Wadi Musa when necessary.[46] (King Hussein had made medical treatment for the Bedouin free in 1979.[47])

42 It was not the only tomb interior with pilasters, although this was rare. When we went around to the next wadi beyond the Tomb of the Roman Soldier, Wadi en-Nmeir, one of the tombs (Gable Tomb 253) also had pilasters inside.

43 See also Bienkowski and Chlebik 1991: 154. The main equipment had changed little since the 1930s when Margaret Murray (1939: 23) described it.

44 Marguerite also hid to avoid tourists in her early years in Petra (van Geldermalsen 2006: 108, 272).

45 Van Geldermalsen 2006: 107. Changes in the Arabic used by Bdoul men with outsiders (as opposed to within the tribe) were evident by the late 1970s and early 1980s, having been learnt from contact with the dialects of the non-Bedouin Levant, Egypt, and Saudi Arabia (Shoup 1985: 287). About thirty years later, by the early 2010s, changes in the Arabic of the younger generation of the Bdoul were notable (Farajat 2012: 153).

46 Marguerite van Geldermalsen (2006: 98–111, 167–68, 171–74) describes her experiences running the clinic.

47 Van Geldermalsen 2006: 103.

Fig. 90. Khasneh, upper order, 2010.

Marguerite and Mohammad's cave was located slightly away from the others, above the east end of the south side of the Colonnaded Street. The outside living area was concreted, with a garden and an awning for shade in summer. It had a view over the city centre across to the Qasr el-Bint and el-Habis.[48] Inside, their cave had a concrete floor and painted walls. Beside their main cave, Mohammad had also excavated a smaller cave, which they subsequently used as a kitchen (fig. 92).[49] Unlike other Bdoul caves, theirs had a stove (cooker) with an oven, run from a gas canister.[50]

One evening when we visited them, Mohammad had finished baking clay "antiques", which included lamps, in this oven. He had an ancient Roman one, of about the second century AD, which he had used to make the moulds for the top and bottom halves of the new lamps. He would press the clay into each mould then join the two halves together to make the lamp, before baking it. The sample he showed us had an erotic scene on it, which was a common motif.

Marguerite and Mohammad showed us colour photographs from their trip to New Zealand when they had tried living there.[51] They had returned to Petra a few months before we arrived. The photographs included those of a country show, with goats with prize ribbons around them, and a Scottish pipe band, with the musicians wearing spats. It was very similar to small-town country shows in Australia. The New Zealand country show reflected an interest in livestock in common with the Bedouin, while, in some other respects, it was a world away from Petra.

A couple of weeks later, an Australian Broadcasting Commission television crew arrived to film a feature on the Bdoul and background for a documentary on archaeology in Jordan. The young journalist, Peter George, went with me up

48 Van Geldermalsen 2006: 185. Their cave is "Household 6" in Bienkowski and Chlebik 1991: figs. 2, 9. That article is their most detailed report, incorporating Bienkowski 1985; 1989.

49 Marguerite van Geldermalsen 2006: 8–9, 184–85.

50 They acquired the oven in 1979 (van Geldermalsen 2006: 136).

51 Marguerite van Geldermalsen (2006: 180–83) describes their experiences in New Zealand and decision to return to Petra permanently.

Fig. 91. Pompeii, House of the Labyrinth, wall-painting depicting a circular pavilion in a court, 1984.

to Marguerite's for a cup of tea. As she had had bad experiences of being treated as a freak by city Arabs, because of a programme on Jordanian TV, she was not willing to be filmed, but agreed to talk to him. Many city Arabs could not understand how she could live such a simple lifestyle and with those they viewed as primitive people.

Marguerite explained why she liked living in Petra. The main reason was because the people were so sociable. People came to visit her each day, and if they didn't she went to visit them. If she felt like it, she went to see them more than once. There was no need to think about how long it was since the last visit or whether it had been an appropriate interval between visits. When she and Mohammad had lived in New Zealand, she went from one end of town to the other going to a different playgroup each day of the week with her small daughter Salwa, but nothing further came of it. The mothers didn't meet up outside of the playgroups, and so she did not get to know any of them, even though to her they did not seem to have any other company.

In New Zealand, Mohammad worked at the abattoirs, doing *halal* (Islamic ritual) slaughtering which was needed for the lamb which New Zealand exported to the Middle East. When they had decided to come back to Petra, Marguerite thought Mohammad was happier, because his work there was more interesting. Every day was different, and he was his own boss. If he felt like being a guide for a day, or going excavating, or coming home early, he could.

We found the pace of life in Petra was completely relaxed because there were no pressures to do anything. If something needed to be done, it was done eventually, but not according to the demands of any schedule. It was always possible to break off from any activity by going and having some *shay* in company. It was the pace of life, even more than being cut off from the world by the surrounding hills and our lack of a vehicle, which made Petra feel quite idyllic.[52]

52 Petra only had four vehicles, including pick-up trucks and Marguerite and Mohammad's car, after everyone from outside Petra had left for the day (van Geldermalsen 2006: 189).

Measuring Tomb 813 with Norma

Tomb 813 is the southernmost Hegr Tomb along el-Khubthah (figs. 44, 93). It is reached by gradually walking up from the area opposite the Theatre (fig. 94), as it is on a level above the valley floor (fig. 95). The first time Angela and I climbed one of these "back streets" of Petra early in the morning, walking past the inhabited caves along it, there were donkeys and a camel[53] tethered outside and chickens running about.[54] We were invited in for tea by a woman sitting under an awning. Later, while we worked, taking theodolite readings on Tomb 813, the smell of burning frankincense came wafting over towards us.

Tomb 813, which is sometimes called the ʿUnaishu Tomb,[55] has a courtyard with colonnades on either side, which no longer survive (figs. 95–96). Inside the tomb, burial recesses, called *loculi*, had been carved into the walls. The *loculi* were ca. 2 m long, and 1 m wide, with graves cut into their floors (fig. 97). To the left (north) of the tomb, there was a banqueting room (a triclinium) with benches around three sides, and three *loculi* in the back wall. As we set off home in the

53 The camel belonged to Musa Salem, but he did not take it to work at the Khasneh often (Marguerite van Geldermalsen, pers. comm. 11 October 2018).

54 Examples of chicken coops: Simms 1988: 206; Bienkowski and Chlebik 1991: 162.

55 An inscription, on a *loculus* slab, referring to ʿUnaishu, brother of queen Shaqilath, was found in Tomb 813 or Tomb 808, but it is not completely clear in which (McKenzie 1990: 37, 167–70, pls. 162–64). Shaqilath was active in the second and third quarters of the first century AD.

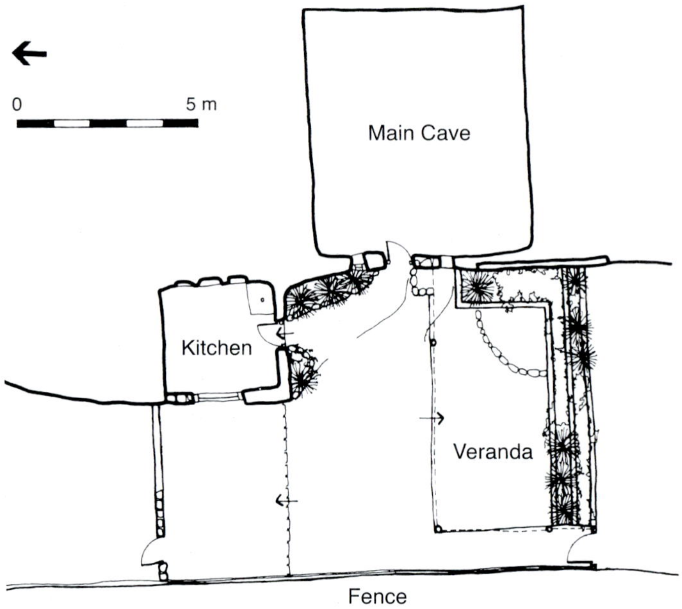

Fig. 92. Plan of cave complex of Marguerite and Mohammad Abdallah [Bienkowski and Chlebik 1991: fig. 9].

Fig. 93. Looking east to el-Khubthah, 2001.

Fig. 94. Theatre, looking towards el-Khubthah, 1986.

Fig. 95. Tomb 813, before sunset, mid-March 2015 [Otto Nieminen].

Fig. 96. Tomb 813, near midday, 1986.

Fig. 97. Tomb 813, interior, with *loculi* and partly excavated floor with layers of compacted dung and ash, 1986.

Fig. 98. View to the Theatre (left), Hajj Salameh's tent and store (near the pickup truck), 1981.

late afternoon, we noticed how the stone was much pinker than it had been in the full sun (fig. 95). We passed the Theatre on the way home. There had been various estimates of its seating capacity. When we subsequently measured it, we found it had ca. 3,860 linear metres of seating (fig. 94).[56] As Hieron of Alexandria's *Stereometry* allows a Ptolemaic foot of 0.35 m per person,[57] this gives a capacity of 11,000. If more space were allowed per person, this capacity would decrease to 8–10,000 people.

A few weeks later, when Angela was ill, I asked Norma to help me take more measurements of Tomb 813 with the theodolite.[58] Norma was a Canadian nurse who had arrived in Petra not long after us to stay in Nazzal's Camp.[59] She was aged about fifty, with short grey hair and slacks, and she was of particular interest to some men.[60] For the whole of the day I worked with Norma, a few young men hung around on the sidelines watching us. They never tried to start any conversation, as they were too timid. Later, I asked Mohammad, Marguerite's husband, why the young men were hanging around, because this had never happened when Angela and I were working, and Norma was much older than we. He replied that it was obvious: "She is a married woman here without her husband," i.e., she knows what she is missing and will be wanting it, whereas it was assumed we did not know what we were missing, so were not potentially available.

The most simple protection against unwelcome attention was to maintain a reputation for not being interested, so that the Arab men did not make an approach because of the glee other men would take at their loss of face if rejected. Maintaining such an impression was not so difficult, as it was largely a matter of being consistent and taking care to wear suitable clothing. With time, I found that trousers under a skirt was the most effective way of achieving this, along with a scarf which protected my hair from the sand.

The Kodak Film Stand in a Tent

In the open area beyond the Theatre, before turning left into the Colonnaded Street, there was a Bedouin tent where souvenirs were sold (figs. 98–99). After about six weeks in Petra, I wanted to take a picture of it, with the Kodak film sign swaying in the breeze. The owner, Hajj Salameh Moham-

56 McKenzie 1990: 144.

57 McKenzie 2007: 323.

58 Angela Phippen notes: "While neither of us became seriously ill on this trip, we both experienced multiple low-level digestive upsets. We could only carry a small amount of water with us during our daily fieldwork which we used for drinking purposes. …[S]uch illnesses were inevitable." (pers. comm. to A. T. Reyes, 22 September 2019)

59 Angela Phippen notes: "…[F]or one of our visits to Petra, we had to share our cave with her. In fig. 51, I am lying on a bed; in fig. 107, I am lying on mattresses which are on the floor. That is because I had given up my bed for Norma." (pers. comm. to A. T. Reyes, 22 September 2019)

60 Fawzi Zayadine was always interested in women. One day, he invited us up to Wadi Musa for a proper warm shower as there was no such facility in Petra. To accept such an invitation from a man was out of the question.

Fig. 99. Hajj Salameh's souvenir stand, 1981.

Fig. 100. Entrance to Hajj Salameh's store, 1981/2.

mad, put himself in the photograph, then invited me into his shop for tea. His shop, which was in a cave in the rock-face behind the tent, was sufficiently far from our cave that we did not use it as much as Dakhilallah's, although it had much more stock, ranging from packets of biscuits to bags of cement (fig. 100).[61]

Hajj Salameh brought out his passport to show me his name and address in English so that I would be sure to send him a copy of the photograph. This led to his showing me the passport of his son, Abdallah, who was at university. He was very proud of him and even produced his report cards and matriculation certificate. He explained that his son would finish university when he was twenty-two years old. These were the first complete sentences which I had understood in Arabic, and I suddenly felt that I really would be able to speak it if I kept learning. Hajj Salameh's son went on to become a schoolteacher.[62]

Wadi Musa and Back to Amman

Every two or three weeks we would go back to Amman, usually for a week. The first few times Abu Isa came from Amman in the Volkswagen combivan to collect us from our cave. We later took the JETT bus.

We drove back up through the Siq, past the Rest House, then up the hill to Wadi Musa, with its peppercorn trees lining the main street (fig. 101). We passed the shops with roller doors, which stocked vegetables in wooden fruit boxes out in

61 Marguerite van Geldermalsen (2006: 121–23) gives a detailed description of his stock.

62 Marguerite van Geldermalsen, pers. comm. 26 January 2019.

Fig. 101. Wadi Musa, main street, 1981/2 [Angela Phippen].

the street (fig. 102). The range of vegetables was greater than in Petra, but largely limited to potatoes, onions, tomatoes, cabbages, and capsicums. Cucumbers were kept in the cool inside (sometimes in the fridge if the shop had one, so we needed to know the word for them in Arabic). There were also oranges and lemons. Abu Isa bemoaned how there were no eggplants (aubergines) in Jordan at the time, as they were sent to Iraq.

As we wound up the road, we looked back down on the pinkish-red hills of Petra which stood out against the cream hills and new houses of Wadi Musa (fig. 103). One house we passed was indicative of the change in architecture which was occurring. The original part was a single storey high and made of stone. The extension to it, with a water tank and TV aerial on top, was made of cement-rendered breeze blocks between concrete pillars which were reinforced with iron rods (fig. 104). As elsewhere in Jordan, this construction technique was used for the newer houses. In amongst the olive trees on the hillside of Wadi Musa, there were also old stone houses and storerooms (fig. 105). In the terraced wadi at the foot of them, fruit trees such as figs grew.

One day, on the way back from our trip to Shoubak Crusader castle with Marguerite, Mohammad, and Mufleh, we had visited a family in Wadi Musa. Their house consisted of a single room and courtyard, with a kitchen and toilet off it. The whole family lived in one room. In this room, there were five children, their father, and two women, sitting on a few foam rubber mats on the concrete floor. They had a television, a large fridge, and a new china cabinet with fancy coffee cups. The room also contained a wardrobe, a treadle sewing machine, and a pile of bedding and rugs. Like the caves, by day the room served as a living room and by night as a bedroom for the whole family, when they would have spread the bedding out on the floor. They were watching black-and-white westerns broadcast from Israel, which was not so far away. We had noticed that on the official television news broadcasts, "Israel" was mentioned by name, even though in those days the name could not be used in any ordinary conversations for fear of arousing suspicions.

As we left, we met two men going out for a special occasion. They were wearing *thaubs* (full-length men's robes) with their heads covered with *keffiyehs* (head scarves) held in place by *'agals* (black rope loops). The Bdoul called these *mirreers* and *mendeels*, respectively).[63] Each had a gun slung over his shoulder, much as one would have worn a carnation to a party.

As we drove away from Wadi Musa to the Shara Mountains, we passed the small forest, with its sparsely spaced small prickly oak trees (bearing acorns, but with leaves like holly), and some Bedouin tents erected beside concrete houses. The

63 Van Geldermalsen 2006: 278.

Fig. 102. Wadi Musa, shops with vegetables outside, 1986.

Fig. 103. Wadi Musa, looking towards Petra, with the Petra Forum Hotel in the distance, 1981/2.

Fig. 104. Wadi Musa, stone house with rendered breeze block and concrete extension, 1981/2.

Fig. 105. Wadi Musa, stone houses and olive trees, with vines and fruit trees in the terraced wadi in the foreground, 1981/2.

land flattened out as we drove across the desert, passing neither dwellings nor traffic. The line of semi-trailers and lorries marking the Desert Highway came into view in the distance. Its asphalt road crossing the desert only became visible when we reached it. We joined the traffic and headed north to the British Institute at Amman for Archaeology and History, our base in Amman.

The British Institute at Amman for Archaeology and History

The British Institute at Amman for Archaeology and History (the BIAAH, since re-named the British Institute in Amman, run by the Council for British Research in the Levant) was a place for archaeologists in Amman to use when they were doing fieldwork in Jordan. It provided a base at which to stay whilst obtaining permission letters from the Department of Antiquities and assembling equipment before an expedition, as well as between field trips.

Beside a lounge, dining area, and kitchen, the ground floor of the Institute housed a library, with a drawing board, and a darkroom. On the lower floor there was storage for archaeological finds and equipment, and a work area. On the first floor, the archaeologists who stayed in the two shared bedrooms or the very narrow single room (in which I had stayed) shared a bathroom. The director, Crystal-M. Bennett, also had a flat in the building.

The Institute was located in what was then a new, undeveloped area at the edge of Amman, near Jordan University. The centre of Amman could be reached from the Institute from the major road below, by either sharing a group taxi, a service which followed a standard route, or by taking the bus from outside the University. The Department of Antiquities and other government offices were open until 2 pm every day, except Fridays when they were closed (for prayers, according to Islamic custom). Any visits to them were done in the morning, with everyone back at the Institute in time for lunch.

Lunch at the Institute was a formal sit-down affair, as was dinner. It was cooked by Hamsi, the cook, and served at a long dining table, set with silver-plate cutlery from a cutlery canteen on the side board. Lunch and dinner were a mixture of local and English cuisine. Crystal-M. Bennett, who sat at the head of the table, had a dachshund called Marrow. When the fruit course was reached, those sitting at the table had to put small pieces of their fruit into a piece of their orange or mandarin peel and pass these offerings along the table to Crystal, so that she could feed the titbits to Marrow. These were known as "Marrow's boats".

After lunch and dinner, the conversation continued over Arab coffee in the lounge area, with its bamboo furniture. Having to dine together and make conversation meant that different generations of archaeologists came to know each other, establishing contacts and friendships which then lasted throughout their careers.

The limited water supply in Petra meant that we could not wash our hair or our clothes properly there, but water at the Institute was also in short supply, because it was delivered by a tanker to a tank on the roof. The shower was over the bath, common in England, but not in modern bathrooms in Australia. We each had a shower and washed our hair with the bath plug in to save the water. Then we washed our clothes in that water, which went pink from the Petra sand which penetrated everything, like cat fur. We dried our clothes on a line outside, bringing them in as soon as possible, so that they did not fade.

We needed to return to the Institute every few weeks to develop the black-and-white film in order to be sure that the photographs had come out successfully. As the photographs needed to be as high resolution as possible to allow for further magnification, I had investigated the best method of achieving this before we left Sydney. We used the finest grain, slowest Ilford film, Pan F, which we down-rated (increased the exposure time on) to further increase the grain. Perceptol, a fine grain developer, could achieve an even finer grain with long development times. As it came in powder form, I was able to bring it with me from Sydney. For inside the tombs, we used a faster, 400 ASA, film. As the darkroom was fairly warm, and the development times long (sometimes 25 minutes), we had to make a supply of ice to cool the water to the correct temperature before we started.

Shopping in Amman

Each time we returned from Petra, we would go to the Post Office to send a telegram to my parents to let them know we had returned safely. My mother would then ring Angela's parents.[64] To phone Australia from Amman was hugely expensive, so we never phoned our parents, nor did they phone us – not even once. We sent weekly letters, and we also sent a telegram that we were safe if something had happened which we thought might have alarmed them, such as when Abu Nidal had let a bomb off in the Intercontinental Hotel carpark. Its size was calculated to be just loud enough for the journalists who would hang out in the hotel bar to hear it, but not to do much damage. The Intercontinental Hotel was the main international hotel and a good place for a coffee before heading into the noise of downtown Amman.

We bought our food supplies for the next trip at the Rainbow Supermarket near First Circle. Most of the supplies we bought there were tinned fish or tinned meat, but also included other food, such as jam. It was the only supermarket in Amman, and the owner had been killed by a bomb blast because it stocked alcohol. It stocked every imported luxury one might want, from biscuits to Swiss honey and Lindt chocolate for a treat. Years later, when I visited it when Amman had big supermarkets (e.g., Safeways), the Rainbow

64 We could not send a telegram to Angela's parents because, like most people in those days, they associated telegrams with bad news.

Fig. 106. Our equipment and luggage at the foot of the stairs to our cave, with the Department of Antiquities Toyota land cruiser. The new restaurant is under construction on the far right, 1981/2 [Angela Phippen].

Supermarket looked like a corner store. It was necessary to go into the centre of town for notebooks, film, clothes, or other equipment. Most things could be obtained. It was a matter of finding out which shop stocked them. We were even able to buy Fabriano drawing paper and Rotring drawing pens.

One day, when Angela and I were in the centre of town shopping, I noticed stalls with bunches of key-rings with small plastic bank notes on them, like the ones Marguerite's husband, Mohammad, sold in Petra. We heard a voice calling us from behind. It was Mohammad. He led us to an upstairs café for a Pepsi. Then he took us to the souvenir shop near the Great Mosque where he bought the souvenirs he supplied to the other venders of Petra.[65] The shop sold the knives "made by the Bedouin", jewellery from Egypt, and other items. These included fake coins, of which there was an enormous carton on the floor.

Although Amman was a modern city without the narrow streets of Damascus or Jerusalem in its centre, it still partly followed the Arab suq system, where shops selling similar merchandise were grouped together. The gold suq was the most obvious example of this, where the shops had nothing except gold bracelets hanging in the windows. Some of the bracelets had gold coins on them which were English sovereigns or copies of them, with the head of King George on one side and St George on the other.

In the "Mud Suq", near the Great Mosque, there was a shop in the basement which sold bronze objects, such as metal trays and lanterns. As the floor was always covered in about a foot of water, customers were given rubber boots to walk around it, slowly making waves, while above them, the shop was lit by working electric lighting. The safety of this did not seem to be a consideration. I bought two pairs of pierced brass lanterns there, two of which had come from Hejaz railway carriages.

To our surprise, in one of the news-stands, we found a children's book in Arabic with a very familiar animal on the cover. It was about kangaroos, which were shown with background scenery which included other Australian animals and birds. We took the bus back to the Institute. After a trip into the centre of town, with its dust and car horns honking all the time, the Institute provided a quiet, cool, clean respite.

Return to Petra

After our stay in Amman, Abu Isa drove us and our equipment back down to Petra (fig. 106). When we arrived back, it seemed much the same, as if we had not been away. Petra had an atmosphere of timelessness, as if it had been like this

65 Marguerite van Geldermalsen (2006: 126–27) also describes visiting this shop.

Fig. 107. Sharing our cave with confiscated pottery, 1981/2.

for the last 1,500 years, with the birds singing, and nothing happening, so that it was also possible to understand how the ruins had survived. However, work continued on the construction of the new restaurant, which was an augur of changes to come. It was only a single storey high, but built in a very angular style, which was being faced with pinkish stone to match that of Petra (visible on right in fig. 106).

In our cave, we now had to avoid the Nabataean pots laid out on the floor in front of the Museum cases along the side wall (fig. 107). There were reportedly more confiscated objects in the Museum than there were registered pots from official excavations. The pots had been found by illicit digging, especially in al-Katuteh rubbish dump.[66] While they dug there, the Bdoul would post a look-out to let them know when the Inspector of Antiquities was in the valley. The amount of this material was impressive, especially the complete fine Nabataean painted bowls, some of which were probably found in tombs. At the time, the Bdoul would keep their best finds, generally complete pots, for one particular German collector until he was next in Petra. He reportedly had the largest collection of Nabataean pottery outside Jordan. However, we were told that he had been caught with broken pots hidden in his socks in Petra a few months before and expelled from the country. As he had not been back for some months, this created an income problem for some of the Bdoul.

After our trip back from Amman, we woke late (at a luxurious seven o'clock) to the sound of the stonemasons, including Dakhilallah, chipping stone blocks for the restoration of the Qasr el-Bint. This sound broke the silence every day, and reminded us that in Nabataean times, it would not have been as quiet as we imagined. There would have been a continuous symphony of little chipping noises by day, interrupted by the sounds of animals, such as donkeys braying, roosters crowing, and dogs barking. Nabataean masons would have been quarrying, cutting, and carving the blocks for the many stone buildings in the city centre, as well as chipping away to make the tomb facades and their interiors around the site.

How the Tombs were Made

The facades were carved from the top down, as evident from the Unfinished "Tomb" on the side of el-Habis (figs. 108–109).[67] Details of the stages of carving can be determined from unfinished tombs in Petra and Medain Saleh.

66 Marguerite van Geldermalsen (2006: 186–87) describes how fruitful illicit digging could be.

67 Detailed descriptions of how they were carved are given in Rababeh 2005; and, in French, by Bessac 2007: 89–118. Bessac summarised in English in McKenzie 2010: 753–55.

Fig. 108. El-Habis, with remains of rock-cut houses and the Unfinished Tomb, 1986.

Fig. 109. The Unfinished Tomb, 1981/2.

Fig. 110. Remains of stuccoed walls in rooms which have dropped away on the side of el-Habis, 1986.

The masons stood on a platform of uncarved stone as they worked down a facade. They would block out stone and then carve the details before moving their rock-cut platform down to repeat this process. The facades and their interiors also functioned as quarries for building blocks, when they were being carved. Contrary to its name, the "Unfinished Tomb" might not have been planned as a tomb because it was designed with columns in front cut free from the rock. South of it, there are remains of the side walls of rock-cut houses and even the stuccoed walls of some rooms left when the rest of the rooms had fallen off the side of el-Habis (fig. 110).

The Deir

We needed to measure the mouldings on the Deir, which is a large facade high up above the valley at the end of a walk which takes three-quarters of an hour. The name "Deir", which means "Monastery", would have survived from a time when there were monks living near it, in the Byzantine period and later. Crosses were visible in the niche in the back wall in the late 19th- and early 20th-century.[68] How high up it was above the Petra valley was indicated by the silhouette of the urn at the top of it, which could be distinguished in the distance from the platform in front of the Urn Tomb, in the row of "Royal Tombs" (directly above the theodolite head in fig. 111).

We set off for the Deir from our cave, passing the caves to the north of el-Habis along Wadi ed-Deir, where people were preparing for the day (fig. 112–113). Their goats were still hanging around near where they had spent the night. The early morning sun lit the way up to the Deir, with its gnarled trees beside the path with rock-cut steps, originally cut from the rock by the Nabataeans (fig. 114). Where the steps were too worn or had not survived, they had been repaired or rebuilt, under the supervision of Muhammad Khadija (fig. 115). Part of the way up, there is a pretty ravine on the left at the end of which there is a small classical facade, with lions on either side of it, the Lion Triclinium (fig. 116). When we came back on another day to measure the mouldings on this facade with the theodolite, it was very difficult because of the steep sides of the ravine in front of it, where oleander and other shrubs grew.

Near the top of the path to the Deir, looking back, there is a view down to the valley below with the "Royal Tombs" along el-Khubthah (the Palace Tomb, Urn Tomb, and Corinthian Tomb), providing a sense of how high above the valley the Deir is (fig. 117).

The Deir first becomes visible behind the rock outcrop at the end of the path when the top of its urn and Doric frieze appear (fig. 118). It is carved into the east side of the

68 E.g., Musil 1907: vol. 2, part 1, 142, figs. 106–107.

Fig. 111. View from the platform in front of the Urn Tomb, from which the urn on top of the Deir is visible, 1981/2 [Angela Phippen].

Fig. 112. Wadi Deir, Jabal M'aysrah West from our cave, looking north-west, 1981/2.

Fig. 113. Wadi Deir, caves on the west side, early in the morning before the goats have left for the day, 1981.

Fig. 114. Path up to the Deir, looking east, 1981/2.

mountain, facing a clearing on the ridge and rock outcrops (fig. 119). When we climbed there, the location had a very open feeling, with a view from the crest of the ridge to the Wadi Araba and Jabal Haroun (with the white shrine of Aaron's Tomb on top), and of the mountains in each direction. Usually only four to six, if any, tourists made it as far as the Deir in a day, so that the area was quite unspoilt, with an Arcadian feeling.

The facade of the Deir is a plainer, larger, and wider version of the one on the Khasneh and is greyer in colour. The Deir is not a tomb. Rather, inside it has a single nearly square chamber with a large wide niche in the back wall (fig. 120). Later excavations revealed that the chamber had a very low bench along both side walls.

The Deir has simpler decorative details than the Khasneh, with blocked out Nabataean capitals (figs. 121–122). These are in contrast to the ornate floral ones on the Khasneh (fig. 75). The Nabataean capitals are accompanied by a Doric frieze with plain discs on it (fig. 121). The plainer decoration used on the Deir is part of a Nabataean style which had later developed, and from our observations, we demonstrated that it was carved after the Khasneh. We noticed how the facade had remains of a colonnade in front of it, on either side, as indicated by the remains of a stylobate and plastered column drums.[69] We also identified a very weathered rock-cut altar beside it.[70]

69 McKenzie 1990: 161.

70 McKenzie 1990: pl. 143b; fig. 214 here.

Fig. 115. Re-cut Nabataean steps up to the Deir, 2001.

Fig. 116. Lion Triclinium, from the foot of the gorge, 1981.

Fig. 117. View to el-Khubthah from the path to the Deir, looking east, 1981/2.

Fig. 118. Approach to the Deir when the urn on top becomes visible, 1981/2.

The top of the Deir could be reached with difficulty by climbing up the worn rock-cut steps beside the altar. At the top, unfinished details of the friezes showed how the Deir was carved (fig. 121). At the very top there were the outlines of unfinished quarried blocks, and a sense of the size of the Deir could be gained from stepping onto the roof of the tholos (fig. 122). There were no obvious tombs in this area, only cisterns and rooms. In the rock outcrop opposite, there was a rock-cut room (No. 468) with a finely carved ornamental niche in the back wall.[71]

Dakhilallah's Wife, Umm Khaled (Rakhiya)

There was a Pepsi stand in a wide cave which was almost like a rock overhang, facing the Deir (fig. 123). It was run by Dakhilallah's wife, Umm Khaled (Rakhiya).[72] She did not need to commute to work as they had been living up at the Deir for the previous year. They had one main cave for living in, with an outside area for cooking (visible on the bottom right in fig. 119). To make the cave habitable, Dakhilallah had filled the large hole in the roof above the window.[73]

71 McKenzie 1990: pls. 111–12.

72 A woman took the name of her eldest son, once she had one. This was viewed as the respectful form of address. If she were known that way when we were in Petra, her given name is provided in brackets.

73 This is "Household 4" in Bienkowski and Chlebik 1991. The sketch plan of the complex of caves in fig. 7 is not completely accurate.

Fig. 119. Deir, with Dakhilallah's main cave on the bottom right, 1984.

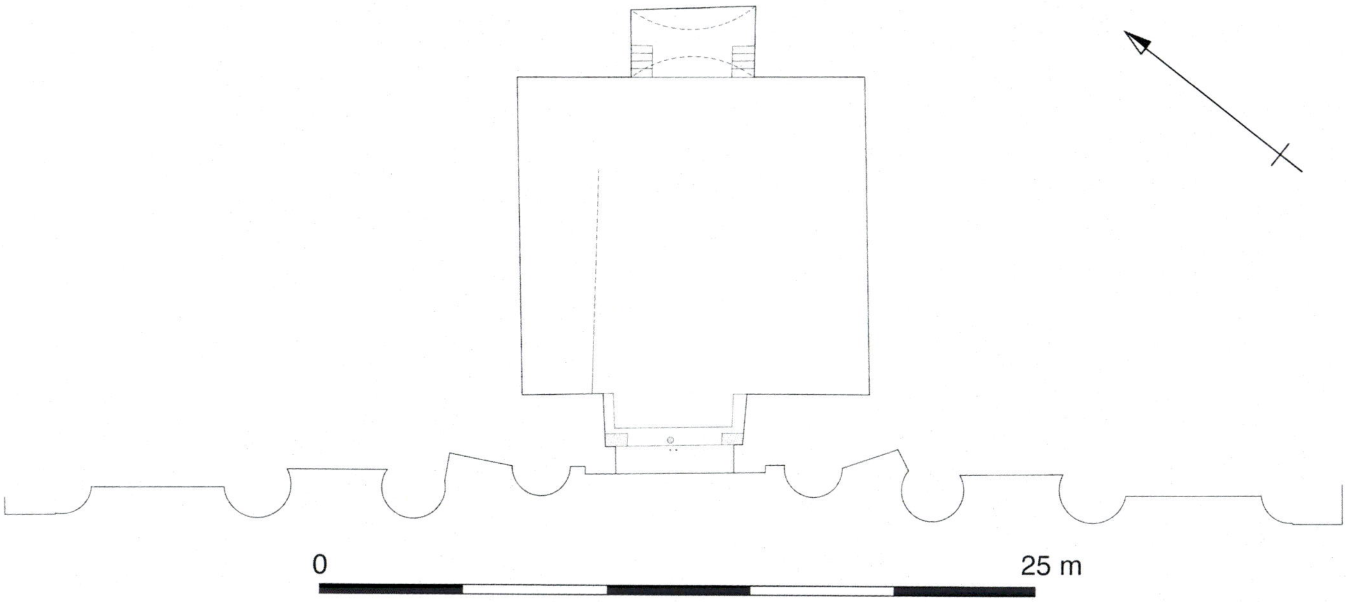

Fig. 120. Deir, plan.

Fig. 121. Deir, Doric frieze on the south side of the top order, with unfinished details, 1986.

We joined Umm Khaled for tea at lunch time (fig. 124). She boiled the kettle on a small fire and poured the tea from the usual blue enamel teapot into the ubiquitous small Duralex tumblers, which she stood on a metal tray to protect them from the sand. The water used to make the tea and wash out the glasses was poured from one of the plastic jugs with a narrow spout designed to minimise the amount of water used (fig. 124). With their flat surfaces, these jugs were based on a metal prototype.

Umm Khaled was dressed the same way as the other older Bdoul women with children. Her long black overdress, called a *mudraga*, was made of a thick, slightly shiny synthetic cloth (figs. 125–126). The yoke had a panel at the front decorated with machine-embroidered flowers and two rows of a related pattern were embroidered around the hem. Her dress had cap sleeves which hung down to a point on each side and were folded back on the shoulder. The dress splayed out towards the bottom, as a result of the piece of cloth inset on either side, and Umm Khaled's arms were covered by the long sleeves of her orange under-dress. She had a piece of black organdie or crepe (*misfah*), which was about 1.5 m long, wrapped around her head and under her chin, then tucked into the yoke of her dress. Over the top of this, she wore a brightly coloured folded scarf round her forehead, rather than the black scarf (*asaba*) used by older women, such as the one who had served us tea in the Tomb of the Broken Pediment (fig. 89). Like the other Bdoul women and older girls, Umm Khaled wore moulded black plastic shoes and had a gold tooth on her right eye-tooth (fig. 127).[74]

74 Marguerite van Geldermalsen (2006: 262–65) describes how eventually she ended up with a gold tooth herself.

Fig. 122. Deir, the urn on top, 1981/2 [Angela Phippen].

Fig. 123. View from the Deir, looking west, with Dakhilallah's refreshment stand on the far left, 1981/2 [Angela Phippen].

Fig. 124. Angela having tea with Mohammad, Umm Khaled (Dakhilallah's wife), baby Khalil, and Ali, 1981/2.

Fig. 125. Umm Khaled with Mohammad, Ali, and baby Khalil, 1981/2.

Baby Khalil was wrapped in swaddling clothes which were criss-crossed and tied with a band of cloth. He was wearing a little yellow pixie cap,[75] the continuation of a tradition seen in photographs of a Bdoul woman and her baby, who lived in a cave on the way up to the Deir in ca. 1940–46, with amulets attached to the baby's cap (fig. 128).[76] The baby's mother has her head covered by a *misfah* with an *asaba* tied over it, and her dress has the same cap sleeves as Umm Khaled's.

On one occasion Umm Khaled enthusiastically persuaded me to try on a *mudraga* and a scarf (fig. 126). It had machined embroidery done with variegated thread, whereas the flowers and leaves on Umm Khaled's were done with different coloured threads. I could not really afford the *mudraga*, but I did buy the scarf (fig. 127). It was blue with colourful flowers on it, like those in photographs of Russian peasants. It was made in Japan of a soft acrylic material which was comfortable as it did not slip on my hair. I found that the scarf, which I still have, was useful to wear to prevent sand and dust blowing into my plaited hair, which I could only wash once a week.

Dakhilallah and Umm Khaled's main cave was around the back of the rock outcrop with the refreshment stand

75 Marguerite van Geldermalsen (2006: 164–65) discusses the amulets which were attached to such caps.

76 This photograph was apparently taken at about the same time as fig. 224.

Fig. 126. Judith in a *mudraga*, with *misfah* and *asaba* (scarf), with Umm Khaled, 1981/2 [Angela Phippen].

Fig. 127. Judith in her new scarf, with Umm Khaled, baby Khalil, Mohammad, and Ali, 1981/2 [Angela Phippen].

cave in it. In the rock outcrop across from their main cave, there was another smallish cave. Affixed to the rock peak above it, there was a television aerial, which Angela observed reminded her of the "Flintstones" cartoon (fig. 123). It was necessary to climb up to enter this cave, which was unusual, but would have kept the goats out. It was set up as a best room for visitors, who were probably largely tourists paying for the experience of a Bedouin feast and living in the cave for a night. This room had an underlay of clean hessian bags on the floor, with a woven plastic mat on top. Around two sides, there were the usual two-foot (60 cm) wide foam rubber mattresses. These were covered with cushions or bolsters with frilled and embroidered cotton pillow covers. On the third side of the room, there were two trunks or chests of drawers covered with a satiny velvet rug with Persian designs. On each wall, there was an 18 by 10-inch (45 by 25 cm) wall-hanging with a Persian design painted on black velvet. It was all very new and the perfect parlour.

As Dakhilallah ran the store under our cave and also worked as the chief mason, I often wondered what he did with his money. It turned out that he had invested some of it in livestock. Up at the Deir, in addition to the usual herd of black-haired goats, he had two of the much larger Damascus goats from Syria, which are used for milk. He also had seven sheep there (fig. 129). Until then, we had seen only one sheep down in Petra, with a large bell around its neck. Sheep were much more expensive than the black goats, and also required more pasture. Besides supplying milk, sheep were a valuable source of income because their wool was used to weave traditional Bedouin rugs. The black goats' hair was used for weaving traditional Bedouin tents, *beit sha'ar*. Most families had a herd of black goats, which were also a source of milk and its by-products, as well as of meat, and could provide additional income if sold.[77]

We noticed that Umm Khaled largely spent the day nursing baby Khalil, or breastfeeding him, and occasionally herding the goats. In households with girls, the older girls prepared and cooked the dinner, but Umm Khaled had to cook the dinner herself, because she only had sons. She also sold soft drinks or souvenirs to the few tourists who had ventured as far as the Deir.

Fig. 128. Bdoul mother and child in Wadi Deir, ca. 1940–46 [American Colony, G. Eric and Edith Matson Photograph Collection, Library of Congress, Prints and Photographs Division, LC-DIG-matpc-21176].

Fig. 129. Dakhilallah's sheep in front of the Deir, 1981/2.

Turkmaniyah Tomb

The Turkmaniyah Tomb is a large Hegr Tomb away from the main tombs in the centre of Petra (figs. 130–131). It is in Wadi Abu 'Olleqa (sometimes called Wadi Turkmaniyah) which runs north-east from the centre of Petra. Because of a flaw in the rock, the lower part of the facade of the Turkmaniyah Tomb had been built of ashlar masonry, which was no longer there. It is the only tomb with a Nabataean inscription on it. The date for this inscription (mid-1st to mid-2nd century AD, based on the style of the letters)

77 Banning and Köhler-Rollefson (1986: 163) mention the sale of young male goats providing the Bedouin at Beidha with some income.

Fig. 130. Wadi Abu 'Olleqa (Wadi Turkmaniyah), looking towards the Turkmaniyah Tomb, 1981/2.

Fig. 131. Turkmaniyah Tomb, 1981/2.

provides an indication of when the tomb facade was carved. The long inscription describes the structures associated with the tomb, which are dedicated to the god Dushara and included a courtyard with benches, together with wells and retaining walls, presumably for gardens.[78] Above the inscription there was a recess with the remains of the lower parts of two busts (probably of the deceased) inset in it.[79] This tomb had an exceptionally large main chamber, with a small tomb chamber in the back wall. A second chamber was very unusual in Petra, because the tombs almost always consisted of a single chamber, with *loculi* carved in their walls or graves in the floors.

When Angela and I had visited the Turkmaniyah Tomb for the first time at the end of the summer, it was not inhabited. A few weeks later, as Angela was ill, I went round to it with the Canadian nurse, Norma, to do the theodolite readings for its mouldings. We arrived to discover there were two small Bedouin tents erected inside it, one on each side (fig. 132). In the tomb chamber at the back, there was a donkey. In between the tents, a woman was washing clothes in the large shallow metal dish the Bdoul used for the purpose, beside the 44-gallon drum in which they stored the water brought from the spring. Clothes were drying on a washing line outside strung from one side of the tomb.

Norma froze on seeing the tomb inhabited, so we could not measure it. If I had been with Angela, we would have taken a leisurely approach. The occupants would have invited us for *shay* with them, and we would have given them a few cigarettes (which we usually carried, though neither

78 Translation of whole inscription: Healey 1993: 238–39.

79 Kühlenthal and Fischer 2000: colour pl. 9.5.

Fig. 132. Turkmaniyah Tomb, with tents of Awwad ibn Juma and his son, 1981/2.

of us smoked). Then we would have asked to measure the tomb, aware that they would have known that they were not supposed to be living in it. The Bedouin were still allowed to live in the caves, but not those with significant larger facades. They had moved into the cave for the greater protection it provided from the winter weather.[80] This kind of relaxed approach and rapport with the Bdoul was an essential ingredient of our success.

Turkmaniyah Tomb Again

When I returned with Angela to measure the Turkmaniyah Tomb in early January, it was still inhabited with the two tents in place as before. When we arrived, the occupants' herd of goats was standing in front of it, having spent the night there (figs. 133–134). There were many baby goats and a light brown foal (fig. 135). The cooler weather made January the time of the year for the arrival of the baby goats, and their multiplication rate appeared to be fairly good, suggesting the Bdoul had a good supply of goat meat.

As it was so early in the morning that the men, Awwad ibn Juma and his son Sliman, were still there,[81] we were invited by Sliman for *shay* in his tent (on the right). He later explained that his father's house was the tent on the other side (fig. 134). Sliman's tent had no roof. Rather, the "tent" consisted of a wall of traditional Bedouin tent material woven from black goat's hair with stripes of white cotton (fig. 134), with canvas tacked on to it as well. The tents were needed in this tomb in order to provide protection from the exposure to the elements, as the tomb was open on one side because the front wall was missing.

Sliman worked at the Khasneh selling souvenirs and told us that he would be leaving for work at eight. While we had *shay*, we offered his wife a cigarette, as we normally did by way of returning the hospitality of being offered tea.[82] Nearly everyone smoked then. He told us that she did not smoke because: "If your wife smoke, it cost you much money. She always ask 'gimme cigarette'." Notably, when she poured tea and we said "*Shukran*" ("thank you") he, instead of she, replied "*Afwan*" (an equivalent of "you are welcome"). Sliman explained how one of the small children had had something wrong with his forefinger and had spent one month in Maʿan while it was fixed. Despite being semi-nomadic Bedouin, this suggested that they received some proper medical attention.

80 Marguerite van Geldermalsen (2006: 81, 149–50) describes Hajj Nuwaija, his wife Rakhiya-n and their children camping in the tomb in winter 1980, before going back out of the Petra valley.

81 I thank Marguerite van Geldermalsen and the older Bdoul for their correct names. Marguerite van Geldermalsen, pers. comm. 31 December 2018.

82 We never bought sweets for the children to protect their teeth, although some asked for "bon-bon".

Fig. 133. Turkmaniyah Tomb, at the beginning of the day, with Awwad ibn Juma and goats, 1981/2.

His old father, Awwad ibn Juma, who used a shepherd's crook carved of wood as a stick, fed his white mare and let her feed her foal, before riding off. With his white *keffiyeh* and his *thaub* (robe) of dark suiting hanging down on either side, he looked like someone in an old depiction of Biblical scenes. The baby goats and the foal were left at home in the sun with the children, who played with a wheel-less cart made of half a plastic jerry can (fig. 136). After a while, the children sat down and watched while we took our theodolite readings.

The women sat in the sun and were joined by three or four neighbours for the usual 10 o'clock morning tea. They sat around the fire, which they had made on the sand in front of the tomb. They were spinning wool, producing very large balls of yarn. One of them, who was spinning grey wool, held a loosely wound skein around her arm while she spun it with a wooden drop spindle, which was about fifteen inches long. It had a long straight round stem and a wooden cross-bar with a hook at one end. She would twirl the spindle, then stop and wind the spun wool onto the stem, and twirl a bit more. Sometimes, she spun standing up and sometimes sitting down.[83]

83 The spindle was similar to those illustrated in Weir 1976: pls. 36–37. As I was never in Petra in the summer, I did not see black goats' hair being woven for tents, as described in van Geldermalsen 2006: 236–39. Summary of Bedouin spinning and weaving in south Jordan: Weir 1976: 31–40, figs. 7–8 (loom).

The wadi had some retaining walls across it, suggesting that it had supported some agriculture in the past (fig. 130). Further down the wadi (going towards el-Habis), there was a garden, and thick oleander bushes surrounded the concrete school building.[84]

Across from the tomb on the other (east) side of the wadi, the ridge was covered in pottery sherds (fig. 137). From the ridge there was one of the most beautiful views in Petra, with the colours of the sand ranging from red to orange to cream (fig. 138). In the distance, the tombs of Moghar an-Nasara were situated at the north-east limit of the site.

On one occasion, we met surveyors who were surveying this ridge for a road into Petra from the north. The plan had been for the Siq to be widened by blasting it, so that tour buses could fit down it and then drive through Petra to the Basin Restaurant which was being built opposite our cave (fig. 106). After dining in the Restaurant, it was planned that visitors would leave on their buses via the road along Wadi Abu ʿOlleqa.[85] According to Crystal-M. Bennett, the Direc-

84 More detail: van Geldermalsen 2006: 149.

85 Later, once the Siq was paved with concrete, this route had to be used as an unsealed back route into Petra, in order to avoid the need for vehicles to go down the Siq. Vehicular access was necessary to supply the restaurant, Pepsi stands, excavations, and restoration work, to bring in people to work on these, and also to empty the septic tanks. The road was re-graded and sealed in 2017 (*World Heritage Centre–ICOMOS–IUCN* 2017: 30). Figs. 368–369.

Fig. 134. Turkmaniyah Tomb, with donkey, 1981/2.

Fig. 135. Turkmaniyah Tomb, foal waiting while its mother eats, 1981/2.

Fig. 136. Turkmaniyah Tomb, children playing with a jerry-can cart, 1981/2.

Fig. 137. Pottery sherds on the ridge opposite the Turkmaniyah Tomb, 1981/2.

Fig. 138. View from the ridge opposite the Turkmaniyah Tomb to Moghar an-Nasara, 1981/2.

Fig. 139. Looking north-east to Moghar an-Nasara, 1981/2.

Fig. 140. North end of el-Khubthah, with the Tomb of Sextius Florentinus (left) and the Palace Tomb (right).

tor of the British Institute, this plan was stopped in its tracks by King Hussein, who had the wisdom to understand the attraction of the undeveloped natural site to western tourists.

Tuffleh and her In-Laws

The tombs of Moghar an-Nasara were a series of large Hegr Tombs carved in the last red sandstone outcrop in front of the cream mountain where the new village of Umm Sayhoun was being built (fig. 138). The houses of the village were barely visible on the line of the hill, as they were a single storey high (fig. 139). We needed to measure the largest and highest of these tombs, the Tomb with the Armour (No. 649).[86] It was of particular interest because it had a frieze of armour carved on it, with faces at either end, which we later identified as Humbaba, the hideous faced demon of the Mesopotamian Gilgamesh epic.[87] Moghar an-Nasara means the Christian cave(s), suggesting that there was still a Christian population there at some point, before or after the arrival of the Crusaders in the twelfth century. As approaching these tombs from Wadi Abu 'Olleqa involved a steep climb onto the ridge opposite, we found it easiest to reach them further east via Wadi el-Matahah (fig. 226).

Fig. 141. Garden Temple, with a cutting through floor deposit of ash and dung, 1981/2.

86 McKenzie 1990: 168, pls. 160–61.
87 McKenzie et al. 1998.

Fig. 142. Tomb with *loculi*, with an earthen floor, the indent from a fire pit for the hearth, and a row of stones delimiting space for the family and for goats, 1898–1946 [American Colony, G. Eric and Edith Matson Photograph Collection, Library of Congress, Prints and Photographs Division LC-DIG-matpc-05970].

On the way back, when we were walking along the foot of el-Khubthah, before we reached the Tomb of Sextius Florentinus (fig. 140), Tuffleh, Mohammad Abdallah's sister, and Hamdah, Tuffleh's mother-in-law, invited us into their cave for *shay*. Like all the caves in Petra, this one was squared out inside, although it lacked a rock-cut front wall. Bedding was stacked on top of a low wooden cabinet to be put out on the floor when needed at night. There was a locked chest in one corner, which contained important papers. The locks kept the small children out of these chests, for which the women carried the keys around their necks.

The floor was made of hardened compacted dung which was nearly as smooth as concrete but could be distinguished from it by a slightly hollow sound. (Angela had to conduct this test before she was convinced.) In the Garden Temple, there was an 18-inch (45 cm) deep section through the floor showing such a deposit of dung (fig. 141). Photographs of some tombs taken in the first half of the twentieth century have the tell-tale evidence of Bedouin use of them, with a fire pit in the floor of compacted dung and ash, and lines of rocks demarcating space for family use and for young goats (fig. 142).

In the centre of the cave, there was a fireplace dug in the floor, and everyone sat on the floor around it on foam rubber mattresses (fig. 143). The three older girls were very proud because each of them had made part of the dinner. One of them had

Fig. 143. Tuffleh (in the white scarf) with her in-laws (left to right) Irbaya, Toba, Maheela, Uthmaiya, Se'ideh, Aisha, and Khalil, 1981/2.

Fig. 144. Bdoul woman, ca. 1900–1920 (the woman is also in fig. 173) [American Colony, G. Eric and Edith Matson Photograph Collection, Library of Congress, Prints and Photographs Division, LC-DIG-matpc-09428].

made the tea (*shay*), one the Bedouin bread (*shraak*) on a domed iron plate (*sāj*) outside, and one the stew, which was cooked on the fireplace. We were invited to join them for dinner, which consisted of a stew of potatoes, tomato paste, and overcooked pasta, accompanied by *shraak*.[88] They did not have cutlery, but used the traditional method of picking up the stew with small pieces of bread folded to form a spoon for each mouthful. Affluence influenced the diet of individual Bdoul families, so that more income directly resulted in the consumption of more fresh vegetables and meat,[89] which was a luxury.

On this first occasion, there was no sign of the men, and we all ate together. The oldest girl present was Tuffleh, who was married to Hamdah's son Abdallah, but lived with her in-laws when he was away in the army.[90] She was 15 years old, with neatly combed shiny black hair under her headscarf. There were five smaller children. They all fitted in this one room, and it seemed quite normal and everyone content. Hamdah was heavily pregnant, even though to us she looked too old to be bearing children still, like many of the Bdoul women. They were worn out by repeated child-bearing, their faces parched by the sun. We subsequently came to spend much time with this family. Tuffleh's father, Abdallah, lived in a cave which was further along the side of el-Khubthah going north-east. It was a very large cave with *loculi* carved in the walls.[91]

After dinner, Angela and I walked home. We sometimes had to use a torch, which we always carried. However, in the absence of city lights, the moon was also an important source of illumination. Returning home at night was easy by the full moon, which cast along the way shadows of the eucalyptus trees near el-Habis. The paving of the Colonnaded Street would glow in moonlight, so that we could see the direction back to el-Habis and our cave.

Hamdah's New Baby, Atidal

About a week after we first had dinner with Hamdah and her children, one of her daughters, who was riding her donkey down to the spring to collect water, stopped in the Colonnaded Street to tell us her mother had had a baby. She invited us to come and see her.

Beside the small fire, in the centre of the cave, there was a bundle of quilts on the rubber mattresses which occupied about a quarter of the floor. Hamdah was sitting on these, and after a while, she lifted up a bundle and unwrapped it to show us her baby girl Atidal. She was wrapped in swaddling clothes and had a small yellow veil over her face. Hamdah lifted the veil to show us Atidal, who had fairly dark skin and a lot of thick black hair about half an inch long. Usually, a mother would keep the baby's face covered and not show it for about the first three months to avoid the baby being given a sore eye or a cold.[92]

After a baby was born, visitors were supposed to give the family money (about 200 fils, 0.2 of a dinar). This gift was viewed as a debt, to be repaid when the visitor had a baby.[93] Rather than money, we brought a large box of biscuits from Dakhilallah's shop, which was the nicest gift available in Petra and also not particularly inexpensive. The biscuits, which were plain ones made in Jordan, were immediately devoured by the children with great excitement.

Hamdah was also cuddling her two-year-old son, Khalil, so that he did not feel rejected by the arrival of the new baby. It interested me that some modern western problems with small children did not exist in Petra. There was, for example, no problem getting a young child to go to sleep in its room alone at night, because everyone went to sleep together at the same time, on the bedding laid out on the cave floor.

The fathers were also very demonstrative, especially to young children. The older men who had lots of children were quite fatherly, even to me with my plaits and Bedouin scarf which made me look about fourteen years old. Dakhilallah came halfway up the Qasr el-Bint scaffolding one day to make sure I could get down safely, and another time told me how to settle my upset stomach.

About two months later we went to see Tuffleh. She was not there but Hamdah invited us in for *shay*. Atidal was being nursed quite capably by her older sister, who was about six years old. Hamdah then fed Atidal using powdered milk in an unsterilised bottle. This was concerning, as usually we saw the babies being breastfed, and I had thought this contributed to the high survival rate of the children at the time.[94]

88 Marguerite van Geldermalsen (2006: 119–20) describes the simplest form of this one-pot stew as consisting of onion, tomato purée, and macaroni (pasta), to which other ingredients could be added.

89 Margaret Murray (1939: 22) complained that the Bdoul were lazy and did not want to do hard physical work, while also commenting on their poor health (including tuberculosis), probably influenced by a poor diet which left them under-nourished.

90 Marguerite van Geldermalsen (2006: 95) mentions how two years earlier (in 1979) Tuffleh was a goat-herd.

91 Marguerite van Geldermalsen (2006: 176) also comments on its "centuries thick" floor.

92 Marguerite van Geldermalsen (2006: 97, 164) describes how this custom was protecting new babies from the 'evil eye'.

93 Marguerite van Geldermalsen (2006: 149, 163) gives examples of this.

94 Vaccinations and antibiotics in fact probably played a key role in the survival of the children.

Fig. 145. Juma Samaheen playing the *rabābah* in his tent, with Khalil watching, 1984.

One of Hamdah's neighbours came in, wearing a dress decorated with cross-stitch embroidery done by hand. The stitching, which was a fawn yellow colour, used the crosses as fill and was not arranged in rows around the hem. Hamdah had a machined version of the same pattern in the same colours, which suggested that the pattern was probably traditional.

On another occasion, Tuffleh's husband, Abdallah, was home from the army for a few days, and we were invited for *shay*. He said he was sixteen years old, and he looked very young. As he had made the invitation, he himself put out three foam rubber mattresses for us to sit on when we arrived, so that we felt like the princess and the pea. He made an enormous fire, fuelling it with kerosene, rather than just firewood. When we took his sisters' photograph, his brother Irbaya insisted that we include their battery-operated cassette player in the picture (fig. 143).

Tuffleh had shining black washed hair, nail polish, and mascara which was kohl made from soot.[95] Some of the younger girls had also put mascara on, continuing a custom observed on the Bdoul women in the first half of the twentieth century (fig. 144). Tuffleh was usually very vivacious, talking to us in English continuously. On this occasion, she sat in the background dicing potatoes, then went and made the bread, hardly talking to us. Seʿideh, Hamdah's eldest daughter, who was about the same age, was also there to help. The men were the focus of the whole conversation. The four

Fig. 146. Toba playing the flute, 1986.

younger girls, Toba, Uthmaiya, Maheela, and Aisha, sat in a row along one side of the fire, with the youngest one nursing baby Atidal. The goats kept coming in and having to be shooed out. As soon as his father Juma arrived home, little two-year-old Khalil wanted to sit on his crossed legs. When Juma put his white *keffiyeh* on Khalil, it came down to the ground, and he ran round in it with everyone giggling. It was all just like any household at dinnertime.

Juma owned the camel which worked at the Khasneh. One day he invited us for *shay* and played a *rabābah*, a single stringed instrument with a bow, as he had on my trip in 1984

95 Marguerite van Geldermalsen (2006: 20) describes the production of kohl from soot.

Fig. 147. Outside Hamdah's cave, with Khalil, Hamdah, Aisha, Toba, Judith, Angela, and Uthmaiya.

Fig. 148. Corinthian Tomb, 1981/2.

Fig. 149. Tuffleh loading the donkey with chaff, stored in the main chamber of the Corinthian Tomb, 1981/2.

(fig. 145).[96] He held it downwards like a cello, on his knees, and changed the notes by putting his fingers on the string to make the trilling sound of Arab music. The Bdoul also played flutes, as on a later trip when Toba played a flute fashioned from a plastic pipe (in 1986, fig. 146). This was played by blowing across the end of the pipe and fingering the row of holes in it. When we heard a youth playing panpipes in one of the Palace Tomb chambers, the sound he produced created an Arcadian atmosphere.

Tuffleh's in-laws used the space outside their cave, as well as some of the other caves nearby, as living space for activities (fig. 147). They used the Corinthian Tomb to store their animal feed (fig. 148).[97] The entrance to its main chamber was high enough up that the goats could not get into it, but low enough to load the animal feed onto the donkey (fig. 149). The feed was stored in the broad *loculi* (fig. 150).

Chaff on the floor of the Tomb of Sextius Florentinus indicated that it had been used for animals relatively recently (figs. 151–152). It was also very smoke-blackened indicating a long history of past occupation. Beneath the soot on the upper part of the back wall we could distinguish an entablature which was curved upwards in the middle and was supported by half-columns framing the *loculi* along the wall (fig. 152).

One of the caves between Hamdah's home and the Tomb of Sextius Florentinus (fig. 153) was used as a stable for Juma's camel, which he took to the Khasneh each day for the tourists (fig. 70). When we arrived at the Tomb of Sextius Florentinus one morning to work, the camel was in its stable-cave. At the end of one day, when we were working at the Palace Tomb, we saw it walking home unaccompanied. The camel bent its long neck round to look back occasionally but continued to head home. After work one day, as the shadows grew long, Juma let us try the camel out (fig. 154). Juma wore a traditional *thaub*, accompanied by a jacket and a white *keffiyeh* on this occasion.

The children watched us as we were setting up and taking the theodolite readings at the Tomb of Sextius Florentinus. When Angela held the ranging rod up against the facade, five children raced over to her and stood facing the theodolite. They thought I was taking her photograph and wanted to be in it. We had to defend the theodolite from being bumped by goats, as well as the children. Initially, we used lengths of the smooth twigs of sea squill with stones around them to mark the theodolite stations (the exact positions of the theodolite, which had to be measured with a tape measure). However,

96 See also Weir 1976: pl. 17.
97 Barley and wheat chaff, and barley grain: types of feed clarified by Marguerite van Geldermalsen, pers. comm. 11 October 2018.

Fig. 150. Corinthian Tomb, main chamber, with animal feed stored in *loculi*, 1981/2.

when the children began to copy these, we had to change to using lengths of wire cut from coat hangers and making sure we kept track of them.

The Palace Tomb was in the area of space Juma and Hamdah's family used, which extended from their cave to the Corinthian Tomb. One day when we were photographing the Palace Tomb (fig. 155), Maheela carefully made a pile of stones under the camera tripod, with a twig, like we did with the theodolite (fig. 156). I had a strong telephoto lens which required a large tripod in order to photograph details which were high up. Like the telescope of the theodolite, the telephoto lens revealed details such as the painted dentils on the Palace Tomb (fig. 157). The top part of the Palace Tomb was free-standing, and we were able to see on the side that timber had been used above the vaulting (fig. 158). To photograph such details, we had to take into account the position of the sun for the best shots, and often had to go back to tombs at a particular time of day.

The children would hang around and help us when we were measuring near the Palace Tomb (fig. 155).[98] One afternoon, they carried the staff and ranging rod. Following along behind Angela, they looked like the shoemaker's elves with their scarves, and they were so small that three of them

Fig. 151. Tomb of Sextius Florentinus, 1981/2.

98 The Bdoul called the Palace Tomb *Umm Sanadeeg* ("The Mother of Boxes"): Canaan 1930: 9, 34 (es-Snêdîq); van Geldermalsen 2006: 57–58.

Fig. 152. Tomb of Sextius Florentinus, back wall, 1986.

Fig. 153. Juma Samaheen's camel in its stable, 1981/2.

Fig. 154. Testing Juma Samaheen's camel in the late afternoon, with Aisha and three other girls in 1981/2 [Angela Phippen].

Fig. 155. Palace Tomb, 1986.

Fig. 156. Photographing the Palace Tomb with the telephoto lens, while Maheela sets up a stone and a twig to imitate a theodolite station, 1981/2 [Angela Phippen].

carried the great big long staff together (fig. 159). We would share our lunch with them, giving them bread and cheese, which they liked.

For morning or afternoon tea, or tea in between, we would sometimes join them in the sun outside their cave, for *shay* made by Hamdah, sitting on foam mattresses placed on the sand (fig. 160). They would patiently wait while we said we had to work for an agreed length of time or until an agreed time when we said we could stop for tea. Tuffleh and Hamdah both had watches. *Shay*, which was also called "Bedouin whisky", refreshed us as a quick source of energy, due to its high sugar content.

On one occasion I had a skirt on, without trousers (fig. 147). Hamdah indicated that I needed to also wear trousers under it (like the girls in Jordan did when they went to school). After that, I usually wore my army trousers under my skirt in what became a distinctive style. The pockets of the army trousers were useful for carrying things like my passport, and also a small torch, toilet paper, and matches which we carried with us all the time.

Playing Skippy the Kangaroo

One day, we went round to Hamdah's place to pay a visit. The children were there, but she was out, having left baby Atidal with them to be bottle-fed. The girls' method of feeding her, which we also saw used by some mothers, involved laying her on her side, balanced on a mound of cloth, and

Fig. 157. Palace Tomb, detail of lowest entablature with painted dentils, 1986.

leaving her to suck from the bottle. This method lacked the cuddles and attention which normally accompanied breast-feeding.

We sat out in the sun and again showed them the picture book we had about Australia. They were fascinated by it and wanted to look through it many times, so that they formed a tight cluster with their heads over the book. This cluster became even tighter when they were looking at hundreds of ant-sized, but scantily clad or half-clad bathers on Sydney's Bondi beach (fig. 161).

They were well acquainted with how the goats fed their young and were intensely interested in the kangaroo's arrangements for this. We explained how the baby kangaroo lived in the mother's pocket (pouch) when it was small and drank the milk from the teat in the pocket. As the kangaroo with its pocket fascinated them so much, I did a demonstration of how the kangaroo Skippy "the bush kangaroo" jumped.[99] This was a hit and became a game with me jumping along with my hands curled over in front of me like paws with about five or so children doing the same (fig. 162). They thought it was great fun, but it would give me a stitch if I did it for too long.

99 Skippy "the bush kangaroo" was a kangaroo who featured on Australian television in a series of adventures with a young boy, initially in the late 1960s.

Fig. 158. North side of the Palace Tomb showing vaulting supporting a bed of timber, 1986.

Fig. 159. Hamdah's and other children helping Angela carry our levelling staff and ranging rod, 1981/2.

Fig. 160. Tea in front of Hamdah's cave, with Khalil, Hamdah, Aisha, Toba, Uthmaiya, and Angela, 1981/2.

Fig. 161. Examining a book on Australia with photographs of sunbathers on Bondi Beach, 1981/2 [Angela Phippen].

Fig. 162. Playing Skippy the kangaroo outside Hamdah's cave, with the Tomb of Sextius Florentinus in the distance on the far right, 1981/2 [Angela Phippen].

Playing Dolls at Moghar an-Nasara

We had to return to Moghar an-Nasara for further readings on the Tomb with the Armour (No. A649). We got up at five o'clock while it was still pitch dark, had breakfast, and then left by the first morning light, walking along the Colonnaded Street to the Nymphaeum and then along Wadi el-Matahah and up the sandy slope to Moghar an-Nasara.

While Angela and I were working at the Tomb with the Armour, three little girls, all about six years old, arrived (fig. 163). Each was carrying a little sling-crib (*muzferr*) like their mothers used to carry their babies, such as Hamdah and Umm Gasim (figs. 163, 165). The *muzferr* consisted of a hammock-like crib formed by a square of cloth folded in half lengthwise and hung from two pieces of narrow cloth or rope across the mother's forehead. The mother carried the baby in the *muzferr* behind her back, so that she had a clear view of the path and rocks ahead of her.[100] The

Fig. 163. Three girls playing dolls outside the Tomb with the Armour at Moghar an-Nasara. The dolls are made of rocks, each in a *muzferr*, 1981/2.

100 Marguerite van Geldermalsen (2006: 175–76) explains the advantages of a *muzferr*.

Fig. 164. Hamdah going home with her children, with her baby in the *muzferr* hanging down her back, 1982.

Fig. 165. Umm Gasim (Agaela) carrying her toddler in a *muzferr*, 1986.

little girls playing dolls had blankets covering the baby and even yellow netting over the face, like that covering the face of Atidal when she was newborn. The girls used rocks as the dolls.[101] (Once, we saw Hamdah heading home with five of her children and the donkey, and she carried baby Atidal in a *muzferr* [fig. 164]. Moghar an-Nasara is seen in the distance).

The next day, two of the girls reappeared, along with an older girl, and played making *shraak*, unleavened Bedouin bread (fig. 166). They first collected twigs for the fire, including broken squill stalks. They put these in a pile with three rocks around them and balanced a larger flat rock on top (for the domed iron plate, *sāj*). The eldest girl dusted the area in front of her, the way Bedouin women do with the flour when preparing the dough (in a round tray). She threw a rock, which was the dough, from one hand to the other, copying their mothers when they stretch it out to make it thin. Then she put it on the flat rock, drawing her hand back quickly, as if the metal plate rock were hot. She bent her head down and sideways and blew on the sticks. Sitting cross-legged, she shook her skirt at the "fire" to help it cook the bread. Her movements were identical in every detail to those used by the girls' mothers and older sisters to make bread (fig. 167).[102]

101 Marguerite van Geldermalsen (2006: 222–23) describes little girls playing dolls with rock-babies.

102 Marguerite van Geldermalsen (2006: 77–81) on learning to make *shraak*, which also requires the correct firewood (juniper). Bdoul women used the same traditional Bedouin method when Margaret Murray (1939: 24) was in Petra in 1934. Pink oleander survived in the wadis of Petra (when not removed to make routes easier for vehicles) because it would not be used for firewood or eaten by goats. Nor were the sea squill edible. Wormwood also made good firewood.

Fig. 166. Three girls playing making *shraak* (bread) at Moghar an-Nasara, 1981/2.

Dinner at Abu Shaher's Cave

Mohammad Abu Shaher invited Angela and me up to his place for dinner. He was known as Abu Shaher (father of Shaher), because Shaher was the name of his oldest son. His home was up on the eastern ridge of Jabal Mʿaysrah (fig. 168).

Abu Shaher had three caves in a row. The first one, the largest, was the main cave for entertaining and sleeping, while the middle cave was used for cooking and family meals (fig. 169). His family also used the space in front of the caves, which had a view across to others on Jabal Mʿaysrah (fig. 170). The third cave was used as a pen for his sheep and goats (figs. 171, 172).

The front wall of the main cave was made of stone rubble stabilised with cement. It had a lockable door, with a square window on either side, and one above the door. The windows had panes of glass. The frames of the door and windows were outlined in blue paint (fig. 169). Inside it had a polished concrete floor and white painted walls. It was very spacious with a high ceiling, with none of the claustrophobic feeling of the smaller more cramped caves. The room was lit by a Tilley lamp. (Tilley lamps cast a surprising amount of light when they worked. The Bdoul also used kerosene lamps.)

In the back wall there was a large recess, with a curved ceiling and a large synthetic carpet of a lion hanging on the wall.

Fig. 167. Umm Gasim making *shraak* (bread), 1982.

Fig. 168. Eastern ridge of Jabal Mʿaysrah, looking towards Abu Shaher's caves, 1983 [Piotr Bienkowski].

Fig. 169. Abu Shaher's main cave and "kitchen cave", 1981/2.

Fig. 170. Abu Shaher, with children, including his daughters Zahra, Abla, Fatima, and Miriam outside his caves, 1981/2.

Fig. 171. Abu Shaher's sheep and goat pen cave, 1981/2.

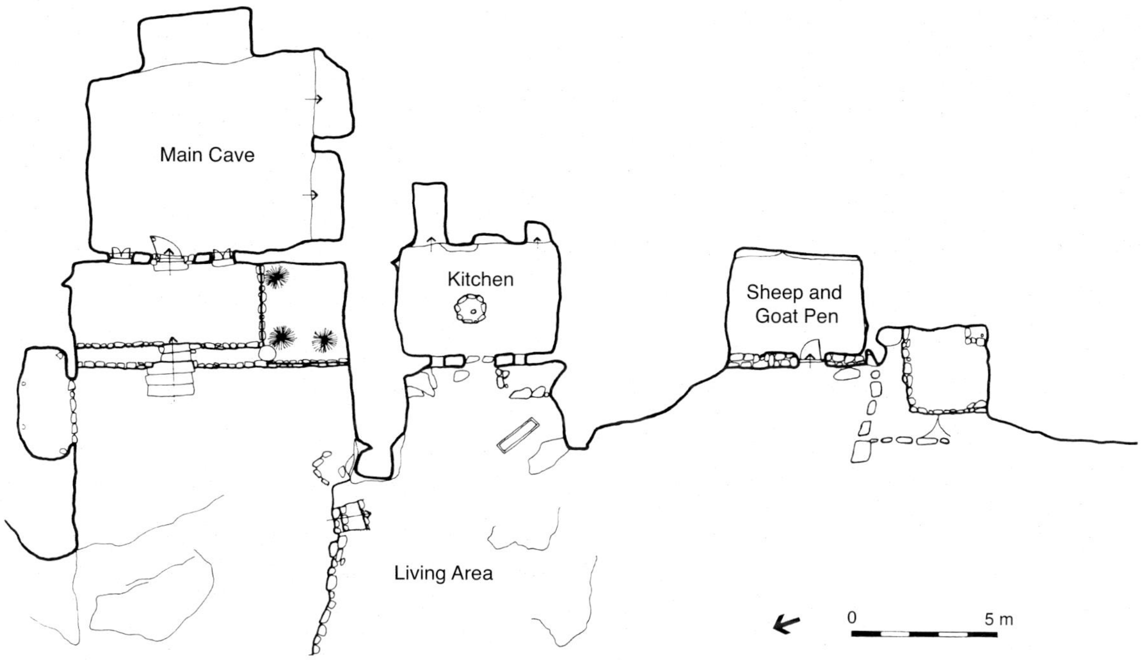

Fig. 172. Abu Shaher's caves, plan [based on Bienkowski and Chlebik 1991: fig. 5].

The bedding (foam rubber mattresses and quilts) was piled up neatly on one side of the room. In one back corner, there were a small table and an iron frame bed, which Shaher used. In another corner of the room, there were a table and shelves with food on them. Hanging on the walls, there were studio portraits taken a long time ago. Framed in glass, they included a formal family portrait of Abu Shaher and his wife Ghlal, and a portrait of Abu Shaher in his army uniform wearing a *keffiyeh*.[103] There was also a large portrait of King Hussein taken in about 1953, wearing western-style military uniform.

When we arrived, the room was ready for guests. Inside near the doorway was a large flat basin (about one meter in diameter). This was to collect water, when washing hands or feet, under the flow directed from a water jug with a very narrow spout (like the one in fig. 124). Shoes were left just inside the doorway. Towards the middle of the room, three foam rubber mattresses formed a U-shape on a handwoven wool rug with a brazier (portable metal fireplace) in the centre.

The brazier had been prepared beforehand, with a woodfire made in it outside.[104] When the fire had burnt down to hot coals, so that it no longer created smoke, the brazier was brought inside. It was used for heating and making the tea. It was much cleaner than having a smoking fire in the middle of the cave.[105]

The breadmaking and cooking for our dinner were done in the smaller cave next door, which had a fireplace in the centre and firewood piled high. The front wall of this cave was made of a dry-stone wall with a doorway and windows in it (fig. 169). In warmer weather, the cooking and breadmaking were done in the area in front of the kitchen cave.

When it was time to serve dinner, the brazier was moved out of the way, and a circular platter with *mensef* was put in its place. The one-metre wide platter was lined with Bedouin bread (*shraak*) surrounding a pile of rice with chicken on top of it. The delicious juice from the cooking was poured over it, which had been flavoured with reconstituted hard, salty dried goat's milk yoghurt balls (*jamīd*). The *mensef* was accompanied by two bowls of yoghurt and a bowl of tomato salad. Everyone sat around the large platter and ate from it. Each had a spoon for the rice and used fingers for the meat. When there were no spoons, skill was required to eat the rice. A ball of rice had to be formed by squeezing enough juice out of it, in order to get it into your mouth without grains of rice spreading all over your face. Although it was traditional to eat with your right hand, they did not mind that I was left-handed. We ate first, with the men.[106] Then when they had finished, deliberately not having eaten all of the food, the platter was moved across the room, where Umm Shaher (Ghlal) and her daughters ate what was left.

The Bdoul usually used chicken for *mensef*, only having goat on special occasions.[107] On a subsequent occasion when

103 Marguerite van Geldermalsen (2006: 168–69) also gives a description of Abu Shaher's caves. She also mentions that he had another large cave with water drums and where they tethered the donkey (2006: 169). Abu Shaher's is "Household 2" in Bienkowski and Chlebik 1991.

104 Marguerite van Geldermalsen (2006: 141, unnumbered colour plate 3) describes making the fire for a brazier.

105 Caves with earth, not concrete, floors could have firepits at the centre of them.

106 Margaret Murray (1939: 25) noted that the Bdoul women and children also ate last when she was in Petra in 1934.

107 Banning and Köhler-Rollefson (1986: 164) noted, from their observations at Beidha in 1982, that chicken bones would have appeared less in the archaeological record than goats' bones due to dogs eating the bones. In other parts of Jordan, *mensef* is more commonly made with lamb, which is considerably more expensive than chicken. When Margaret Murray worked in Petra in 1934, the Bdoul did not keep chickens (Murray 1939: 22).

we ate at Abu Shaher's, the *mensef* was made with goat, which they slaughtered for that purpose. Helpings were also given to neighbours to ensure that it was all consumed that evening, as there was no refrigeration.

After dinner, Abu Shaher served tea twice, each time with a different herb such as mint added to it.[108] He explained that there was a new drink called "half-coffee". This turned out to be Nescafé granules, with the word "Nes" misheard as *nusf*, which means "half" in Arabic. He also sometimes served cocoa.

Abu Shaher showed us his "wife's work". Umm Shaher made hand-woven Bedouin rugs from the wool of their sheep. The traditional colours of these rugs were deep red, with some white and black lengthwise stripes. The wool was spun with a spindle like those used by the women at the Turkmaniyah Tomb. They were woven with the warp threads, rather than the weft, being long. Umm Shaher also made small hand-woven bags, with the wool dyed a variety of colours, to sell to tourists. Abu Shaher had a pocket book full of addresses of visitors to Petra.

Abu Shaher was good at maths. We played parlour games with match sticks and glasses, and his contribution was to combine eight 8s, so that they came to a total value of 1,000 (888+88+8+8+8). He read out a hand-written letter he had been sent. He was one of the few men of his generation of the Bdoul who could read and write. (Dakhilallah also could, but he was younger.) Abu Shaher had learnt when he was in the Arab Legion. He was from Petra originally, but had spent twenty years in the army. He had travelled all around Palestine with Glubb Pasha and had a medal from King George for it. The Bedouin had a history of serving in the Jordanian army and were intensely loyal to King Hussein.

Abu Shaher invited us to stay the night, because it was too far to walk back to our cave, especially if there was not much moonlight. We agreed, and he produced two sleeping bags. The next morning, Umm Shaher made *shraak* (bread) for breakfast. Abu Shaher served the *shay* with condensed milk. The addition of the syrupy sweet condensed milk was a luxury which most of the Bdoul could not afford. His army pension and salary from the Jordanian Department of Antiquities gave him greater affluence. He had been a night-guard for the Department of Antiquities part of the time we were there.

Family Life at Abu Shaher's Home

When Angela and I were working in Petra, we had visited Abu Shaher's home as dinner guests, but later I had the opportunity to see how Abu Shaher's family lived the rest of the time. I stayed with them when I went back by myself for a week to take photographs at the end of February 1982.

When the family was alone, without guests, I ate dinner with them in the second (middle) cave, which they used for cooking and also for eating breakfast in winter. They used it in preference to the larger, main one with the concrete floor, which they used for sleeping and serving dinner to guests. At that time of the year, the middle cave was also used at night to keep the baby goats safe and to keep an eye on them. When Umm Shaher and the baby had a cold, she and the baby also slept in it, so as not to disturb the rest of the family sleeping in the main cave.

In the main cave, the bedding, which consisted of foam rubber mattresses and large quilts, was laid out on the floor at night. In the daytime, the bedding was stacked away with a cloth over it. The use of space in the main cave of a family in Petra was flexible. Like Abu Shaher's, most families lived in a single main cave (where they entertained, ate, and slept), and often had a second "kitchen cave", for cooking and some other activities. They also used the area outside as an extension of their daytime living and cooking space. At Abu Shaher's, as in some other households, this area also had a tent erected in it in summer.

The day I arrived, I went with them for dinner at the home of Abu Khaled (Hassan), Abu Shaher's brother, who lived in the cave above. Reclining on foam rubber mattresses set up on three sides around the *mensef* reminded me of how the Nabataeans would have used the rock-cut banqueting rooms called triclinia, with benches carved along three sides.

On another evening, Abu Shaher and I went to the house of Salameh al-Muktar (Salameh Aid Suleiman Alfageer) for dinner. He was the Petra mayor or *Muktar*. As an elected official, the mayor played an important role within the community. To be more precise, we went to the cave of his Egyptian wife.[109] She was 18 years old with a small child, very pretty and cheerful, teasing her husband. She had been in Petra for three years. By then, because of the shortage of Bdoul women relative to the number of men, there were a total of fourteen Egyptian girls who had married Bdoul men. This had only happened in the last few years.[110] The mayor's Bdoul wife occupied another, larger cave.

As an "honorary man", I ate with the men. Caspar Weinberger, the United States Secretary of Defense at the time,

108 In all my visits to Petra, 1981/2, as well as 1984 and 1986, I was never served traditional Arab coffee by the Bdoul. Marguerite van Geldermalsen (pers. comm. 11 October 2018) explains that this was because it was made by the men for weddings, circumcision parties, and other special dinners. It was usually served to the men only. It is depicted in a photograph from 1934/5, fig. 29.

109 At this time (February 1982) the *Muktar*'s Egyptian wife occupied his smaller cave and his Bdoul wife (Maryam) his larger cave. By May and June 1983, when this living area was studied as "Household 1" by Bienkowski and Chlebik (1991), the *Muktar* had moved to Wadi Musa and his cave was occupied by Ali Metluk. Because of the *Muktar*'s role, as elected community leader, his cave complex included a lavatory, as it was his cave in which foreign visitors were most likely to stay when visiting. On Salameh, his wives, and houses, see also Shoup 1985: 289 n. 2. He moved to Umm Sayhoun ahead of the rest of the tribe: van Geldermalsen 2006: 258.

110 As far back as the late 1950s the Bdoul, who then only numbered 150, had fewer women than men. Marguerite van Geldermalsen (2006: 209–11) explains how Mohammad al-Jamadeh (al-Jimedy) married the first Egyptian girl in 1978 and then took other Bdoul men to Cairo to also bring back wives, usually to be second wives. A few of these marriages were unsuccessful.

had been to Petra on an official visit to Jordan and had given the *Muktar* a Parker pen and a gilt tie-pin inscribed with "Secretary of Defense, United States of America". I was handed this to examine, as the *Muktar* wanted to know whether or not it was solid gold.

The next day, at breakfast time, Abu Shaher turned on the radio for my benefit to listen to Alistair Cooke's *Letter from America* on the BBC World Service. It was surreal listening to it crouched on the sand in a cave in Petra.

Fatima's House

Although Abu Shaher's eldest daughter Fatima, who was 16 years old, was married, she still lived in her father's house and ran the household because her husband was away in Bahrain in the army.[111] In Tuffleh's case, in the equivalent situation, she stayed with her in-laws, so there was no hard-and-fast rule for a woman having to stay in her father's house, rather than with in-laws in her husband's absence.

One afternoon, when I came back early from the southern graves and the Snake Monument, Fatima decided to show me her house. It was a cave on the next level above Abu Shaher's caves. It was locked, with the contents of the whole cave all neatly packed away inside. Fatima carefully showed me that there were six large and six small mattresses. She also had fancy glasses and cups for serving visitors. The items included decorative ones for her, including a handkerchief which she had edged in coloured beads, as well as a necklace of cloves, a supply of henna, and the black kohl women put around their eyes. A Bdoul woman photographed early in the first half of the twentieth century also wore kohl and a necklace of cloves, in addition to her jewellery (fig. 173).

Fig. 173. Bdoul husband and wife, 1900–1920 [American Colony, G. Eric and Edith Matson Photograph Collection, Library of Congress, Prints and Photographs Division, LC-DIG-matpc-22011].

Wadi Siyyagh

Two days before, I had accompanied Fatima on the donkey to the spring at Wadi Siyyagh to fetch water, which took about one hour. It was not very strenuous, since we rode the donkey, and it carried the two 20-litre plastic jerry cans filled with the water which gushed out of pipes at the spring (fig. 174).[112] The spring is fed by the perennial water supply from ʿAin Musa, the spring in Wadi Musa, which runs into Petra underground. The Bdoul in the caves did not have a water tank, like our kitchen, but usually stored their water in a large 44-gallon metal drum or used it directly out of the jerry cans.

The trip to the spring was quite a social outing as it provided the opportunity to meet people who were not immediate neighbours. It also gave the young men a chance to view the girls of marriageable age.

Wadi Siyyagh had a large garden, which was also a refreshing green haven, where Dakhilallah grew fruit trees (producing figs, guavas, apricots, lemons, and pomegranates), as well as olive trees, grape vines, and vegetables (marrows and tomatoes) (fig. 175). The green plants contrasted with the stark reddish walls of the sandstone on either side, and with its contrast to the dry surrounds, it brought to mind a walled garden.

111 This is the Fatima from whom Marguerite van Geldermalsen (2006: 25, 168) took her Arabic name.

112 Marguerite van Geldermalsen (2006: 84) describes the process of children filling their jerry cans.

Fig. 174. Wadi Siyyagh, the outlet of the spring, 1981/2 [Angela Phippen].

Fig. 175. Wadi Siyyagh, garden, 1981/2.

Trip to Beidha with Abu Shaher

Near the end of our final field trip together, Angela and I needed to venture further afield to the two main Nabataean areas on the outskirts of Petra to the north and south, Beidha and Wadi Sabra. We arranged to go to Beidha with Abu Shaher as our guide. He brought his shotgun in the hope of seeing some birds to shoot (although we did not come across any).

We went along a narrow gorge between Wadi Deir and Wadi Abu ʿOlleqa. At first there were many tombs in the rock faces on either side, until the gorge narrowed. Then the gorge widened out, and there were traces of the old rock-cut Nabataean road, which led to roughly furrowed agricultural land (fig. 176). Abu Shaher showed us a simple single plough (*ard*) which the Bedouin used, pulled by two donkeys. The soil was still devoid of growth, as the seasonal spring rains had not come. There were retaining walls running across the wadi to collect and hold the runoff when it rained. Areas such as this would become very green after seasonal rains, as we later saw (fig. 177). The land opened out into a plain with the cream mountain to the east and the last few red drips of Petra sandstone in front of it as small rounded rock outcrops. After crossing this plain, we entered a wadi with yellowy cream sandstone hills on either side and many more small shrubs, not at all overgrazed like Petra. At the beginning of this wadi, there is a solitary small facade with Assyrian crowsteps.

Fig. 176. Beidha, ploughed land, 1981/2.

The archaeological site of Neolithic Beidha had been exposed when the side of the site had fallen away across Wadi Siq al-Ghurab. The remains at Beidha date from the Pre-Pottery Neolithic B period, when people had stone tools but did not make pottery. The remains were directly below the surface, and it was quite thrilling as we could distinguish the house plans clearly from the three feet (ca. 1 m) high stone walls. They included a circular house with gaps for posts in the stone walls all the way around. There were also oval-shaped and square houses. One house had a set of steps leading down into it. There were traces of plaster on the walls, and the floors were reportedly plastered. Many flints littered the ground, including sickle blades for harvesting grain. There were also many stone querns lying around, used for grinding wheat. We imagined that the occupants would have had lives similar to those of the Bedouin, but using stone, rather than metal, implements.

Fig. 177. Cereal growing near Beidha after rain, 1986.

Siq el-Barid and the Painted House

At Beidha itself, the rock-cut remains were Nabataean. They included a very large cistern which was still in use. The main Nabataean monuments at Beidha are in Siq el-Barid, which is a narrow gorge. To the right of the entrance to Siq el-Barid, Facade 846 is cut in the cream rock face (fig. 178). This facade does not have a large chamber behind it, but only one as high and wide (ca. 1.75 m) as the doorway, and about 10 or so feet (3.3 m) deep when the doors open. There are recesses for double doors at its entrance,[113] suggesting that it probably contained something like a cult statue of a god, rather than being a *loculus* for a burial.

Beyond Facade 846, the small narrow siq opens out into a chilly narrow gorge – hence its name Siq el-Barid (*barid* = cold). Inside this siq, which only has one entrance, there is a very beautiful monument on the left with four columns, which are carved free. The tops of the columns are as crisp as the day they were carved, providing a sense of how Petra must have looked when the carving was fresh. There were also many cisterns, but the whole siq did not have any tombs, indicating it was used only by the living. Further along, the gorge narrowed a little, and there was a row of wide entrances opening into banqueting rooms (triclinia) with benches around three sides for dining (fig. 179).

Beyond the triclinia, on the right, a flight of steps leads up to the so-called Painted House 849, which was

113 McKenzie 1990: pl. 106a.

Fig. 178. Facade 846 before the entrance to Siq el-Barid, 1986.

Fig. 179. Siq el-Barid, triclinia (banqueting rooms) with Abu Shaher, 1986.

Fig. 180. Painted House in Siq el-Barid, with painted vault in large recess, with Alex Cresswell and Abu Shaher, 1986.

a *biclinium* (i.e., with two benches, fig. 180), with the remains of a painted ceiling decorated with ivy, grape vines, and flowering vines, with birds and chubby figures in them (fig. 181).[114] The figures include cupids (with wings) (fig. 182) and a young Pan (the god of shepherds, with a goatskin back and cloven feet) playing a long flute (fig. 183). Their full beauty was revealed when they were subsequently cleaned (figs. 184–185).[115] There are the remains of stucco imitation ashlar masonry on the walls, held in place by the neat tooling in the rock (fig. 180).

The Painted House provides a sense of how the insides of banqueting rooms and some tombs would have looked when stuccoed and painted, when all that remains now are the diagonal stone dressing marks which keyed the stucco.

114 The carbon deposits on the wall-paintings were removed by conservators from the Conservation of Wall Painting Department of the Courtauld Institute of Art, London, commissioned by the Petra National Trust with funding from a variety of sources. The work, completed in 2010, was carried out by Stephen Rickerby and Lisa Shekede as consultants (Stephen Rickerby, pers. comm. 16 September 2018). The technique used is unusual, and the materials include gold leaf (Akrawi and Shekede 2010; Alberge 2010).

115 Plan: McKenzie 1990: pl. 113c.

Fig. 181. Painted House in Siq el-Barid. Detail of ceiling of large recess, 1986.

Fig. 182. Painted House in Siq el-Barid, a cupid on ceiling, 1986.

Fig. 183. Painted House in Siq el-Barid, young Pan on ceiling, 1986.

Occasionally, traces of stucco in the upper corners of tomb facades and chambers are visible in Petra.[116]

Siq el-Barid was very cold and damp when we were there in late January. The far end of the siq was blocked and had a stairway going up to a look-out. The extensive traces of carbon on the triclinia walls and ceilings indicated that the Bedouin had made use of them until recently. The dark colour of the soil and sand along the bottom of the siq caused by goats' droppings (still evident on my trip four years later, fig. 179) indicated that it had been used relatively recently for their herds, providing them with protection from the elements.[117]

Bedouin Tents at Beidha

When we came back out of the horribly cold siq, we were invited across to a black Bedouin tent nearby to have tea and lunch. The tent was pitched facing the rock, forming a small yard in which was a pile of firewood, some chickens, and a few baby goats nibbling the firewood. The Bedouin at Beidha were largely from the ʿAmmarin tribe, and some were Bdoul.[118]

We were invited into the endmost compartment or "room" of the tent, which is traditionally the men's section and used for entertaining. This "room" was very neat and clean, with woven mats. Covered mattresses were laid out for us to sit on round the hearth, which was built with rocks in the ground and indicated many years of use. The arrangement was the same as in a cave, but the walls were of woven black goats' hair. Abu Shaher told us that a tent lasts around twenty years.

Tea was put on the fire, and the young wife went to the next room of the tent, which was used by the women for cooking.[119] She returned with a pile of bread and a bowl of egg scrambled in buttery oil, which was the first time

116 E.g., McKenzie 1990: pls. 102c, 105b, 150b; Shaer in Kühlenthal and Fischer 2000: figs. 1–2, 7, 9, 16, colour pl. 9.

117 Banning and Köhler-Rollefson (1986: 161) noted that the ʿAmmarin moved next to, or into, Siq el-Barid in winter (although we did not observe them in the siq), and that some of the Bdoul spent winter near the prehistoric site. Their work revealed that Beidha had a very mild micro-climate, protected from season climatic extremes, resulting in the Bedouin not moving far from it in the course of a year, unlike those in other areas (Banning and Köhler-Rollefson 1986: 165–66).

118 Banning and Köhler-Rollefson 1986: 161.

119 A traditional tent has the men's section or compartment/room for visitors at one end, and the women's section for food preparation in the middle, with the third section for goats at the other end. Description of the parts of traditional Bedouin tents and division of space: Weir 1976: 1–3, 7–8, 17, figs. 1–3, pls. 3–5, colour pl. 2; Layne 1987: 356–61 (in the Jordan Valley); van Geldermalsen 2006: 169; Banning and Köhler-Rollefson 1986: 161–62.

Fig. 184. Painted House in Siq el-Barid, detail of painting on ceiling of large recess after cleaning, 2018 [Sean Leatherbury].

Fig. 185. Painted House in Siq el-Barid, young Pan on the ceiling, after cleaning, 2018 [Maria Lidova].

we had been served eggs by the Bedouin. It was delicious and very rich. There was a fantastic rapport between the forty-year old husband and his young smiling Egyptian wife, who seemed to be wrapped in each other. As the Bedouin at Beidha lived in their tents all year round nearby, the government had erected a concrete school there.

On the way back to Petra, we stopped at another tent for tea. This was a distinct contrast. We sat out in the sun in front of it on the foam rubber mattresses, with baby goats sunning themselves around us. The area in front of the tent was carpeted with goat droppings. Clothes and various possessions were shoved in the bushes around. The tent, which was open along one side, was divided into two rooms, one twice as long as the other. The longer one, which was two thirds of the length of the tent, was used for the goats at night. The other room, which occupied one third, was used for sleeping and cooking.

There was much variation between the affluence of the owners of the two tents, as there was between some occupants of the caves in Petra. These two examples also showed how the configuration of the compartments of a tent could be varied according to a family's requirements. If a family did not have a nearby cave for a goat pen, then they used their tents traditionally, accommodating their goats in part of them.[120]

Dinner at Abu Nawas's Cave

For our second journey further afield, we arranged with Mohammad Abu Nawas[121] to go to Wadi Sabra, where few people ventured. Abu Nawas's children and their friends often came to watch us when we worked in Wadi Farasa (figs. 186–188). Late on the day before our journey, we went round to his place to check what time we would be leaving the next morning. His home was in Wadi Farasa, on the west side of Jabal al-Madhbah which has the Theatre carved into the east side of it.

His home consisted of two caves at right angles to each other forming a courtyard, which had a rock face on the third side and was open to the west on the fourth side (fig. 189). The cave at the back of the courtyard was a Proto-Hegr tomb (No. 192), which was used as a stable for his horse and donkey. They apparently did not own any goats. Abu Nawas made his income from his horse, taking tourists down the Siq and on day trips. The front wall of their main cave (on the north side), in which his family lived, was built up of rocks with a wooden structure with a door beside it. The cave was only about twelve feet (4 m) by twelve feet square, with an earthen floor.

In the centre of the floor, there was a fire with a small pot on it, in which a thin stew of the usual potatoes, noodles (pasta), onion, and tomato paste was simmering. They moved it to one side and made *shay* for us. While the *shay* was brewing, Abu Nawas went outside. There was much clucking and squawking of chickens, then silence. This was repeated. The children also had gone outside. We enquired what was

Fig. 186. Abu Nawas's children keeping us company in Wadi Farasa, 1981/2.

Fig. 187. Girl with a flute and her friend in Wadi Farasa, 1981/2 [Angela Phippen].

120 Van Geldermalsen 2006: 169.

121 Abu Nawas was a nickname (Marguerite van Geldermalsen, pers. comm. 3 October 2018), instead of his being called Abu Gasim, after his eldest son.

Fig. 188. Abu Nawas's children and a friend in Wadi Farasa, 1981/2 [Angela Phippen].

Fig. 189. Abu Nawas's caves in Wadi Farasa, 1982.

Fig. 190. Breakfast at Abu Nawas's cave, with *shay* and *shraak* made by Umm Gasim, 1982.

Fig. 191. Angela on the donkey with Abu Nawas, followed by his son Gasim, heading for Wadi Sabra across Stouh an-Nabi Haroun, 1982.

Fig. 192. View down to Wadi Sabra, 1982.

going on. His wife, Umm Gasim (Agaela), explained to us, with great pride, that her husband was killing chickens for us.

When we employed one of the Bdoul as a guide for a day trip, they would always spend part of what we had paid them on inviting us for dinner with their family afterwards, normally *mensef* made using a chicken bought in Wadi Musa. This was the only time we were given such a meal before the trip or that chickens were slaughtered for us.

Mohammad brought the two chickens inside, and Umm Gasim put them in a large saucepan on the fire, after the stew had been moved to the primus (kerosene pressure) stove in the corner. When the chickens were ready, Abu Nawas took them to one side and plucked them. Then, with a rather blunt knife and great difficulty, he cut them up. Umm Gasim fried the pieces in a deep saucepan and then simmered them in water. She lined a shallow metal dish with Bedouin bread (*shraak*) and put the cooked chicken on this. They did not have any rice with which to make a proper *mensef*. The result was put before us with great pride.

I picked up a piece of chicken and felt it to pull some meat off, but it was so hard that I could not tell if it was flesh or bone. I bit into it and discovered there was some flesh on it, but it was so tough I could not pull it off even when I gripped it with my molars. The chickens were clearly very old, reflecting the rarity of their offering such hospitality. Abu Nawas then began pulling pieces of flesh off for us and putting it on the dish in front of us. The bread which had soaked up the juices was very tasty. The two chickens made just enough for Abu Nawas, Angela, and me. Umm Gasim, Abu Nawas's brother, and the children ate the stew instead. Umm Gasim explained how their eldest son, Gasim, had been injured when their primus stove had exploded. He still had scars on his face.

Having chickens killed in our honour for dinner felt like an adventure out of the tales of the old explorers and was a decided ego trip. (At each stage before the chicken was put on the dish, I thought we were being given the chickens to take away, as it was very late in the day to be preparing them for dinner.)

Trip to Wadi Sabra with Abu Nawas

As arranged, we went to Abu Nawas's home early the next morning, ready for the adventure we had been looking forward to for a few days. The ruins of Wadi Sabra were at the southern extent of Petra where the mountains narrowed beyond an area of agricultural land. Wadi Sabra was rarely visited, other than by the Bedouin. Outsiders could only go there with a guide because the Bedouin there were likely to use their guns first and ask questions later.

Umm Gasim made bread for breakfast, which we had with *shay* (fig. 190). Like all of the women, she made fresh

Fig. 193. Ancient road to Wadi Sabra with a retaining wall, 1982.

Bedouin bread (*shraak*) for breakfast. She patted a ball of dough in flour on the metal platter, then threw it from side to side in her arms until it was about 18 inches (45 cm) wide, then quickly cooked it on the domed iron sheet (*sāj*). Over breakfast, she told us, as we were all women, that we were to make sure her husband collected firewood on our trip and that he was taking the donkey for this purpose. The women would go to Wadi Sabra to collect firewood, as the supply in Petra had been depleted by both the Bdoul using it and by grazing goats. Umm Gasim saddled the donkey, Musa, with the old-fashioned wooden frame the Bdoul used as a saddle, with blankets over it. She put our lunch and camera gear into the dusty hessian saddlebags.

We set off. Gasim followed us for long enough that, in the end, his father allowed him to accompany us (fig. 191). In the early morning light, the journey began with a steady climb up the Nabataean road which was still visible in places cut out of the deep reddy-brown rock. Looking back, there was a view across Petra to the new Bedouin village, under construction. We then reached flat agricultural land which was being cultivated. Some stone terrace retaining walls across it were still visible. On our right, Jabal Haroun towered above, with the small white shrine of Aaron's Tomb glowing in the sun.

After walking across the flat plateau, Stouh an-Nabi Haroun, for a while, there was a view down into Wadi Sabra for its full length (fig. 192). It was very beautiful with the dark reddish-brown cliffs rising steeply on each side, and mountains of orange, pink, cream, and even white stone. Across the end of the wadi, there was a cream limestone mountain similar to the mountains of Wadi Musa. The colours of the rock and sand contrasted with the green in the wadi itself, creating a very beautiful view.

As we descended into the wadi along a fairly steep old road of limestone rocks which was built up with a retaining wall along the side (fig. 193), we met a woman with a camel coming up it in the opposite direction (fig. 194). Once the level of the wadi is reached, there are many old trees with gnarled trunks where the Bdoul come to collect firewood. After walking for two and a half hours, we reached Wadi Sabra, which was full of large oleanders. There were a few wells, as the water table was just below the surface of the wadi. Further along the wadi, beyond the small theatre, water was flowing, making a very pretty sight as it sparkled in the sunlight (fig. 195). Not having had running water for three weeks, such a small pleasure gave us great enjoyment. There was a solitary date palm growing, but sufficient water to have supported many more.

There are no rock-cut tomb facades on the way to Wadi Sabra, only agricultural land. There are no ruins of buildings until those at Sabra itself, which included some blocks that were the remains of what was obviously Nabataean

Fig. 194. Woman and her camel we passed on the way to Wadi Sabra, 1982.

Fig. 195. Wadi Sabra, with its perennial water supply, 1982.

Fig. 196. Wadi Sabra, small theatre for water ceremonies or entertainment, 1982.

architecture, and some substantial retaining walls.[122] The most complete ruin is the small theatre partly carved in the side of the mountain and partly built free-standing (fig. 196). It had a reservoir above it which provided water to fill the area in front of the seating (the orchestra), when used for water performances or festivities.[123]

Wadi Sabra is the entrance for the southern trade route to Petra, leading out to the Wadi Araba. It has a perennial water supply, and it is situated where the wadi is fairly narrow, beyond the agricultural land between it and Petra. Wadi Sabra probably served as a defence post for that southern route.

Abu Nawas made a fire and *shay*, and we had lunch with the donkey, Musa, close by (figs. 197–198). Abu Nawas was very nervous, wanting us to stay close to him. When I went behind the hillock to the back to answer the call of nature, he became very agitated because he was worried that the "people with guns" would take a shot at me in his absence.[124] A few months later, when I was in Jerusalem, the Nabataean archaeologist Avraham Negev told me that young Israeli soldiers would try to come across the border to see Petra.[125] Between the foundation of the state of Israel in 1948 and the

Fig. 197. Abu Nawas and Gasim at Wadi Sabra, 1982 [Angela Phippen].

122 A new project at Wadi Sabra, since 2014, has recorded baths, a temple, and houses. Tholbecq 2016: 666–67, fig. 24.

123 Lindner 1986: 146–54, figs. B, 5–8.

124 When Marguerite van Geldermalsen (2006: 156–57) visited Wadi Sabra in early 1980 with her husband and Bdoul friends, they were frightened away at gun point, even though they were obviously Bedouin.

125 Similarly, Shoup (1985: 279 n. 1) refers to several Israelis crossing the border illegally being killed.

Fig. 198. Having lunch at Wadi Sabra with Abu Nawas, Gasim, and his donkey, Musa, 1982 [Angela Phippen].

Oslo peace accord in 1994, Israelis were not allowed to visit Jordan, so Petra gained the status of an impossible destination amongst them. He told me that half of the young men who attempted the trip to Petra did not return.

As Wadi Sabra was little visited and there was no vehicular road there, it was a completely undisturbed wilderness, totally away from mankind. Consequently, it was much nicer than Petra itself, which was spoiled by the presence of vehicles, Nazzal's Camp, and the restaurant under construction in the wadi below our cave.

We walked back along the wadi in the sand, noticing how, at one point, it cut through a green vein of metallic copper which had been mined further north at Wadi Faynan, especially under the Romans. Angela and I took it in turns to ride the donkey (fig. 199). Walking along with Abu Nawas and Gasim, with Angela on the donkey in front, I felt like a nineteenth-century explorer (fig. 200). This trip was about the biggest thrill of our whole stay in Petra.

When we arrived back, Umm Gasim was not pleased with Abu Nawas because we had not collected any firewood (fig. 201). He viewed that as women's work. We paid him (adding enough to cover the cost of dinner), and he promptly handed the entire amount over to her to manage. This was not the only time we saw men give all of the money to their wives, who managed the household budget.

Awwad and his Bedouin Supermarket

One evening, we went into Musa al-Smadi's office-cave to ring Crystal-M. Bennett, to let her know when we were returning to Amman. Awwad Hammad al-Faqir was having dinner with him. Awwad owned the "Post Office Bedouin Supermarket", which was under the caves to the north of ours (fig. 202). Awwad criticised us for not having had anything to do with the Bedouin, but rather working all day and keeping to ourselves. We refuted this accusation, pointing out that that day we had had seven tea breaks with various Bdoul. In his opinion, there was no point in coming to Petra unless we saw the Bedouin lifestyle, which was different to ours, so that we could understand it.

Awwad said he never could understand the world from which the tourists in his shop came, until he went to Germany for three months to stay with a German friend. His greatest delight, when he was there, seemed to be that he was trusted to go to the supermarket alone with his friend's wife. He was also very proud that he could "work" their kitchen. Hence, the sign on his shop in fact meant: "Come and see what a Bedouin supermarket is like".

Like Dakhilallah's shop and Hajj Salameh's behind the tent opposite el-Khubthah, Awwad's was much like an old country town store in Australia, with the walls lined with

Fig. 199. Judith riding Musa in Wadi Sabra, with Abu Nawas and Gasim, 1982 [Angela Phippen].

shelves consisting of wooden fruit boxes stacked sideways, bags of flour and other dry goods leaning against the walls, and a set of scales. We felt disloyal to Dakhilallah if we went there. Awwad's shop also contained the telephone exchange for the three phones in Petra, two in the Department of Antiquities caves above him, and one in Nazzal's Camp.[126]

Awwad considered the European way of life superior to the Arab one, not because it was more affluent, but because things in Europe, like the telephone, always worked. He explained this in terms of a different attitude by citing the example of what had just happened to him. He was talking on the phone to Amman (which was about equivalent to trying to ring Australia from Petra), putting all his emotion into it, when the line was cut because the girl operating the exchange in Amman decided to talk to her boyfriend. He described Muhammad Khadija as a "European person" because he got things done, and considered that he should be respected for this. Ironically, we had been told not to post mail at the "Petra Post Office", as it would take up to three months for it to get as far as Wadi Musa.

I asked Awwad how long the Bdoul had been in Petra. Awwad said that in his grandfather's time there were ten or fifteen families in Petra.[127] In his father's time, there had been

126 Muhammad Khadija, pers. comm. 27 September 2018.

127 Margaret Murray (1939: 21) gives the number in 1934 as 35 families or 150 people.

Fig. 200. Heading back to Petra from Wadi Sabra, 1982.

Fig. 201. Umm Gasim, who was unimpressed when we returned from Wadi Sabra without a supply of firewood, 1982 [Angela Phippen].

Fig. 202. Awwad's "Bedouin Supermarket" at the foot of el-Habis, 1981/2.

five to ten families; many people had left because there was not enough to eat. Awwad considered there were now, in 1982, one hundred and fifty families in Petra.[128] He explained that when there were fewer of them, they would have been less likely to have been seen. He said they were like goats up in the mountains: "They see you, but you do not see them." This was very like our experience of Mufleh following us, but us not seeing him, and how, like Harriette Martineau, we had only noticed that some tombs were occupied because of the fires visible in them at night.

Awwad related how the name Bdoul comes from the Arabic *badala* which means "to change", because the Bdoul are the Nabataeans who converted to Islam. He also believed that all Arabs were descended from the Nabataeans, and that the Nabataeans originally came from Yemen. At the time (in 1982), there were two views about how long the Bdoul had been in Petra. The view held by the Bdoul was that they had been in Petra for centuries – possibly since the time of the Nabataeans. Others, such as the Jordanian archaeologist Fawzi Zayadine, argued that the Bdoul had only been in Petra since the end of World War I, because the specific name "Bdoul" was not mentioned by any nineteenth-century explorers, nor did they mention any Bedouin living in the caves. Some officials used this as an argument to justify

128 Farajat (2012: 152) gives the total number of families as 166, including those near Jabal Haroun at the time of the move to Umm Sayhoun in 1985. Shoup (1985: 284) gives 100 households.

moving the Bdoul to the new village of Umm Sayhoun, on the grounds that they did not have a historic right to live in the caves. I thought the Bdoul could have been there but not seen. I later found references to the caves being inhabited in the nineteenth century and concluded that it was possible to identify their occupants as the Bdoul,[129] I have presented an abridged form of this argument at the beginning of this book.

The nineteenth-century descriptions provided a picture of the Bdoul occupation in Petra related to the one we saw. Some of them occupied the caves only in the winter but pitched their tents in the valley and on the surrounding hills in summer. Others lived in the caves all year round. They were sufficiently few in number that not all visitors saw them and were less likely to do so in the summer. Like their modern counterparts, the nineteenth-century occupants had herds of black-haired goats and grew wheat and barley, most commonly on agricultural land between Petra and Jabal Haroun, in the valley of Petra, and at Beidha. The success of the crop, however, was dependent on adequate rainfall. During the twentieth century, with the growth of tourism and related archaeological work, the amount of time the Bdoul spent in the caves and valley of Petra gradually increased.

Leaving Petra

When I rode out through the Siq on Abu Shaher's horse for the last time of my 1981/2 field season, I was still struck by how amazing it was. The Siq was so tall and narrow with a bed of river pebbles at the bottom of it that it was completely silent except for the echo of the horses' hooves, creating a sense of timelessness. The shoes were not horseshoe-shaped ones, but solid so that pebbles did not catch in them. The ride down the Siq and glimpse of the Khasneh were fantastic enough to justify the trip for the tourists who did not usually go past the point where they could see the Urn Tomb and the Colonnaded Street, or the surrounding mountains which made Petra a world in itself.

I returned to Amman in the JETT minibus on the day nine university students had been killed when the coach in which they were travelling came off the road and crashed just outside Wadi Musa. When we drove past the coach lying on its side, everyone, including the JETT driver, had grave faces and said how terrible the accident was. Despite this, he drove back to Amman like a maniac. When asked to go more slowly by some of the female students who were frightened because of the accident, he refused.

His lack of any concern that he would have an accident was influenced by his belief in the predetermination of Allah's will. "God will provide": Allah would look after them. The most incredible risks were taken because of the belief that if something went seriously wrong, it was Allah's will which no human action could influence. The centrality of Allah to fortune is expressed in the word which always follows the expression of hope that something will happen, *Inshallah*, "God willing". If something which has gone well is mentioned, it is accompanied by *Alhamdulillah*, "Thank God" or "Allah provides". Thus, whether a man was rich or poor was also Allah's will.[130]

129 McKenzie 1991.

130 While there is still a strong belief in Allah and his benevolence, since my first trip to Petra, an acknowledgement of the relationship between dangerous driving and accidents has developed, along with a realisation of the relationship between hard work and education and affluence. This difference was very obvious when 21 people, 18 of whom were children on a school trip, were drowned in a flash flood at the Dead Sea in October 2018. There were calls at all levels for accountability over the human errors that had led to the trip going ahead, and much national soul-searching as to why there were not adequate precautions in place to avoid such a tragedy.

CHAPTER 4

1984

After returning to Sydney and analysing the material we had collected in the 1981/2 field trip, I made a field trip to Petra in early 1984 to check details and to take further theodolite readings and photographs. For that work, I borrowed a theodolite in Amman from Wimpey, the construction company. It had aluminium legs, as opposed to the wooden legs of the old model I had used previously. The aluminium made it harder to keep level in the cold wind and warm sun. When I had visited the engineering faculty at Jordan University to see if I could borrow one there, I noticed many of the students studying in that department were women. For the 1984 work, my assistant was Pamela Watson, a mature-age PhD student, who had been working on the Australian Expedition to Jerash (the Roman city in the north of Jordan).

Arrival in Amman after Two Years

It was two years almost to the day since I had left Jordan, but on arrival in Amman, the rapid pace of change in that time was evident. On my previous visit, passengers alighted from the plane down steps to the tarmac, then waited surrounded by armed soldiers until the bus arrived to drive them to the terminal. The terminal was not very large, so that passengers came straight outside into a noisy chaotic area where everyone was waiting, with taxi drivers pressing for fares by trying to grab the luggage of new arrivals. By contrast, the new Queen Alia Airport had moveable gangways which ran from the planes to the terminal. The airport was much larger, with a waiting area inside for arrivals, providing a much more orderly welcome to Jordan. As the new airport was so far out of town, I took the local bus to Abdali and then a taxi from there to the British Institute at Amman for Archaeology and History (the BIAAH).

Many new buildings had appeared in Amman in the past two years, especially out near the Institute and the University. These buildings exhibited considerable creativity. New styles of architecture were being developed, sometimes with eclectic combinations of features. The most interesting structures which had appeared in the previous two years were large houses and apartment blocks. Each was a rectangular multi-storey block, but on the top was a small building with a steeply pitched, red-tiled roof, with a line reminiscent of that of a Swiss chalet. Other variants involved the use of architectural features with no consideration of their original structural purpose. They used arches much more than we did in the West, although the arches were usually curved in shape rather than the pointed ones of traditional Islamic architecture. One building had small arches across the top of the windows, but with no vertical supports between the arches. Another had windows in the shape of upside-down arches. It was possible to make windows these shapes by making a wooden frame of the desired shape and pouring concrete into it. The concrete was then faced with limestone. If ashlar masonry with stone blocks had been used, the arches would have had to have vertical supports and be the correct way up.

Seeing these buildings, it was easy to understand how the Nabataean architecture could be stylistically eclectic and how the classical elements came to be used with no consideration for their original structural purpose. When the Nabataeans carved the facades out of the rock faces at Petra, their designs were not limited by what would stand up if they had been built free-standing from stone blocks. On the Palace Tomb, the Nabataeans designed lots of cornices, one on top of the other and supported by very short columns, maximizing the decorative effect over the surface of the facade (fig. 155). The Nabataeans also combined classical pediments and columns with Near Eastern features, most notably Assyrian crowsteps and Egyptian cavetto cornices (figs. 95–96).

At the British Institute, Crystal-M. Bennett had retired, and the director was a young prehistorian, Andrew Garrard. The ground floor had been re-arranged so that the open-plan arrangement had been broken up. The former dining room had been separated off and turned into the library and was very good for working in. The sound did not travel nearly so much, and so there was more private space. The old library area had become the dining room, and the lounge area remained in the corner. The atmosphere was much more relaxed.

I went into the Department of Antiquities, and Maha Jayhousi, the secretary of the Director, Dr Adnan Hadidi, gave me a royal welcome, kissing me on the cheek and giving me coffee. Going down to Petra and continuing my work was no problem. Everything seemed much more relaxed than last time. With the Jordanians, it was easier because they already knew me and were really glad I was back again. The noise and chaos of Amman did not seem as bad as I had remembered it, perhaps because I arrived expecting it.

A Jordanian archaeologist, from Jordan University, Dr Nabil Khairy, who studied Nabataean pottery, worked in the Institute library until 11 pm in the evening many days. He

Fig. 203. Old part of Wadi Musa, with stone houses and store rooms, and olive and fruit trees, 1984.

had done his PhD in London with the Nabataean expert Peter Parr. When Andrew Garrard had told Nabil that I was working on the tomb facades at Petra, he naturally wanted to know if I was trying to date them. When I confirmed that I was, he grinned at my naiveté and pointed out that everyone else working on Petra had tried to do so and not succeeded, and it was not possible. His reaction was similar to that of the Abbé Jean Starcky, a very distinguished Near Easternist, whom I once met.

I explained that many of the tombs at Medain Saleh, unlike those at Petra, had inscriptions on them from the first century AD mentioning the date and the name of the stone cutter and his father. At Medain Saleh, I found that, using only dated evidence and not assumptions about which tomb type came first, I could detect changes over time in the characteristics of the work of individual stonecutters. Brünnow and von Domaszewski had photographed and recorded the facades at Petra in 1897 and 1898 and divided them into types of tombs (whether they had one or two rows of crow-steps or were crowned by facing pairs of steps or had primarily classical features). They had then placed types into an evolutionary sequence, while also taking into account where the tombs had been carved.[1]

At Petra, I was able to divide the classical facades into groups based on the details of their classical features, such as cornices (which we had measured with the theodolite) and capitals (which we photographed). These groups of monuments could then be placed in a sequence, based on the monuments in them dated by evidence excavated in the 1960s and 1970s (such as the Qasr el-Bint, which was in the same group as the Khasneh).

When I had finished my explanation, Nabil was kicking himself for studying Petra for ten years and never solving the problem. It made me realise that I had come nearest to solving the mystery of dating the tomb facades of any scholar since Brünnow and von Domaszewski.

To Petra

Pam and I took the JETT tourist bus down to Petra. Tourism had increased sufficiently in two years that it was now a coach rather than a minibus, and so there was plenty of space for our equipment and supplies. The Desert Highway had become a four-lane divided highway all the way to the new airport. Beyond the airport, a phenomenal speed of construction was achieved by different companies each building a stretch of road and working day and night.

Most people on the coach were only going to Petra for the day, having been collected from their hotels. The coach went once per day, leaving Amman at 6:30 am and arriving

1 Brünnow and von Domaszewski 1904: 137–88. English summary of von Domaszewski's argument for the chronology of the tombs: McKenzie 1990: 2–4.

Fig. 204. Remains of paving in the Siq, 1981/2.

at Wadi Musa at about 10:30 am. It returned to Amman from Wadi Musa in the late afternoon the same day. This allowed the 15 to 30 or so tourists on it to ride down the Siq on horseback and see the Khasneh, then continue as far as the Theatre, and glance across to the "Royal Tombs" (the Urn Tomb, Corinthian Tomb, and the Palace Tomb). After about two hours in Petra, they returned for lunch at the Rest House (from 1983, at the Forum Hotel) in Wadi Musa, before leaving to get back to Amman.[2] Tourists on tours arrived by coach and had a similar experience. Usually, there were about 100 tourists per day. About once a week, if a cruise ship came into Aqaba, there were about 400 tourists.

Two years before, I had left Petra just before the growth which follows the arrival of the spring rains. I arrived at about the same time of year as I had left previously, which meant that my 1984 trip continued the cycle of the seasons. There was now a tinge of green on the desert after the spring rain. When we looked down on Wadi Musa, the terraces were very green with crops of wheat and barley about 12 inches (30 cm) high (fig. 203). The new road bypassed the main street of Wadi Musa with its peppercorn trees. In the distance, the way the knobbly red sandstone mountains of Petra stood out against the undulating cream limestone ones still struck me as remarkable.

The Petra Forum Hotel in Wadi Musa

As with the airport and the Desert Highway, the changes in Wadi Musa indicated rapid modernisation. The new Petra Forum Hotel (later Crowne Plaza), which had been under construction when I was there in 1981/2, was now open. As we wound down into Wadi Musa, we could see the hotel, with the cream hill behind it. It was two storeys high and fairly long, standing out because of its angular shape, rather than its colour (fig. 34). It was faced in very pale pinky cream sandstone dressed in imitation Nabataean style. In front of the new hotel, the cream sandstone landscape was scarred by an asphalt car park and a helipad for visiting dignitaries. The style of the hotel was similar to that of the Basin Restaurant in Petra, which was under construction opposite our cave in 1981/2 (fig. 106) and designed by the same Jordanian architect, Jafar Tukan.

On entering the foyer of the new hotel, it was obvious that it was a five-star hotel of international standard. It was part of the Intercontinental hotel chain. It had very pleasant décor. The foyer was paved in polished pale pink marble, with heavily tinted windows on each side to keep out the glare. Each pane of window glass was decorated with a large decal of a Nabataean coin. In the lounge area, large old engraved *mensef* dishes were used for coffee table tops. Most of the staff were from the Indian subcontinent.[3]

There was a piazza at the back of the foyer, with a blue-tiled swimming pool. This amount of water glistening in the sun was an amazing sight. The back of the hotel had a very good view of the pale cream sandstone hills which mark the beginning of Petra. The hotel was well placed for the view, but the location meant that it stood out. However, the view from the restaurant was blocked by the apparent afterthought of a Bedouin tent, lit with pierced brass Damascene lanterns, which had been erected on the piazza beside the pool and enclosed in a white air-conditioned shell.

The restaurant was very tastefully decorated in an Arab style. On the walls there were local Bedouin rugs and some extremely nice old brass vases, plates, and swords. It had deep blue carpet and chairs. The tablemats had a photograph of part of a Bedouin rug in deep red, with a touch of black and white. The menu also had a rug printed on the cover. The dishes were named after parts of Petra. The entrée was

2 By 1984, the hiring of the horses was organised into a queuing system, with each horse being given a number, so that they were hired in that order, without pestering the tourists. Most, but not all of the horsemen, were Wadi Musans. Some were Bdoul (e.g., Abu Shaher, Abu Nawas).

3 Shoup (1985: 282–83) provides further information about the staffing arrangements of the hotel when it opened.

Fig. 205. Dakhilallah and Haroun outside their shop, 1984.

called "Bab el-Siq" (entrance to the Siq). This course could be followed by choices such as "Lamb Temenos" and "Theatre Club Sandwich". Desserts included "Coupe Petra". For me, the idea of having meals with butter for the bread was as amazing as seeing the swimming pool full of water, as there were no fridges in Petra.[4]

Arrival in Petra

As the Department of Antiquities Inspector, Niazi Shabʿan, said he would drive our equipment in, we walked down the Siq (fig. 204). On the way, we met Musa al-Smadi, who remembered me. When we reached the Khasneh, I was still impressed, even though I had seen it many times before.

Beyond the Khasneh, after the Outer Siq, and slightly before the Theatre, Mohammad Abdallah had set up his stall, separate from the other vendors.[5] He looked thinner in the face than two years before. The souvenirs he now sold included Jerusalem (Armenian) pottery plates with the Khasneh on them. On the Colonnaded Street, we met Abu Nawas who was delighted to see me. He shook my hand, then kissed me on each cheek.

We reached Dakhilallah's shop below our cave, where we met him and his son Haroun (fig. 205). The tree which Dakhilallah had planted just before we left was now quite big, and he had planted two more. He had expanded his shop out in front with an area covered by concrete for a lot of chairs outside. Inside his shop, little had changed. The photograph of King Hussein was still there, stuck behind the glass of the dresser with glass doors on the right-hand side. Now, on the left-hand side, there was the article from the Ansett Airways journal about camel races in Australia, which my mother had sent me to show them in 1981/2, because they would not believe that there were camels in Australia. The boomerang I had given him on that trip had been lost when one of the children threw it.

As our old cave was now the Museum storeroom, for this trip we were to use the one beside it, which used to be a Department of Antiquities office. It was a little lighter, as it was square with two windows. Inside, there was one brass Museum cabinet and a table. Our first task was to furnish the cave and equip the kitchen. We put some foam rubber mattresses from Nazzal's Camp on the floor to use as beds. Niazi told us to pay the guard to fill the water tank above the kitchen. Niazi also had the gas hot plates and gas canister moved back into the kitchen from Nazzal's Camp.

4 Marguerite and Mohammad eventually had a kerosene-fired fridge for his insulin (van Geldermalsen 2006: 268).

5 Marguerite van Geldermalsen (2006: 201) explains that this move was partly a result of what Mohammad had learnt when they were in New Zealand.

Fig. 206. Dinner at Abu Shaher's, with Abu Shaher, Abdallah, Pam, Zahra, and Shaher, with King Hussein's portrait in the wall, 1984.

The biggest change in Petra was the new restaurant which was now operating. It was not as much of an eyesore as it appeared it was going to be while it was being built. It had gardens planted around it with oleanders and pink pigface, which was thriving as it tumbled over the edge of the harsh angular concrete. The greeny yellow roof was now pink. The restaurant had a piazza beside it with tables and beach umbrellas. The waiters and kitchen boys were all dressed in neat uniforms, with red or blue and black decorated jackets. Abu Shaher's son, Shaher, was one of the kitchen boys there.

Dinner at Abu Shaher's Place to Repair his Photographs

Shaher told us that Abu Shaher no longer took tourists on his horse down the Siq, as it was too tiring going into the Rest House every day. Shaher must have told Abu Shaher of our arrival, because the next day, while I was working at the Qasr el-Bint, he came along to greet me. He was not clean-shaven, and his whiskers were quite white so that he looked a lot older. After he had finished work, Shaher came to collect us to take us up to his father's house. Climbing up the winding path, I recognised each twist and turn of the path. We arrived after the family had had dinner.

As the family photographs, which had been there two years previously, were not hanging on the niche in the back wall of Abu Shaher's cave, I asked him about them (fig. 206). While we were drinking *shay*, Abu Shaher took out a square bundle which was carefully tied up. After cutting the string, Abu Shaher opened it to reveal all the photographs in their frames piled up. The black-and-white portrait of Abu Shaher in his Arab Legion *keffiyeh* (fig. 207), which was taken when he was about twenty years old had been torn by Abdallah, his little three-year-old son (fig. 208). Consequently, Abu Shaher had put the rest away for safekeeping, because he was so heartbroken about it. I offered to re-photograph it for him to make a new one, and he invited us for dinner the next day.

What pained me the most when thinking about the idea of the Bdoul all being moved to the new village was the idea of Abu Shaher's picture gallery being removed. With its studio portraits, it provided a link with the past, which showed that thirty years ago, the Bdoul were not uncivilised when living in the caves.

The next evening, we went up to Abu Shaher's. While there was still sufficient light, I set up the tripod to photograph Abu Shaher's picture (fig. 207). I had framed it slightly smaller than the viewfinder and weighed it down with coins. Abu Shaher looked through the viewfinder and instantly noticed that it was not lined up exactly with the photograph.

We sat outside while dinner was cooking. Abu Shaher was removing the stones from a bag of grain so that it could be ground in Wadi Musa, using flat metal *mensef* dishes. The

Fig. 207. Abu Shaher when he was in the Arab Legion.

large hessian bag of grain was then sewn up by his daughter-in-law Wath-ha and daughter Miriam, ready for taking to Wadi Musa.

In the area in front of the cave, there was a whole household worth of mattresses, quilts, pots, and pans piled up. Near it, an old woman was sitting. Abu Shaher said that she was his sister who was unmarried and did not have any children, but he did not explain why she had moved all her things out of her house.

We went inside for dinner. The whitewashed walls had simple patterns painted along them. The large lion carpet hanging, which had been hanging on the wall before, was draped over Shaher's iron frame bed (fig. 206). Stacked along the side of the cave were piles of bedding, including one with Abu Shaher's prayer mat on it (fig. 210). There was also a locked blue metal chest, as in most other main caves. The cave had been set up for dinner, as before, with foam rubber mattresses and pillows as bolsters stacked up high on which to recline (fig. 206). The top pillow had a frill and an embroidered pattern on it. The dinner was chicken *mensef*, which was placed in the centre, and everyone, Shaher, Abu Shaher, his brother Abu Khaled, Abu Shaher's young son, Abdallah, Pam and I, moved around it to eat, by the light of a Tilley lamp (figs. 209–210). Abu Shaher explained that his son Atallah, who was about fifteen years old, had gone to Amman for his schooling.

Fig. 208. Abu Shaher with Aisha and Abdallah, 1984.

Fig. 209. *Mensef* at Abu Shaher's, with Pam, Judith, and Shaher, 1984.

Fig. 210. Dinner at Abu Shaher's, his brother Abu Khaled (Hassan), son Abdallah, Abu Shaher, and Pam, 1984.

Fig. 211. Abu Shaher's main cave, kitchen cave, and his son Khalil's cave (far right), 1983 [Piotr Bienkowski].

Fig. 212. Cave of Khalil, Abu Shaher's son (with blue door), 1983 [Piotr Bienkowski].

Fig. 213. El-Mudhlim tunnel at the entrance to the Siq, 2010.

On my trip in 1981/2, whenever we took photographs of them, the Bdoul asked us to send them a copy, but they hardly ever received them. We had sent mail to Wadi Musa Post Office, but it rarely found its way to them.[6] To avoid the problem on this trip, we had brought a Polaroid camera, which we called "the five-minute camera". This meant that we could give them their photograph five minutes after taking it, having waited for the shot to develop. I took some photographs with the Polaroid of them having dinner. When Umm Shaher saw the "five-minute photographs", she wanted hers taken and was quite delighted by it. I was surprised because I would never have had the nerve to ask to take her photograph, but her demanding one was another matter.

The third cave, which used to be a pen for sheep and goats (figs. 171–172), had been converted into Khalil's house for him and his wife Wath-ha (fig. 211). He was Abu Shaher's second eldest son and was in Bahrain in the army. The front of the cave had been built up to accommodate a doorframe and door (fig. 212). To the right of the door there was a small garden bed built of stone, which contained pigface with pink flowers, indicating influence from the restaurant. Inside, the cave was painted white, and the back wall was decorated with the same sprayed-painted pattern as in Abu Shaher's, with paper decorations strung from the ceiling. The conversion of this cave from animal husbandry to domestic use showed that not only did short-term arrangements for the use of space in the caves and outside change (e.g., living room by day, bedroom by night), but also that longer-term changes were made when demanded by circumstances.

Exploring a Back Entrance to Petra along Wadi Mudhlim

On the way back from working at the Bab el-Siq Triclinium, near the entrance to the Siq, Pam and I decided to see if it were possible to reach Petra via the tunnel which led to Wadi Mudhlim (Muzlim). In theory, the Siq, which approached Petra from the east, was the only entrance. In fact, Petra could also be approached from the south from the Wadi Araba, via Wadi Sabra. From the north, Petra could be entered from Beidha, or along Wadi Abu ʿOlleqa (Wadi Turkmaniyah) from Umm Sayhoun, where the new Bdoul village was being built.

Unchecked, the winter rains cause flash floods down the Siq, sometimes with a wall of water, sand, and pebbles high enough to drown people, as had happened to over twenty tourists in 1963. Consequently, when the Nabataeans paved the Siq, they raised the roadway at the entrance to it and made a dam. As part of the project, they carved a large tunnel to divert the water which would have flooded the Siq from the Wadi Musa catchment so that it flowed down Wadi Mudhlim into Petra (fig. 213).

6 Marguerite van Geldermalsen (2006: 81–82) had similar experiences.

Fig. 214. Deir, with rock-cut altar in foreground, 1986.

Fig. 215. Umm Khaled (Dakhilallah's wife), in front of her refreshment stand in the cave opposite to the Deir, with her first daughter, Fatima, and Ali, 1984.

We set off by going through the tunnel, past a dead donkey. This led to a wadi bed which went into another siq, with many oleander bushes blocking the way, much as there would have been in the Siq in the nineteenth century. Eventually, we came to a drop of about 15 feet (5 m). I would not agree to scramble down this, as I knew I would never be able to climb up such a height, if we had to go back because the route later turned out to be impassable. I had done much bushwalking in Australia, and my rule was never to continue along a route without knowing there was a reliable way back. I retraced our path, but Pam said she would continue along the wadi.

I headed back down the Siq and arrived back at our cave by about 5 pm. There was a note stuck on our cave door, saying "Gone to Wadi Musa, Steve". Steve Hart was an Australian colleague from the British Institute, who was coming down to Petra. I simply assumed that Pam had come back successfully along the Wadi Mudhlim route and gone to meet him in Wadi Musa. I thought nothing more of it, made dinner, and went to bed.

At about 9 pm, there was a loud banging on the metal door of our cave. It was Pam totally exhausted and a nervous wreck looking as if she had seen a ghost. It turned out that she had reached a point where the route was completely impassable, then had to turn back. By the time she reached the tunnel, it was dark. She had to walk past the dead donkey. The Siq walls were just distinguishable in the night light. She continued through the Outer Siq, and past the Theatre. Once she turned the corner beyond the Theatre, the slight glinting of the Colonnaded Street paving guided her way back to our cave on el-Habis. Pam had been intensely concerned about the embarrassment that would have resulted if I had sent out a search party. She was unaware that due to Steve's note, I was calmly tucked up in bed.

When I related this event to Andrew Garrard, he immediately wanted to know exactly where the donkey was so that he could go and collect it to boil down the bones for the reference collection of animal bones he was building up at the Institute.

Dakhilallah's Daughter, Fatima

One day, we walked up to the Deir (fig. 214). In the absence of the annual maintenance organised by Muhammad Khadija, the stepped path had deteriorated noticeably as a result of the seasonal rains washing away some of the repairs which had been made to it.[7]

7 In 1982–84, rain was the main cause of the damage, as there was not nearly as much donkey traffic as there was when tourist numbers greatly increased, along with the use of larger donkeys and mules.

Dakhilallah had expanded his shop up at the Deir (fig. 215). The TV aerial on the hillock opposite was gone. His wife, Umm Khaled, was nursing their daughter Fatima, who was their first girl after six boys. Umm Khaled was absolutely crazy about her, kissing her all the time. I took a Polaroid photograph of her with Fatima, and she was ecstatic. The Polaroid photographs gave our Bdoul friends an incredible amount of pleasure, so they were worth the expense.

At the end of the next day, we sat outside Dakhilallah's shop below our cave, as usual. He was as delighted as Umm Khaled about Fatima being their first girl and was busily building a new storeroom beside his shop. While he was dismantling the wall between them, he found a black scorpion, which he was taking home to burn. His wife would put the ashes on her breast when she fed Fatima, which was thought to protect the baby against the effects of a potentially fatal scorpion sting.[8]

Dakhilallah had an old black *mudraga* for sale, embroidered in red cross-stitch, which had belonged to his mother-in-law. It was sleeveless, and she would have worn a long-sleeved underdress beneath it. I would have liked to buy it but could not afford it. He also had a machine-embroidered one, made by Umm Khaled, who had a treadle sewing machine.[9] She would sew together the pieces of a thick black synthetic material like polyester, and then the machine embroidery was added in Wadi Musa. The pattern on this one consisted of flowers around the hem and yoke. It had folded back cap sleeves which came down to a point. I bought it. That evening when I put it on to show Mohammad, the night guard, he was most impressed, exclaiming "*Mabrouk*" (congratulations), which was everyone's response when they saw me in it.

On my trip in 1981/2, Mufleh had been one of the people who would hang around outside Dakhilallah's shop at the end of the day. This time, he was in Europe with his wife Nawal and their daughter. In his absence, we met his mother, Umm Mufleh (Bekhita), drinking tea outside Dakhilallah's shop. She lived alone and seemed to be getting a bit senile but was still quite a character. She had smooth green tattoos on her face, a gold tooth, some teeth missing, and a ring through her nose.[10] She always wore a sleeveless black wool sheikh's cloak draped over her head and carried her things in a baby's sling-crib (*muzferr*), with the sheikh's cloak underneath it. Whenever Angela and I saw her, on the previous trip in 1981/2, she would always wave enthusiastically at us and give us a big grin (minus one top tooth), as if she had heard about us from Mufleh, although we had never had *shay* with her.

One evening, when we were sitting out on the verandah of our cave, talking to the night guard Mohammad, I asked if Umm Mufleh had any other children, because we had never heard of anyone else being related to Mufleh, and she was always by herself. It turned out Mufleh was an only child. When her husband died, before Mufleh was born,[11] Umm Mufleh came back to Petra from Beersheba, which would have been in about 1944.[12] She did not remarry.

Another woman who had moved back to Petra was Abdallah's mother-in-law. Marguerite van Geldermalsen explains that Mohammad Abdallah's father, Abdallah, came from al-Manajah tribe at Ras-a-Nagb.[13] Abdallah's mother-in-law was from the Bdoul and his father-in-law from al-Manajah. When his father-in-law died, his mother-in-law had moved back to Petra, so that his wife had grown up there. Abdallah moved to Petra on account of his wife.

Two Wives in One Cave

I was photographing the Urn Tomb with the telephoto lens on the ridge above Marguerite and Mohammad's house, when I was invited into a cave for *shay*. The old woman outside, Fathiya, looked a bit like Mufleh's mother with a wizened tattooed face and a nose ring in her left nostril. She was blind with the lenses of her eyes clouded over white with cataracts.[14] Inside the cave was very poor, which made me wonder if the father had two wives. One woman was breastfeeding a new baby. She had six children, although she did not look very old. Another woman brought the tea in. She was much better kept and was wearing a gold bracelet and earrings. She had only one child and told me that she was the second wife.[15] They both lived in the same cave. Usually, when there were two wives, they lived in separate caves.

Their husband was Mohammad al-Jamadeh, who drove the Department of Antiquities truck (fig. 81). He dressed in a dashing style, which included a velveteen jacket, so that Angela and I had called him "the guy with the velveteen jacket".

Wadi Farasa

Two days later, we went round to Wadi Farasa to work on the Renaissance Tomb. It had a small baby goat penned inside by some rocks placed across the entrance (figs. 216–217). The floor was completely covered in sand and goats' droppings (fig. 217), and the ceiling was level with the top of the doorway. Unusually, this tomb did not have any *loculi* in the walls, although it did have the outline in the back wall for a

8 Paradise 2016: 218 also describes a version of this custom.

9 Marguerite van Geldermalsen (2006: 133–35) also had a treadle sewing machine, as did some of the other women, such as Umm Auda in the cave beside the Tomb of the Broken Pediment.

10 Margaret Murray (1939: 28–29) also describes women with facial tattoos, when she was there in 1934. Hamdah had faint tattoos.

11 Van Geldermalsen 2006: 93.

12 Based on Mufleh being 73 years old in 2017 (Sewell 2017). If his mother was 16 at the time, she would have been born in about 1928.

13 Marguerite van Geldermalsen (2006: 53) provides more detail.

14 Van Geldermalsen 2006: 96, unnumbered coloured photograph opposite p. 153.

15 She was Egyptian. Marguerite van Geldermalsen (2006: 208–211) describes Mohammad al-Jamadeh, his series of wives, and his domestic arrangements in more detail. In 1978, he was the first Bdoul to marry an Egyptian woman, leading to further marriages.

Fig. 216. Renaissance Tomb in Wadi Farasa, 1981/2.

wide recess, which had not been carved. When we met the young owner of the goat, Salman, he told us that it was his "sheep tomb".

Further along, Wadi Farasa narrows so that the Tomb of the Roman Soldier is carved on the west side of what had been a courtyard with a large ornate banqueting room (Triclinium 235) on the east side. The tomb was named after the middle figure on it, which is dressed in a cuirass, the body armour of a Roman soldier (fig. 218). As the soldier was probably a Nabataean, it is sometimes called the Soldier Tomb.

While we were working there, Salman came along with a *sayara* (car), which consisted of a pair of wheels and a steering stick made of wire (fig. 219). I later saw a more complex example at Wadi Rumm with a full car body made of wires (fig. 279).[16] Salman's mother, Umm Auda (Thanwa), invited us for *shay*. Their tent was pitched in front of her home, which consisted of the Tomb of the Broken Pediment and the cave beside it which lacked a decorated facade (fig. 220). The tent was pitched with the open side facing the mountain, as was the custom (fig. 221).

As we were intending to work in Wadi Farasa the next day, we left the levelling staff, ranging rod, and

16 Marguerite van Geldermalsen (2006: 188) also describes such wire cars, and how her husband, Mohammad, had also made them as a child.

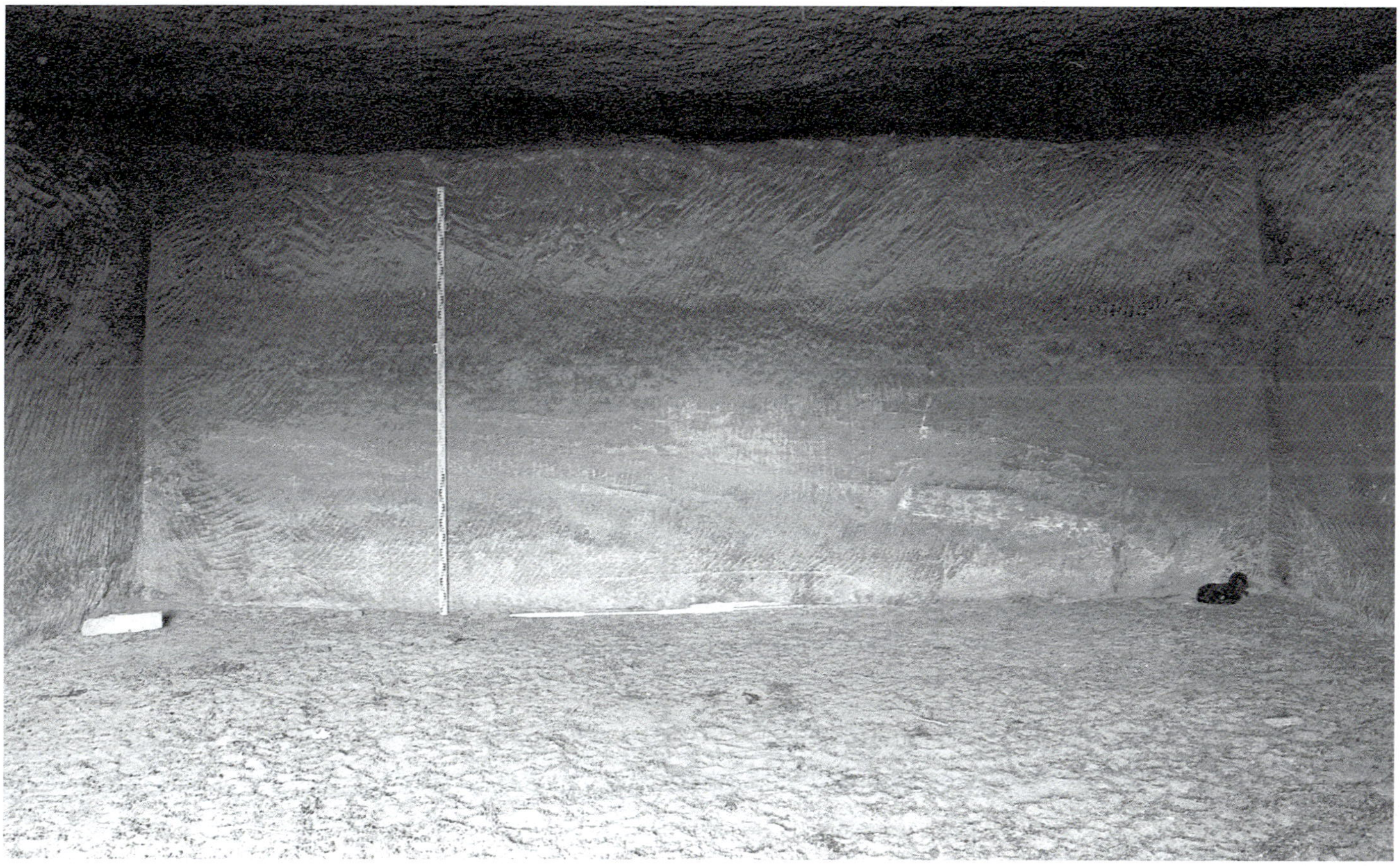

Fig. 217. Renaissance Tomb, with Salman's tiny goat in the corner and the floor completely covered in sand, ash, and dung, 1984.

Fig. 218. Tomb of the Roman Soldier, 1984.

theodolite legs in a nearby cave, as we did if we were going to work near the same place the following day. We never had any problem with theft. Neither the children nor anyone else interfered with our equipment when we left it.[17]

When we arrived in Wadi Farasa the next morning, Salman asked if we would take a photograph of him with his baby brother. He was quite fussy about it and wanted the doorway of the Tomb of the Roman Soldier with the sun on it in the background. When we had satisfactorily taken the picture, he told us that we could photograph inside his mother's house, i.e., the Tomb of the Broken Pediment.

His mother, Umm Auda, served us tea in the cave beside the tomb, the cave which had been the first cave into which I ever went for *shay*. Along the back wall there was a low cupboard with bedding stacked on it and covered with a cloth. In one corner she had a treadle sewing machine. This was their main cave for sleeping in. The Tomb of the Broken Pediment functioned as their kitchen cave, with a hearth, table with kitchen equipment, water drum, and firewood in it. To the left of this cave, there was a cave used as the stable for their donkey. As Umm Auda had made the tea in the Tomb of the Broken Pediment, it was full of white smoke when we went in to photograph it. While we were photographing, she went down to their tent to do the washing. The tent extended

Fig. 219. Salman with his wire car in front of the Tomb of the Roman Soldier, 1984.

17 In those days, the few tourists were not a problem as they were there so briefly, and the Bdoul would have noticed anything they did.

Fig. 220. Tomb of the Broken Pediment, 2003.

Fig. 221. View from the Tomb of the Broken Pediment to the tent erected in front, 1984.

Fig. 222. Umm Gasim, with her baby son, 1984.

Fig. 223. Tomb in Wadi Farasa, 1984.

Fig. 224. Bedouin living in the caves on the left of fig. 223, ca. 1940–1946 [American Colony, G. Eric and Edith Matson Photograph Collection, Library of Congress, Prints and Photographs Division, LC-DIG-matpc-13494].

Fig. 225. Sheep in front of the Palace Tomb, 1984.

their outdoor living space in the warmer weather, while they also used the two caves.

After we had finished work, Umm Auda fried us some potato chips, which were delicious. They were very large and cooked in a large (jam boiler sized) pot on the fire. She served them with very coarse salt, which made them even tastier. They were also nice with *shraak* (Bedouin bread) wrapped around them. We took a photograph of Umm Auda with her youngest baby.

We went round to the next wadi, Wadi en-Nmeir, which had a large tomb (No. 258) with a facade similar to the Tomb of the Roman Soldier, but without the figures.[18] One of the women in Wadi en-Nmeir had obviously seen Umm Auda's photograph because she wanted one the same, with only her and her baby but no one else in the photograph. This composition became the favourite shot with the women, as with Abu Nawas's wife, Umm Gasim (fig. 222). We noticed that if any of the older boys were in the photograph, they would end up keeping it. If it had only the mother and her child in it, then the woman managed to retain it.

With the coming of the warmer weather at the beginning of March, a number of the Bedouin had erected their tents in Wadi Farasa (fig. 223). One tent was pitched facing the caves which they occupied in winter. A photograph taken in ca. 1925–46 reveals that the Bdoul had also been living in these caves earlier in the century (fig. 224). Earlier the previous day, Pam had seen some of the women sitting together in the sun drinking tea and churning goats' milk using a goatskin suspended from a wooden tripod.

Tuffleh's In-Laws and their Tent near the Palace Tomb

With the approach of summer, tents were beginning to appear across the valleys of Petra.[19] Tuffleh's in-laws and some of the other Bdoul had moved out of their caves completely into tents which they had pitched beyond the Palace Tomb (fig. 225), out of sight from the Corinthian Tomb (and of most of the tourists) (figs. 226–227). Another tent was set up further down in the wadi. On the hill above the Temple of the Winged Lions, there were signs of a few more tents being set up. Quite a few other families had pitched their tents in close proximity to their caves, in order to provide additional living space, as in Wadi Farasa.

When we reached the tent of Tuffleh's in-laws, the children recognised me and called us across for *shay*. When she saw us, Tuffleh's mother-in-law, Hamdah, immediately recognised me (fig. 228). The look of sheer delight that came into her face when she did was very gratifying. Her husband Juma was loading his camel with hessian bags of firewood (fig. 229), because he was going away for a few days. He left behind the coloured blankets he put on it for the tourists.

Hamdah and Juma's long black tent was divided into two rooms or compartments. The compartment on the left had the hearth in it and was used for drinking tea in. The room on the right had the bedding in it and was used for cooking. These tents are amazingly cool, as they provide heavy shadows. In addition, the tent was positioned on the ridge to catch the breeze, which could be increased by pushing up the back wall with a pole. We could imagine the Nabataeans using the ridges of the mountains around Petra to catch the breeze, just like its later inhabitants.[20]

Hamdah's children remembered playing Skippy the kangaroo, which surprised me as it was two years ago, and I only remembered playing it a few times. The children also remembered that Angela and I had given Hamdah a large box of biscuits when their little sister, Atidal, was born. As the children clearly rated being given such a box of biscuits as a special event, it was obvious that it did not happen to them every day. Atidal had been bottle-fed then and had looked poorly, so it was pleasing to see that she had survived and was now apparently quite healthy (fig. 228). Hamdah

18 McKenzie 1990: 149–50, pls. 106–108.

19 Also described by Marguerite van Geldermalsen (2006: 169–70). She marked tent sites in the main valley of Petra on the map at the front of her book (no page number).

20 Canaan (1930: 80), who was in Petra in 1929, mentions that the Bdoul also pitched their tents on the mountain tops around Petra.

Fig. 226. Wadi el-Mataha, looking north, with the tombs of Moghar an-Nasara on the top right, with a tent on the lower left, 1986.

Fig. 227. Seʿideh (Tuffleh's sister-in-law) with her neighbour, Heyaiyeh, in front of their tent, 1984.

Fig. 228. Hamdah and Atidal, 1984.

Fig, 229. Juma Samaheen and Auda al-Jamadeh on their camels, 1984.

explained that Maheela, aged twelve, was now her eldest daughter living at home. Maheela had a bobby-pin decorated with a filigree pattern built up of tiny glass beads, with all different colours mixed in together, which could be seen sticking out from under her scarf. Tuffleh no longer lived with them but was just past (south of) the Urn Tomb. We had met her at Mohammad Abdallah's new souvenir stand opposite the Theatre. She did not look any older. She had a baby girl, Nejah, who was about one year old, whom she adored, giving her much attention.

Although they were living in their tent for the summer, Tuffleh's in-laws still used the Corinthian Tomb to store their animal feed in the *loculi* (fig. 230). On the walls beside them, we could distinguish the neatly carved names and dates of earlier visitors, such as "Ibraim 1846".

While we were working at the Corinthian Tomb, Maheela appeared wanting to play Skippy the kangaroo. We played Skippy again (fig. 231). We took a photograph of Maheela and the other children playing it with the Polaroid camera. She spent ages having it labelled by Pam with everyone's names. She put the photograph in the little bag she carried, along with her bits of pottery. She also remembered Angela's name and her singing.

We needed to take extra theodolite readings of the cornices on the Palace Tomb. I told Pam that she was not needed for a few minutes while I set up the theodolite. In no

Fig. 230. Corinthian Tomb, with bags of animal feed and 19th-century graffiti in the main chamber, 1984.

Fig. 231. Playing Skippy the kangaroo with Maheela in front of the Corinthian Tomb, 1984.

Fig. 232. Abdallah playing his *rabābah*, 1984.

time at all, she appeared on el-Khubthah near the top of the Palace Tomb. She was an experienced rock-climber, so when I was doing something which did not require her presence, she would climb to the top of the nearest rock outcrop. A discussion with some of the girls revealed how, even wearing their moulded plastic slip-on shoes, they could reach the free-standing top part of the Palace Tomb (fig. 155). Doing so entailed jumping across a crevice, which they were able to do because, as children, they were light enough, whereas Pam, an adult, could not do so, although she did climb very high up.

On one occasion, when I went past Tuffleh's in-laws' tent, I was invited in for *shay* and her father-in-law, Juma, was at home because he had a headache. He decided to play the *rabābah*, the single stringed instrument, to relax, and he even sang to it (fig. 145). They had an English travel magazine with a feature on Petra in it which they were examining closely to see if they could see or recognise any of the Bdoul in the photographs. It was quite amazing seeing views of Petra in a glossy magazine being examined by the participants in it.

Girls' Education

The law that girls, as well as boys, should go to school until they were twelve years old was now being enforced, with more teachers appointed to the school in Wadi Abu 'Olleqa, which went up to age twelve. There were now four teachers instead of one. On my previous visit in 1981/2, I had seen a photograph of the school class which consisted of about seventy children of whom only about six were girls. A few of the boys continued on to high school by going into Wadi Musa each day.

In the morning, we would now see the little girls all going to school along with the boys. Many of the girls were in uniform, which consisted of a blue knee-length dress (tunic) with trousers underneath, which they only wore to school. Being able to write was obviously a novelty in which the girls took great delight. If we were talking about names of things or people, they would write them in the sand or on any available scrap of litter, such as a film carton. They coveted any pens and pencils they saw. The little boys did not take such an interest in showing off their writing.

BBC Recordings for Queen Elizabeth II's Visit – Mohammad and Abdallah

Mohammad Abdallah was the guard at the Qasr el-Bint,[21] and his father Abdallah would sit near the Colonnaded Street or in the Temenos area in front of the Qasr el-Bint, playing the *rabābah*. He had a few souvenirs for sale, such as necklaces and Bedouin knives (*shabriya*), and the excellent volume on Petra from *Le Monde de la Bible* (fig. 232). While he sat there, he also made *rabābah* instruments to sell to tourists. They were made from goatskin and wood, with horse hair bows.[22]

A couple of weeks before Queen Elizabeth II's visit, which was to be on 30 March 1984, BBC radio came to record background tapes in Petra, as they would only be able to broadcast from Amman while she was there.[23] We accompanied the two BBC journalists down to Petra by taxi, at the request of Andrew Garrard. They rode down the Siq on horseback, recording the sound of the horses' hooves. Once in Petra itself, they needed to record other sound tracks. An obvious candidate to record was Abdallah playing his *rabābah*. I negotiated the price for a ten-minute performance, which was the same as a whole day's pay.[24] Abdallah was very pleased, pointing out afterwards that I was one of the Bdoul.

The two BBC journalists also needed to interview someone about how the Bdoul lived in the caves. Although quite a few of the men had sufficient English to make themselves understood, it would not have been good enough for a radio interview because of their accent. I suggested that Mohammad Abdallah was the best person to interview, although I knew his lifestyle was not exactly typical. They asked him how they cooked. He replied that they had a gas stove. When asked what they did for water, he replied that they drove to the spring to collect water. His cave also had a shower,[25] a kerosene heater, and a gas light.[26] The result was perfect from the point of not portraying the Bdoul as having a "primitive" lifestyle, about which the Jordanians were very sensitive.

Abu Nawas's Home

On the way to Wadi Farasa to work on the Renaissance Tomb and the Tomb of the Roman Soldier, we passed Abu Nawas's home. There was no sign of his wife, Umm Gasim, but the children dragged us to the stable to show us a very young foal which was probably about a week old. A mare which produced foals would have provided an additional source of income.

On the way home, when we went past their house again, the children stopped us for *shay*, and Umm Gasim appeared with a new baby. She was also pregnant and looked older. They were now living in one of the tombs above their old home (fig. 189). It had an intact front wall, unlike their cave on the level below, which had been open on the side. Their new home faced due west, so that it was bathed in the last rays of the setting sun. From it, we could see the very thin

21 Marguerite van Geldermalsen 2006: 206.

22 Marguerite van Geldermalsen (2006: 112–13) describes an earlier *rabābah* player.

23 We were not in Petra on the day when the Queen came with King Hussein. Her visit is described by Marguerite van Geldermalsen (2006: 245–51), who met her.

24 This was a very small amount compared with what they had paid (excessively) for the taxi hired to go to Petra. They had agreed to pay double the agreed price when it was decided that Pam and I accompany them in it.

25 Van Geldermalsen 2006: 198.

26 Van Geldermalsen 2006: 215.

old moon setting over the mountains beside Umm el-Biyara, making a beautiful view.

They invited us to stay for dinner. As they had four boys and two girls aged between about one and eight, there were small children everywhere. Two of them went to school. Their eldest son, Gasim, with whom Angela and I went to Wadi Sabra, could now write. When we left Petra in February 1982, Angela had given them her sleeping sheet. On this visit, I noticed it had made a nice mattress cover and two pillow covers which were still going strong. Abu Nawas gave me a photograph of himself taken in Wadi Musa the previous year. It was a small black-and-white one with a wavy cut white edge (fig. 233). The flash made his skin look smooth, so that he looked much younger, and with his mouth closed, his missing teeth were not visible. We walked back to el-Habis in the near dark after a most enjoyable day.

Trip to Wadi Sabra, Again

Pam and I arranged to make a day trip to Wadi Sabra with Abu Nawas, as he had taken Angela and me there in 1982. I needed to look at the evidence there again, especially the small theatre for water performances or rituals. Pam, who was a keen horse rider, rode his horse. She cantered across the undulating flatland of the plateau Stouh an-Nabi Haroun, while I rode his donkey (fig. 234). We could see Jabal Haroun in the distance, with Aaron's Tomb at its highest point (fig. 235). Beyond the plateau, I was struck again by the beauty

Fig. 233. Abu Nawas, 1984.

Fig. 234. Pam cantering over Stouh an-Nabi Haroun, ploughed for cereal crops, 1984.

Fig. 235. View across Stouh an-Nabi Haroun to Jabal Haroun, with Pam on Abu Nawas's horse, 1984.

Fig. 236. View to Jabal Haroun.

Fig. 237. On the ancient road to Wadi Sabra, Abu Nawas on his donkey, with Pam on his horse and his son, Gasim (taken further south along the road than fig. 193), 1984.

Fig. 238. The shrine of Aaron's Tomb on Jabal Haroun, freshly whitewashed, 1990 [Jane Taylor, photo-archive of American School of Oriental Research, Amman, JT_J_2_09a_018].

Fig. 239. Abu Shaher and Pam with the guard of Nabi Haroun and his son, 1986 [Pam Watson].

of the view (fig. 236). His son, Gasim, also came with us (fig. 237).

Trip to Jabal Haroun with Abu Shaher

The great day for our expedition to Aaron's Tomb on Jabal Haroun arrived. This was the white shrine which could be seen in the distance on the highest peak when approaching Wadi Musa (fig. 34). In those days, the whole shrine was whitewashed on the outside making it more visible (as after a subsequent coat of whitewash, fig. 238).

Shaher had intended to take us, but he had to work in the restaurant, and so he went and found his father to be our guide. Abu Shaher turned up at Dakhilallah's shop with his donkey, which was a nice big one, with a blanket over the wooden frame. Shaher had not mentioned to his father that we also needed a horse for Pam, and so, when we reached al-Katuteh, the "bush telegraph" method of passing the message by shouting from one cave to the next was used. Eventually, it was ascertained that Abu Nawas had already left for the Rest House in Wadi Musa with his horse. A white mare was found instead. It was heavily in foal and sway-backed with a bony rump. After much haggling, the price for the horse was lowered to what my research funds could afford. Pam was thrilled at the prospect of a horse-ride.

Off we rode, Pam on the horse and I on the donkey, with Abu Shaher walking. There was quite a climb after going past the southern graves. Then the land levelled off to Stouh an-Nabi Haroun, much of which had been ploughed. Pam cantered the horse across it. Eventually, Abu Shaher agreed to also ride the donkey with me, as there was plenty of space for two, and I was worried about him getting too tired as he would not agree to take it in turns with me to ride it. To speed things up, he made the donkey trot across the plain, bumping up and down rather uncomfortably, and he had to hold on.

We noticed the Bdoul cemetery, which was in sight of Jabal Haroun. In 1981/2, Dakhilallah had told us that some of the Bdoul used to bury their dead in the caves.[27] Early in

27 Ohannessian-Charpin (1987: 387, pls. 93) gives examples on Umm el-Biyara.

Fig. 240. Interior of Aaron's shrine, with Aaron's cenotaph on the right, 1990 [Jane Taylor, photo-archive of American School of Oriental Research, Amman, JT_J_2_09a_015].

the twentieth century the Bdoul had cemeteries between the Qasr el-Bint and the Snake Monument, with burials facing Nabi Haroun.[28]

Immediately before the foot of the mountain, there was a slight dip in which there was a large black tent. Abu Shaher told us to go quietly as this belonged to the guard who would demand money if he saw us. Further along, on the other side of the path, there was another tent. Both looked quite prosperous, probably because, unlike Petra, the area is not overgrazed.

About one third of the height of Jabal Haroun, relative to Petra, was climbed by the time its base was reached. Jabal Haroun has dark brown to reddish sandstone with quite a bit of iron ore in it. The mountain itself was quite steep, but the path wound up slowly so that it was possible to ride the whole way up on the donkey, but not the horse. A donkey is more sure-footed than a horse on a rock patch. A donkey can always smell a path, even over rock, whereas a horse has to be guided. Thus, the donkey would normally be used to lead the way, with the horse following it.

When we were about halfway up, the guard met us. He appeared from nowhere. He was quite fierce-looking with one bad eye. He was probably aged about fifty. He was accompanied by his young son, who had three keys to the shrine, which were each about six inches (15 cm) long and hung down on both sides of his neck (fig. 239).

28 Crawford 1930: 289, 291–92.

Fig. 241. Aaron's shrine, remains of inlaid marble paving of the Byzantine church, over which the Islamic shrine was built, 2015 [Marlena Whiting].

Fig. 242. Aaron's tomb in the crypt of Aaron's shrine, 2015 [Marlena Whiting].

We reached the plateau at the top of the mountain, before the peak. This level area had been ploughed for cereal crops. From there, we had a view of the Wadi Araba and beyond. In the other direction, towards Petra, it was possible to see the top half of the Deir quite clearly, as well as the new village of Umm Sayhoun, to the north. The guard had a pair of 70× magnification binoculars, which were so strong that it was possible to see the Doric frieze at the top of the Deir. He obviously used them for guarding the mountain.

The shrine is at the top of a steep knoll, approached by a narrow, steep rock-cut staircase. At the foot of the shrine, there is a large cistern, with a roof supported by arches, which appeared to have originally been Nabataean. The shrine itself is not very big, especially considering how obvious it is from the distance.

We had a letter of permission to enter the shrine, which Abu Shaher showed to the guard. We sat in the sun to eat lunch. As it was our custom to share our lunch, we offered some to the guard, but he refused to eat with us. This was the only time our hospitality was ever refused. It was a bad sign of what was to come.

An inscription over the doorway indicated that the present shrine was built (or rebuilt) in 1338/9 by the Mamluk sultan, al-Malik or Nasir Muhammad ibn Qalawun, the successor of Sultan Baibars. The guard let us into the shrine, which was whitewashed inside (as still in 1990, fig. 240).[29]

Fig. 243. Abu Shaher in a *thaub*, with Abdallah in his soldier outfit, 1984.

29 The whitewash was subsequently removed, except for in the crypt.

The cloth-covered cenotaph of Aaron was inside the door. Mats on the floor of the shrine obscured an area of marble paving which belonged to the former Byzantine church on top of which the Islamic shrine had been built (fig. 241). In the crypt below, the reputed Tomb of Aaron was in a recess behind an iron grille (fig. 242).

As the price for having allowed us into the shrine, the guard demanded an enormous amount of *baksheesh*. This led to an unpleasant argument, as the amount he wanted was considerably beyond my means. Eventually, with Abu Shaher's help, we settled on a mutually agreeable figure.

Dinner Again at Abu Shaher's Cave

Abu Shaher had invited us for dinner again. He was dressed in a new grey *thaub* (men's robe) and tailored jacket, along with his white *keffiyeh*. The star of the evening was his little son, Abdallah, who had been given a small soldier suit by his older brother, Khalil, who was in the army in Bahrain (figs. 243–244). The soldier suit, which fitted Abdallah perfectly, was complete with cap, medals, and a holster for his gun. It was fortunate that I had decided to wear my new *mudraga* as

Fig. 244. Abu Shaher and Abdallah, 1984.

Fig. 245. Abdallah, Abu Shaher, Judith, and Aisha, 1984.

Fig. 246. Abdallah, Abu Shaher, Aisha, and Pam, 1984.

they were dressed for a special occasion (fig. 245). Pam and I had an enjoyable evening with the family (fig. 246).

The army not only provided the Bdoul (like other Bedouin in Jordan) with a steady source of income, but also with experience of the world beyond Petra. When Abu Shaher served in the Arab Legion, under Glubb Pasha, he had travelled around Palestine (before 1948). His time in the army had also provided his family with the chance to experience life in Amman.[30]

While Abu Shaher was away in the army and afterwards, the proportion of the year that the Bdoul spent in or near Petra gradually increased. He was born at a time when they still planted cereal crops within the city centre of Petra, at Stouh an-Nabi Haroun and at Beidha, while herding goats.

They lived in the caves of Petra for two to three months in the winter, and in summer they moved into their black tents which they erected within the valley of Petra, near their crops, and on the surrounding ridges. After 1948, following the foundation of the state of Israel, they could no longer travel as far as Gaza for trade.[31] As the Bdoul's income from sources related to tourism increased, they spent an increasing amount of time in the caves of Petra, or camped in the valley of Petra. With the move to the new village to come in 1985, Abu Shaher would see the greatest change for the Bdoul during the twentieth century.[32]

30 Marguerite van Geldermalsen (2006: 168) mentions that when his family was young, they lived in Amman, where the studio portraits on his walls were taken.

31 Simms (1988: 200) suggests that, as a result, they increased their agricultural efforts.

32 Simms (1988: 201) notes of Dakhilallah's father Qublan: "During Qublan's life, the Bdoul settlement and subsistence pattern has apparently changed many times, from wide-ranging camel and goat pastoralism, to semi-nomadism and even near sedentism constrained by dry farming and the tourist economy." As Qublan was 72 years old in 1986, he would have been born ca. 1914.

CHAPTER 5

1986

Field Trip to Record the Tomb Interiors

After the 1984 field trip, I completed my PhD thesis back in Sydney. As it might be of interest, its basic argument can be summarised here.

It began with a detailed examination of the tomb facades at Medain Saleh (Mada'in Saleh), ancient Hegra, the southernmost outpost of the Nabataeans in Saudi Arabia. The facades there are of similar types to those at Petra, except there were no classical facades. They are also much less weathered than those at Petra. Unlike those at Petra, about one third of the ca. 90 facades at Medain Saleh have inscriptions on them.[1] These inscriptions are dated to AD 1–75 and give the name of the stonecutter and his father, as well as the name and occupation of the owner. These texts, which are like legal titles, also give the penalties for re-use of the tombs and revealed that Nabataean women had property-owning rights. The family trees of the stonecutters showed that there were two schools of them. I was also able to detect characteristics of the work of individual stonecutters, whose average working life was 25 years. I found that there was a general tendency for the classical details on the facades at Medain Saleh to become simpler over time, and their proportions more squat.

Developments in the Nabataean capital of Petra would not necessarily have been identical or taken place at the same pace, but my discoveries did provide a framework for approaching the evidence there. I found it was possible to group the classical facades at Petra based on details on them, and I was able to suggest a chronological sequence using dated monuments in each group based on the results of excavations and other evidence.[2] This study revealed that the Khasneh (fig. 68) and the Qasr el-Bint (figs. 59, 335) were dated to the late first century BC or early first century AD, while the Urn Tomb (fig. 252) and the Tomb of the Roman Soldier (fig. 218) dated to the mid-first century AD. The Deir (fig. 119) and the Palace Tomb (fig. 155) were later.

The second part of the thesis concerned the sources for the designs of these facades. The main source of classical influence was the architecture of Alexandria, in particular details such as the circular structure between two half pediments on the top half of the Khasneh (fig. 90). Similar scenes were also depicted on Roman wall-paintings (fig. 91).[3] The Nabataeans decorated their most ornate buildings with floral capitals (fig. 75). They developed their own style using blocked out forms, in particular for capitals and the Doric friezes with discs on them, as on the Deir (fig. 121). They also created completely new tomb designs by combining other features with these classical ones to create the distinctive tomb types, with facing pairs of steps on a cavetto cornice (fig. 96) or one or two rows of Assyrian crowsteps (fig. 45).

As I had collected a detailed record of all of the classical facades, I decided to add a catalogue of them for the publication of my thesis. For the catalogue, it was necessary to add detailed descriptions of the facades and their interiors, with floor plans. This would complement the record provided by the photographs of the details and the cross-sections of the mouldings made from the theodolite readings.

There were some limitations to what could be done when measuring the floor plans and describing them. Many of the floors of the tombs had not been cleared down to their rock-cut floors, but still had layers of compressed dung and ash hiding any graves in the floor. Another difficulty was caused by the fact that the front wall of a tomb was not necessarily the same thickness the whole way along, unlike on free-standing buildings, because the interior was sometimes carved at an angle relative to the facade. In order to orientate each interior relative to its exterior, I had to develop a method using trigonometry.[4]

On the 1986 field trip, I became ill and, because of the resultant delay caused by the time taken for my recovery, I had three different assistants. The first one was Jane Lydon, an undergraduate who had finished the first three years of her Archaeology degree at the University of Sydney. She was followed for two weeks by Kathleen Boswell, the wife of a diplomat at the American Embassy in Amman. For the final week, I was accompanied by Torla Evans, an archaeological photographer.

When I worked in Petra in 1981/2 and 1984, the new village for the Bdoul was under construction, but they still lived in the caves. Petra would be different this time because the move to the new village of Umm Sayhoun, which the Bdoul called al-Wahdat (= the [housing] units) had taken place at

1 McKenzie 1990: 11–31, pls. 2–20. A comprehensive record of the tombs at Medain Saleh has since been published: Nehmé 2015.

2 McKenzie 1990: 33–59. Since updated with important corrections in light of discoveries after 1988: McKenzie 2014.

3 McKenzie 2007: 96–105. Earlier discussion: McKenzie 1990: 85–104.

4 McKenzie 1990: 128, diagram 3.

Fig. 247. Snow on the mountains above the plain of Beidha, 1985 [Phillip C. Edwards].

Fig. 248. Tomb 813 in the snow, 1986 [Phillip C. Edwards].

the end of April 1985, eight months earlier. After the houses in Umm Sayhoun had been completed, the Bdoul's move to them had been delayed by endless months of arguments about the number of family members required for a family to be given two, rather than one, of the semi-detached houses. By early 1985, there was an urgency for the Bdoul to move out of Petra in time for Jordan's second attempt to have it listed by UNESCO as a World Heritage Site. In late April 1985, those families who had been allocated houses were told by the Department of Antiquities to move within a week or they would lose them.[5] By 30 April, following an intense week, seventy-eight families had moved into the available units.[6] This left a further 52 families in Petra and Beidha for whom more houses were then built.[7] Completed in 1987, these additional houses did not include provision for the 34 families near Jabal Haroun,[8] for whom there was a further phase of building.

Arrival in Petra on a Snowy Day

Our field trip to Petra in 1986 was timed earlier in the year than last time. On 19 January, we drove via Shoubak Crusader castle. There was snow on the ground, which had

5 Van Geldermalsen 2006: 266.

6 Van Geldermalsen 2006: 268. Farajat (2012: 152) gives the figure as 80 families.

7 There was also a small village in Beidha, from which the ʿAmmarin were moved to a new village (Twaissi 2016: 342, fig. 10).

8 Van Geldermalsen 2006: 268; Farajat 2012: 152.

Fig. 249. Mufleh, Judith, and Haroun, in front of Haroun's shop, 1986.

fallen earlier in the day. The limestone hills around Wadi Musa had snow on them (fig. 247). It had also snowed in Petra, but the snow melted more quickly on the sandstone there (fig. 248).[9]

Petra was overcast and horribly grey, windy, and cold when we arrived. The next day was much the same, so we did not do any measuring. There was virtually no one around. As most of the Bdoul had moved to the new village the year before, I feared this had made Petra totally dead. To our great relief, once the sun came out the next day, there were more people around – mostly tourists and some Bdoul.

We met Mufleh, who described how "one day the new village was empty and the next day it was full," with Mohammad al-Jamadeh spending all night moving them in the Department of Antiquities truck. However, not all of the Bdoul had moved, because not enough houses had been built for them. Mufleh was living in his old cave around the back of el-Habis, having come back from Switzerland without his wife and daughter. His mother, Umm Mufleh, still lived in Petra. Dakhilallah's family continued to live up at the Deir. When the weather became warmer, in April, Dakhilallah's father, Qublan, erected a tent for his family near el-Habis.[10] Judging by the smoke in the evening visible from our cave, two families were still living on the hill opposite it, Jabal Mʿaysrah. We later noticed that there had also been some changes in occupation at the edges of the valley, in the areas away from the city centre. Some of the Bdoul had moved into these areas, such as Hamdah and her family, who had moved to Moghar an-Nasara. According to Mufleh, there had also been some changes to the south. When families in Wadi Farasa had moved to Umm Sayhoun, some families from Jabal Haroun had moved further in. This explained why I did not recognise some of the children we met in Wadi Farasa.

Dinner with Mufleh

We met Mufleh and Haroun at the end of the day at Dakhilallah's shop, as on my previous trips (fig. 249). Mufleh invited us a few times for dinner at his home. It consisted of two caves at right angles to each other, which formed a courtyard in front (fig. 250). When he had previously invited Jane and me, we ate inside as the weather was cool. By the time Kathleen and I were in Petra, the weather was warmer, so we ate outside with him and Abu Shaher (fig. 297). On each of

9 Banning and Köhler-Rollefson (1986: 161) noted how at Beidha, in 1983, heavy snow settled on Jabal el-Hīshe, but not on the plain at the foot of it.

10 Recorded in June 1986 (Simms 1988: 201).

these occasions, there were variations in what Mufleh served and how he served it, which reflected the ability of the Bdoul to adapt. These occasions also illustrate their flexibility in the use of space, dining indoors or outdoors depending on the weather.

On the first occasion, in late January, when Mufleh had invited Jane and me for dinner, we ate together in his smaller cave, his main cave at the time. He had whitewashed the walls again, but not the ceiling which was still black. He had a steel-frame bed with a bedspread. A stone bench was built across one corner. A little niche in the wall had a candle in it, but the main lighting was a Tilley lamp. Woven plastic matting covered the floor. He had the room set up for dinner with foam rubber mattresses, with pillows or cushions on them, aligned around three sides. In front of these, he had set three places on the floor with placemats from the Forum Hotel restaurant in Wadi Musa, which were decorated with a photograph of part of an old red Bedouin wool floor rug. Each place was set with two bowls, a spoon, and a fork. Mufleh used the room to serve the meal, but it had not been cooked there.

When Mufleh brought in the *mensef*, he brought the meat and rice in separately. The rice, which was on a platter, was yellow from being cooked in saffron. He served the chicken in its yoghurt sauce in a separate bowl. He then told us to serve the rice onto our plates, and to put the chicken and sauce on top. We ate with a spoon and fork. He also served a bowl of salad, which consisted of the usual tomato and cucumbers, but with the addition of pickled cucumber and white cabbage cut in thick strips. I commented that the cabbage was like sauerkraut, and he agreed, so presumably the influence came from his time in Switzerland. He served the chicken with Wadi Musa bread (ordinary Arab bread, not Bedouin *shraak*). After the chicken and rice, we had *hummus* and *labaneh* with bread, and ate the salad. This course was followed by a bowl of apples and oranges, with Pepsi for us and *shay* for him.

Mufleh told us all about a place in the Australian outback, Coober Pedy, where people also lived in caves, which he had seen in a film about Australia when he was in Switzerland. He was really impressed by this opal mining town where people had carved their homes underground to avoid the desert heat.

On another occasion, about a week later, Jane and I ate in Mufleh's other, larger cave which was situated at right angles to the first. He was working on it and was proposing putting some dividing walls inside. He had a table with chairs. It was set for three, with a plastic tablecloth and Forum Hotel placemats on top. Each place was set with an enamel bowl sitting on a paper plate. There was a bowl of Arab bread cut in quarters, *laban*, and a bowl of tomatoes. Mufleh first served a very nice soup made with tinned clear broth, rice, a small amount of onion and a few yellow beans. This was followed by boiled potato and cauliflower, and bully beef fried with onion. The meal was completed with a piece of fruit.

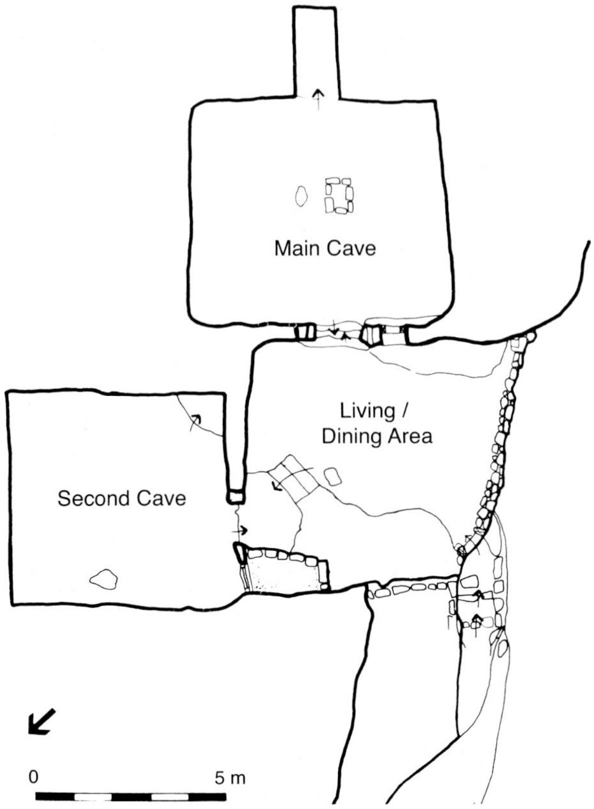

Fig. 250. Mufleh's caves, plan [based on Bienkowski and Chlebik 1991: fig. 8].

Mufleh had received a postcard from his wife which he wanted translated. She said that his daughter hoped that he would come, and she had been playing in the snow and made a snowman. He said that he did not want to go. When he was in Switzerland, he had worked weighing flower seeds and putting them into packets. He also told us tales about his time in Switzerland. He claimed that when he was in Lucerne he had seen an excavation in which Nabataean coins were found. I would have doubted this, if I had not known that Nabataean coins had been found as far away as Switzerland.

The Urn Tomb – A Tomb Converted to a Church

Whereas my previous two field trips had been focused on the architectural decoration, this time the focus was on the interiors behind the facades. Just as the larger classical tombs have very varied designs on their facades, so too the designs of their interior chambers vary.[11] By contrast, interiors of the tombs with the most common types of facades, decorated with a pair of facing staircases or rows of Assyrian crowsteps, almost all had recesses (*loculi*) for bodies cut in their walls, as in Tomb 813 (fig. 97). Some tombs had graves cut in the floor,

11 E.g., McKenzie 1990: pls. 81 (Khasneh), 100 (Tomb of the Roman Soldier), 117 (Corinthian Tomb), 124 (Obelisk Tomb), 147 (Palace Tomb), 153 (Tomb of Sextius Florentinus).

Fig. 251. "Royal Tombs" at foot of el-Khubthah, with the Urn Tomb on right, 2015 [Marlena Whiting].

Fig. 252. Urn Tomb, 1986.

but we could not detect these in those still covered in a thick deposit of dried dung and ash. Even if originally carved in the third, second, or first centuries BC or AD, the tombs were often re-used for burials until at least the fourth century AD. There were also rock-cut houses at Petra, but as these did not have decorated facades, we were not measuring them.

We needed to plan the Urn Tomb. It was in the row of "Royal Tombs" at the foot of el-Khubthah, to the south of the Palace Tomb and the Corinthian Tomb (fig. 251). It had a colonnaded forecourt in front of it, of which the two rock-cut side colonnades survived. They were probably joined by a free-standing colonnade, which no longer survived but would have been supported by vaulting across the front (fig. 252). The Urn Tomb had a very large chamber which originally had wide recesses and *loculi* carved in the walls. It had a high ceiling, level with the tops of its large windows.

The conversion of the Urn Tomb into a church showed how former funerary space was later used by the living. When it was converted for use as a church in AD 446/7 (recorded by the painted inscription which was still visible on the north end of the east wall), wide flattened semidomes were carved above the *loculi* and wide niches in the back (east) wall (fig. 253). In the rock-cut floor, which was already cleared of any debris, holes had been cut in it for the posts for the chancel screen, an altar, and a pulpit. By plotting all of these holes on our plan it was possible to see how the church was configured.[12]

12 McKenzie 1990: 147, pls. 93, 97.

Fig. 253. Back (east) wall of Urn Tomb with apse heads carved for church, 2010.

Fig. 254. Abu Shaher watching Mohammad Abdallah making sand bottles, 1986.

Fig. 255. Mohammad Abdallah making sand bottles, 1986.

The Facade That Fell Down in the Night in 1847

On our way to photograph Facade 66 near the Khasneh we passed Mohammad Abdallah in his stall. He was making sand bottles, which required skill, but the makings did not cost anything (fig. 254). Different coloured sandstone provided the different coloured sands when crushed. The glass bottles were small spirit bottles used on aeroplanes, in hotel minibars, or in hip flasks (fig. 255). His wife, Marguerite, explains in her book how Mohammad made the first one to present to Queen Elizabeth II on her visit to Petra in 1984.[13]

We reached Facade 66, which had had a Greek inscription on it (fig. 256). In this inscription, Arrianos, who was born in "sacred Petra … the metropolis of the land of Arabia", died at age 27 of a disease, and expressed his regret: "One thing alone stings my heart, and that is that I have left my aged mother everlasting grief".[14] The inscription was recorded by Leon de Laborde in 1827, before all of the left hand facade and most of the right hand facade fell down after rain on 22nd March 1847, when Harriette Martineau was camping in Petra (fig. 257). About eighty years later, in 1929, when Taufiq (Tewfiq) Canaan was working in Petra,

Fig. 256. Facade 66 before it fell down in 1847.

13 Van Geldermalsen 2006: 247.

14 McKenzie 1990: 38, 59 n. 98 (references for inscription), pls. 168a–b.

Fig. 257. Facade 66, right-hand part of fig. 256, in 1986.

Fig. 258. Abdallah making a *rabābah*, 1986.

Fig. 259. Haroun, 1986.

this event, which was nearly within living memory, was part of the oral history related by the Bdoul. They described how one evening a European woman, who they concluded was a sorceress, began reading aloud while incense was burnt, then there was a loud noise like a thunderclap and the facade fell down.[15] Many of the Bedouin were living in the caves at the time. As she noted, "Row beyond row of the caves gave out yellow gleams; and in the moonlight rose little pillars and wreaths of white smoke."[16] The next evening she noticed them "even in some very distant caves."[17]

Dakhilallah and Haroun

Mohammad Abdallah's father, Abdallah, still sat on the ground at the edge of the Qasr el-Bint, making *rabābah* instruments for sale to tourists (fig. 258).[18] At the end of the day, as on my previous trips, we would sit outside Dakhilallah's shop below our cave, to have a Fanta or Pepsi or to drink *shay*. As Dakhilallah had stopped working as a stone mason carving blocks for the Qasr el-Bint, his second eldest son, Haroun, now ran his shop (fig. 259).

15 Canaan 1929: 8–9; Martineau 1848: vol. 3, 29, 32.
16 Martineau 1848: vol. 3, 28.
17 Martineau 1848: vol. 3, 32.
18 Abdallah died in 1987 (van Geldermalsen 2006: 50).

Dakhilallah and his family still lived up at the Deir, where he now had a generator and a TV aerial again. Although, like the Bdoul, tourists were not allowed to sleep overnight in Petra, they still did so at Dakhilallah's, which by 1984 had the special guest room we had seen for the purpose. When the parents of a young colleague and those who accompanied them stayed there, there was also an ambassador there. When Dakhilallah, a strict Muslim, went out of the room, the two men both immediately pulled out their hip flasks, and offered each other a sip of whisky.

First and Last Light on the Lion Triclinium and the Deir

Early one morning, we went to measure the plan of the Lion Triclinium, which was located in a picturesque ravine on the way up to the Deir. Positioning the plan of the facade relative to the chamber with the theodolite was difficult because of the ravine in front it (fig. 260). We found that although it had a classical facade, inside it was not a tomb. Rather, it had rough benches on three sides, and a roughly cut, unfinished niche in the centre of the back wall. Jane noticed that the first place the light hit in the morning was this niche, with the rays of the sun coming through the circular window at the top (fig. 261). At the time, it was only one month from

Fig. 260. Lion Triclinium, 1982.

Fig. 261. Lion Triclinium with the early morning sun hitting the niche in the back wall, near the shortest day of the year, 1986.

the shortest day of the year.[19] Originally, the facade had a circular window above the door, but the bottom of the opening had weathered, so that it now joined the top of the door. The circular hole must have been deliberately cut to achieve this effect and the position of the monument chosen to make it possible.

We continued our climb up to the Deir to measure its floor plan. Its interior consisted of a single plain, nearly square chamber (fig. 120). In the back wall, there was a wide niche decorated with an arched top with cornices. This niche was positioned slightly off centre relative to the doorway, contrary to what would have been expected (fig. 120). At the end of the day, the reason for this arrangement became apparent. The last rays of the setting sun shone in a valley between two peaks, so that they hit the niche in the back wall of the Deir last, because of its slightly asymmetrical position (fig. 262).[20]

19 McKenzie et al. 2012 [2014]: 396.

20 McKenzie et al. 2013: vol. 1, 250. This effect is further illustrated in Belmonte and García 2017: 146–49, figs. 4–5. Some scholars (such as Belmonte et al. 2013; Paradise and Angel 2015; Paradise 2016; 2016b) have suggested that the position of all the monuments in Petra was related to the sun. However, the fact that they were also carved following the cleavage plain of the stone was a major consideration in the orientations of the facades, even if other details were influenced by the sun (such as the position of the niche in the back wall of the Deir).

An ornate niche had been carved in Room 468 in the hillock opposite the Deir. From this hillock one could look down on the large circular area between it and the Deir (fig. 263).[21] The steps to the Deir had been worn in antiquity and re-cut by the Nabataeans, suggesting that large numbers of people went up there on festival occasions (fig. 115).

The High Place

In contrast to the Deir, the High Place was approached by a steep and narrow staircase from Wadi Farasa to the peak of Jabal al-Madhbah. At the end of Wadi Farasa, stairs led up from the courtyard in front of the Tomb of the Roman Soldier to an idyllic green area in front of the Garden Temple, before climbing past the rock-cut Lion Fountain to the top. The steps led back down on the other side of Jabal al-Madhbah. When Angela and I had first climbed up to the High Place in 1981, we were amused to find a refreshment stand even up there, when there would have been only a few visitors in a day.

21 We had thought that it was an assembly area for a large crowd, but excavations in 2015 revealed it was what was identified as a 60 m diameter catch pool, possibly for ritual purposes (Finlayson in Corbett et al. 2016: 662). However, the floor of this structure reveals quarry marks, as if it is unfinished.

Fig. 262. Deir, with the setting sun hitting the niche in the back wall, near the shortest day of the year, 1986.

Fig. 263. Circular area in front of the Deir.

Fig. 264. Obelisks (Zibb ʿAtuf) below the High Palace, at the top of Jabal al-Madhbah.

The High Place, which is at the top of the ridge, is a large recessed rectangular area with an altar beside it. Jabal Haroun could be seen from it. The most striking feature was the mountain top below the High Place, from which two obelisks (the Zibb ʿAtuf) had been cut free from the rock (fig. 264).[22] The cuttings made to quarry the blocks followed the cleavage plane of the stone, but with our prismatic compass we found that the two obelisks are orientated exactly east–west.[23] This meant that the shadow of one would hit the other at sunrise and sunset on the vernal and autumnal equinoxes when the sun rises and sets in the exact east or west. The vernal equinox marked the beginning of the Nabataean year.[24]

Hamdah at Moghar an-Nasara

We needed to go to Moghar an-Nasara to measure the floor plan of the Tomb with the Armour (No. 649) in the last week of January. On the way, we passed the old cave of Tuffleh's in-laws where they were no longer allowed to live (fig. 265). Instead they had moved to Moghar an-Nasara (fig. 266). We found Hamdah in Tomb 652, the third tomb along from (south of) the Tomb with the Armour (No. 649). Tomb 652 is a very large cave with a Hegr tomb facade (fig. 267). It still had a hearth. The interior was smoke-blackened from fires over many years. It had a beautiful view over Petra, particularly as the sun set in the evenings. Inside, the living area was delimited by stones, with the earth swept clean. The bedding was piled at the side. The baby goats seemed to have the run of the rest of the cave, as the floor was covered in their droppings and chaff.

The younger children had noticeably grown: Aisha (who now looked like Maheela), Khalil (the little boy), and Atidal (the little girl) (fig. 268). Aisha still remembered that Angela and I were there when Atidal was born, and we brought them the large box of biscuits. She also remembered playing Skippy the kangaroo. Hamdah said that Atidal was her last child, and there would not be any more. Hamdah had a bad chest, and her glands seemed very swollen. She told us she had eleven children, including one married into the Saʿidiyyine tribe. Tuffleh was now living up in Umm Sayhoun and had one boy and one girl. Maheela was married

22 That the fortress-like structure opposite (Qasr al-Qantara) is not Crusader has since been confirmed (Sinibaldi 2016: 94). Pringle (2005: 245) suggests that the fortress might have been Byzantine of the "later sixth century onwards", rather than Nabataean as McKenzie (1990: 172) suggested.

23 McKenzie 1990: 172. Belmonte and García. (2017: 145–46) treat this as a new discovery.

24 McKenzie et al. 2013: vol. 1, 250.

Fig. 265. Cave of Hamdah's family, 1986.

Fig. 266. View to the site of Umm Sayhoun, beyond Moghar an-Nasara, 1986.

Fig. 267. Hamdah's cave, Hegr Tomb 652, 1981/2.

and also lived up in Umm Sayhoun, but she did not have any children yet.

When the weather became warmer, Hamdah and her children moved out of the cave at Moghar an-Nasara into a tent. We could see her near Wadi el-Matahah with a tripod churn and her two smallest children (fig. 269). I was relieved to find that she was much better. In fact, she seemed in good health. The churn consisted of a goatskin suspended from a tripod. Using the churn was hard work, as a goatskin full of goat's milk had to be pushed backwards and forwards (fig. 270).[25] Hamdah was kept company by Atidal and Khalil, who was playing with the baby goats (fig. 271).

Measuring the Palace Tomb

When we had been working on the Palace Tomb and the Corinthian Tomb on the 1981/2 and 1984 trips (fig. 272), Aisha and some of her sisters were always around. They appeared again to help us this time.

We started planning the Palace Tomb. Both Aisha and Toba helped us by holding the other end of the tape measure when we needed two or three people for short periods, which

Fig. 268. Khalil, Aisha, and Atidal, 1986.

25 On the processes for the production of butter, yoghurt, and the hard dried yoghurt balls (*jamīd*) from goats' milk: Weir 1976: 20–21, pl. 22, colour pl. 4; Banning and Köhler-Rollefson 1986: 163; van Geldermalsen 2006: 90.

Fig. 269. Hamdah churning, 1986.

Fig. 270. Hamdah using a goatskin supported by a tripod for churning, helped by Atidal, 1986.

Fig. 271. Khalil playing with baby goats, while Hamdah churns, 1986.

Fig. 272. Palace Tomb and Corinthian Tomb [Sarah Norodom].

Fig. 273. Aisha listening to Jane's Walkman, 1986.

was very useful.[26] While I was drawing, Jane was listening to her Sony Walkman. When she gave Aisha a turn, the look of sheer delight on her face was amazing (fig. 273). Toba was about to have a turn when two male Jordanian tourists appeared walking towards the Palace Tomb. The girls suddenly did not want a turn, nor their photographs taken, and ran off. When the men had gone, they reappeared. Uthmaiya and Toba had a turn with the volume up so loud Jane and I could hear it.

Aisha drew our attention to some Arabic graffiti written with charcoal inside the Palace Tomb, explaining that it was her name and Uthmaiya's. This was a continuation of the fascination the Bdoul girls had with writing which was evident on our 1984 trip when they first started to attend school in large numbers and were so proud of their new skill.

A Trip to Wadi Rumm

As I did not have a vehicle when working in Petra on my previous two field seasons, I had not been to Wadi Rumm. The opportunity arose to go with members of the Sydney University archaeological expedition to Pella. It was a bit of an anti-climax, as I had been told the mountains towered much higher than those around Petra. It had been very

26 If there were details to be planned along a wall, we needed two helpers to hold the tape measure along the wall. Jane needed to hold a plumb bob and read off along it where each detail occurred, while I marked these measurements on a sketch plan for drawing up later.

Fig. 274. Approach to Wadi Rumm, with morning haze after a windy night, 1986.

Fig. 275. Wadi Rumm, tents, 1986.

Fig. 276. Wadi Rumm, tent beside houses, 1986.

Fig. 277. Wadi Rumm, police station, 1986.

Fig. 278. Wadi Rumm, Desert Patrol soldier, 1986.

windy the night before, so that when we drove towards it at 8 am, the mountains were only visible as a series of shadows, each a little darker than the others with a sandy flat in front of them (fig. 274). The sand had blown into ripples, like in photographs of the Sahara Desert. Beside the tarred road along the wadi, reddish brown mountains of rock towered on either side with sand in between (fig. 275). The scenery on the way to Wadi Sabra and Jabal Haroun was more impressive and beautiful.

Some of the Bedouin had settled in houses just before the police station, while keeping some tents (fig. 276). The beginning of the site was marked by the police fort, which had crenellations (fig. 277). It was manned by the Desert Patrol, who wear a red *keffiyeh* as part of their uniform with the badge pinned to their *'agal*, like Abu Shaher when he was in the Arab Legion (fig. 207). The soldier wore a *thaub* (full length robe) instead of trousers. He had a cartridge belt to supply his rifle, which had a bayonet. He was proud to let us all take his photograph (fig. 278). Beyond the police fort, there was only one building. It was built in a similar style to the fort, with crenellations along the top. All the other habitations were tents.

The Bedouin in the tents at Wadi Rumm were not excessively friendly. I took a Polaroid photograph of a little boy with a wire car and gave it to him (fig. 279). Usually, this was a source of delight, and the whole family looked at the photograph. However, his mother announced she did not want the photograph, but half a dinar for the privilege of us

Fig. 279. Wadi Rumm, boy with a wire car with tin cans for wheels, 1986.

taking the photograph. I had never struck this before. There were some older boys who wanted a photograph of them with their camels, and they were much friendlier after I had taken it.

We saw three families of Bedouin moving house with their tents, mattresses, quilts, dogs, women, and children all loaded in the back of a trailer. The trailer had truck wheels and was pulled by a tractor, with very heavy wheels for traction in the desert sand (figs. 280–281).

Ahmad from Wadi Musa

Ahmad Moamaar Nawafleh invited Jane and me for lunch with him in Wadi Musa. He was twenty-seven years old and had spent two months in the United States, and so his English was quite good. His worked for public relations in the Ministry of Tourism in the Petra Visitors Centre and was trying to enter the Department of Antiquities. Eventually, we found him, and we had tea together at the Rest House, and then we took a lift up to his family's house which was fairly high up the hill in Wadi Musa.

The house was cement-rendered concrete and breeze blocks, painted white and brown. It was L-shaped with the rooms on two sides of a courtyard, which was at the back. The family were sitting out at the back on a concrete veranda, which ran along the edge of the house. The side of the house into which we went was an extension, which was only eight months old.

The first room we entered was set up Bedouin style. It had bright orange wall-to-wall carpet with a long pile, and two layers of foam rubber mattresses and pillow-shaped bolsters or cushions arranged along the walls.

We were ushered into a second room for tea with Ahmad and his sisters (fig. 282). This room was furnished in western-style with huge new brown velveteen padded lounge chairs with carved wooden arms. It contained eight armchairs and two three-seater sofas. Like the first room, this one also had orange carpet on the floor. The smooth plastered walls were carefully painted cream, with full-gloss paint used on the bottom half. There was a proper flat electric light fitting, not a naked bulb, in the ceiling. The two small aluminium framed windows were tinted, making the room seem much cooler. In one corner, there was a bookcase with quite a few books, especially on archaeology. In the centre of the room, there was a kerosene heater and a coffee table. It was decorated with gold-painted roses on a glass top and had chromium legs. There were small side tables to match. On the coffee table, there was a very fancy filigree pottery

Fig. 280. Wadi Rumm, Bedouin moving house with their tents, 1986.

Fig. 281. Bedouin moving house with bedding, women, and children, 1986.

Fig. 282. Ahmad Moamaar Nawafleh serving tea in western-style living room in Wadi Musa, with his brothers and sisters, and Jane, 1986.

Fig. 283. Tomb 4, which had been built into the Rest House, and later demolished, 2001.

Fig. 284. Obelisk Tomb and Bab el-Siq Triclinium, 2010.

vase filled with silk artificial flowers, alongside a bottle filled with coloured sand. In one corner of the room there was a stand with a silver tray on top of it and a yellow plastic duck filled with small plastic ducks. I asked if they went in the bath and was told that they did not. Hanging on the wall high up, there was a cuckoo clock with long chains with weights (fig. 282).

We were ushered back into the first (Bedouin-style) room for *mensef*. As usual, a large plastic mat was laid out on the floor to serve as a "tablecloth". Then the circular metal tray with the *mensef* on it was placed in the middle of the mat. The tray was lined with *shraak* (Bedouin bread) at the bottom, on which rice was placed, with lots of roasted pine-nuts and chicken on top. Greek parsley was generously sprinkled over it all. Spoons were provided for the rice, and the chicken was eaten with fingers. I ate it all with my fingers, as it tasted better. We washed our hands at a sink afterwards. It was a very enjoyable meal, but only Ahmad ate with us.

We were invited back into the other, western-style room for *shay*, fruit, and sweet Arab coffee. Ahmad showed us a book in German which was published in 1964 on the Bedouin.[27] It included photographs of Wadi Musa, and some, he said, were of his family.

27 Keiser 1964.

Ahmad said that his family used to live in the tomb (No. 4) which was incorporated into the ground floor of the Rest House (the Rest House was demolished in 1991, leaving the tomb and its courtyard visible again, fig. 283).[28] He said their house was the "first house" in Wadi Musa, as it was built in ca. 1965, by which he meant the first *concrete* house. Two of the photographs in the German book showed Wadi Musa with about twenty houses in it, along with the police fort (e.g., fig. 277).[29]

Ahmad considered that seven times as many people lived in tents at that stage compared with houses. He said some of them also lived in caves right down as far as the entrance to the Siq, including the Bab el-Siq Triclinium, which had extensive carbon deposits on it from fires (figs. 284–286). It had rock-cut benches around it on three sides which would have been used for funerary meals in Nabataean times. Even the chamber beside it, on the right, which had graves in the floor, had blackened walls and ceiling, as did the Obelisk Tomb above it.[30]

28 Date: Suleiman Farajat, pers. comm. 19 December 2018.

29 Keiser 1964: pls. opposite pp. 22 and 25.

30 Canaan (1930: 7, nos. 4–5) indicates that the Obelisk Tomb and Bab el-Siq Triclinium had been occupied by members of the Bani 'Ata (of the Liathneh), after whom they were named.

Fig. 285. Bab el-Siq Triclinium, interior with benches for funerary meals around the walls on three sides, and *loculi* for burials in the back wall, 1986.

Fig. 286. Obelisk Tomb, interior recess in back wall over a grave, with thick carbon deposits on the wall, 1986.

Fig. 287. Ashlah Triclinium 21, with benches around the walls on three sides for dining, located in the hillside opposite the entrance to the Siq, 2010.

Fig. 288. Ashlah Triclinium 21, graffiti of camels and single-wing propeller airplanes, 1986.

The Bedouin of Wadi Musa, the Liathneh, consist of a number of sub-tribes or "clans": Bani ʿAta, el-ʿAlāyā, esh-Shrūr, and el-ʿBēdiyīh.[31] Ahmad said that ten years ago (= ca. 1976), they still married within their own sub-tribe, but now (1986) they married across them. Ahmad was very proud of still being a Bedouin, although the Wadi Musans now lived in houses. Because of their extensive farming activities, most of the Bedouin from the area referred to the Liathneh as *fellahin* (farmers), rather than Bedouin.[32] They still retained some Bedouin customs, such as eating *mensef* seated on foam rubber mattresses, with the *mensef* tray placed on the floor. On the other hand, their Bedouin craft skills, such as making tents and milk products were being lost.

On the way back into Petra, Jane and I visited a banqueting room with three rock-cut benches, the Ashlah Triclinium (No. 21), in the hill which overlooks the entrance to the Siq. As it is not a tomb, it lacks an ornate facade. Like most of the larger tombs, it was smoke blackened inside (fig. 287). Some of the smoke-blackened walls had interesting drawings on them, which included not only a line of camels, but notably two single-wing aeroplanes with propellers at the front (fig. 288). Dating such "petroglyphs" can be difficult and the aeroplanes showed how recent they could be. Although it is not possible to identify the exact type of single-wing single-engine aircraft depicted, they probably date to the late 1930s or the 1940s, which provides an approximate date for these drawings.[33] This banqueting room had a Nabataean inscription in it dated to before 96/95 BC, indicating that the Nabataeans were carving rock-cut chambers by that date.[34]

Back to the British Institute to Recover

We had to return to the British Institute at Amman for Archaeology and History as I had become too ill to work. When I rang the doctor in Australia, it seemed to be amoebic dysentery or giardia, which was not uncommon in Jordan at the time. I had to wait while the medication ran its course. As I was not well enough to do any academic work, Andrew Garrard, who was still the director of the British Institute, employed me making new curtains and covers for the bamboo settees in the lounge, which enabled me to pay the mounting accommodation bill. Ten years after the lounge settees had first been covered, we were able to buy printed cotton with the same pattern, even if in a different colour. Stock in shops in those days in the main shopping street of downtown Amman would sometimes have been there for years. In 1981, I had bought a roll of Agfa film with an expiry date of 1956.

A New Assistant

As Jane had gone back to Australia to start her honours year, once I was recovered at the Institute, I had to find a new assistant at short notice. Andrew Garrard told me to ring up the wife of the British ambassador to see if she knew of anyone who might be interested. The biggest problem was going to be to find someone who would not have an inappropriate liaison with the Bedouin, which would end my work at Petra.[35] I was trying to think of how to say this when the ambassador's wife said, "and of course you'll want someone sensible."

One of the wives from the American embassy, Kathleen Boswell, came to see me and seemed suitable. She had two primary-school aged boys she would be leaving for the ten days or so, to the horror of her mother-in-law. I met her down at the Forum Hotel ready for our adventure after she had spent the weekend sleeping out in Wadi Rumm with her family. She brought with her two weeks supply of bottled water and lots of tinned luxuries: Jacob's Crackers and various instant sandwich spreads. It made a nice change from my usual cave diet.

The Tomb of the Roman Soldier

Kathleen and I had to return to the Tomb of the Roman Soldier to finish measuring it (fig. 289). Unlike most tombs, it did not just have a single chamber. It had a very large main chamber, as well as a smaller chamber off to one side (which probably had burials in the floor, which was covered with deposit).[36] When Jane and I had tried to measure this small chamber, we had been put off by small bats slowly flying around in it. With the absence of the Bdoul, nature was gradually moving back in to Petra. We had also noticed the tracks of small snakes elsewhere in the sand in Wadi Farasa, which was not previously the case when there had been more people around.[37] The ground in front of the tomb was green from the growth after the winter rain. As the area was not as heavily grazed as before, the spring growth had not immediately been eaten by goats. In general, we noticed that there was already more plant growth in the main valley of the city centre as well.[38]

As we needed a third person around all the time, to hold the other end of the tape measure when necessary, now that there were very few, if any, children hanging around,

31 Canaan 1930: 61. Shoup (1985: 290) adds ar-Rawijfa. Details about the sub-tribes and the origins of the Liathneh were recorded by Musil (1908: vol. 3, 57–58), Canaan (1930: 60–63, 79–82), and Peake (1958: 202–3).

32 E.g., van Geldermalsen 2006: 52–53. So too, Canaan 1930: 60; Murray 1939: 4; Shoup 1985: 290.

33 I thank Ernie Wickens and Michael Mockford for this information (pers. comm. September 2018).

34 McKenzie 1990: 34; Nehmé 2012: 33, 163.

35 In those days, the Department of Antiquities frowned upon such involvement as unprofessional because it was viewed as socially disruptive. Authority was very hierarchical, so that an expedition director was answerable for the actions of his or her team.

36 McKenzie 1990: pl. 100.

37 Marguerite van Geldermalsen (2006: 229–30) relates tales of Bdoul encounters in the past with large poisonous snakes.

38 One argument that had been put for the need for the Bdoul to move out of Petra was to prevent the overgrazing which was destroying plant growth which otherwise would have reduced the amount of loose sand which was contributing to weathering the facades when carried by the wind.

Fig. 289. Kathleen and Abu Shaher having tea in front of the Tomb of the Roman Soldier, 1986.

I decided to hire Abu Shaher each day, for the whole day. He also made *shay* for us, so we again had the refreshing tea breaks of "Bedouin whisky" which made work less tiring (figs. 290–291). On my previous trips, we had been kept going by up to about seven tea breaks with the Bdoul women, and the lack of these made a difference.

Abu Shaher also brought his donkey, who enjoyed nibbling at the spring growth in front of the tomb (fig. 292).[39] I sometimes rode the donkey, which had a traditional saddle made of two pieces of curved wood, connected to a fork at the front (fig. 293). At the time, all Bdoul donkeys had this type of saddle (fig. 294). These saddles did not have stirrups, but they were also easy for even an inexperienced rider to mount with the help of a ledge or large rock. The comfort of a donkey-ride depended very much on the donkey being the correct size for the rider – not too big and not too small. Donkeys were excellent because they were sure-footed on the rock paths and not prone to bolt.

Kathleen had been having colloquial Arabic lessons in Amman, and Abu Shaher provided her with someone on whom to practice, which she had not had a chance to do on the embassy circuit. She and Abu Shaher did this while I was drawing the plans. Her Arabic was quite good. I noticed at first that Abu Shaher was listening for "pidgin" Arabic forms leading to confusion. In those days, Bdoul English had a fairly simple structure. It had basic forms such as "I go before" [= past tense], "I go" [= present tense], "I go tomorrow" [= future tense], "I go after tomorrow". It was fairly easy to make oneself understood in "pidgin" Arabic by using the same sentence structures they used in English, but with Arabic words. In our innumerable tea breaks with the women, they had been keen to teach us Arabic. At first, in 1981, Angela and I had pointed at things and asked what they were called. Then we would repeat them the next time and add some more. As a result, we started with a vocabulary of things such as matches, firewood, teapot, female baby goat, and herd. They were happy to correct us until we had the correct word and pronunciation.

The Tomb of the Roman Soldier originally had a colonnaded court in front of it, with colonnades around three sides of the area in front, now green with pasture. On one side of this court, facing the tomb, there was a large banqueting room, Triclinium 235, carved into the mountain side. It was decorated with engaged half-columns, with niches between them. These niches would have had sculpture in them, probably carved in relief on inset blocks, as used for the figures on the facade of the tomb (fig. 289). The banqueting room

39 The donkeys in Petra were all male, i.e., there were no female donkeys (Marguerite van Geldermalsen, pers. comm. 11 October 2018).

Fig. 290. Abu Shaher, drinking tea, 1986.

had rock-cut benches around three sides on which to recline while dining (figs. 295–296), in an arrangement identical to that used by the Bdoul, including at Mufleh's place a few days later (fig. 297).

I noticed that the flat ceiling of the triclinium sloped down towards one corner, relative to the horizontal entablature which ran around the room. I realised that this slope was the result of the masons following the cleavage plane of the stone. The extent to which the positions and orientations of the tomb facades related to the orientation of the cleavage plane of the sandstone later became apparent. The tomb facades were carved following the cleavage plane of the stone so that they also weathered along it (pp. 160, 162, 235–36).

Dinner at Mufleh's Cave, Again

Mufleh invited Abu Shaher, Kathleen, and me for dinner. As the weather was warmer than when Jane had dinner with him, we ate out in his courtyard by the light of a Tilley lamp (fig. 297). He had positioned the foam rubber mattresses around three sides of the court, as in a cave. Our places were each set with a deep plate, knife, and fork. On this occasion, Mufleh had cooked the chicken by roasting it in the ground. In the absence of a wife, this was his preferred method of cooking it. He had used this method before, one day on my trip in 1981/2 when we had stopped on the way back from

Fig. 291. Tea with Abu Shaher in front of the Tomb of the Roman Soldier, 1986.

Fig. 292. Abu Shaher's donkey, enjoying the pasture in front of the Tomb of the Roman Soldier, 1986.

Fig. 293. Traditional wooden saddle on Abu Shaher's donkey, 1986.

Fig. 294. Donkey at the altar of the Qasr el-Bint, with traditional timber saddle made of a stick fork and two carved pieces of wood, 1986.

Fig. 295. Triclinium 235, opposite the Tomb of the Roman Soldier, with benches for dining, 2003.

Fig. 296. Tourists reclining on the benches of Triclinium 235, 1986.

Shoubak with Marguerite and Mohammad. This method cooked the chicken thoroughly, and the flesh came off the bones easily. He made hot coals in a hole in the ground and then put the chicken wrapped in aluminium foil on them. He served it with saffron rice, Arab bread, tomato and cucumber salad, and *hummus* garnished with olive oil and lemon juice.

When Jane and I had arrived in Petra, and Mufleh had described the move to the new village, he explained to us how the families were distributed between the units, giving some examples. As the *Muktar* (mayor) had two wives, he had two houses, with one wife in each. He had moved to the village ahead of the rest of the tribe.[40] Abu Saksuka had three wives, and his Bdoul wife had one house, while his two Egyptian wives lived on the other side, one on the ground floor, and the other directly above her in the extension which he had built on top. As Abu Nawas's family had more than six people, they were given two houses. Those with less than six, like Marguerite and Mohammad, were allocated one house.[41] Some of the social structure of Petra was retained with the distribution of families among the houses so that sons, brothers, or cousins lived next door to each other.

40 Marguerite van Geldermalsen (2006: 258–59) gives a vivid description of her first impression of the houses from visiting his. The *Muktar's* is "Household" 1 in Bienkowski and Chlebik 1991.

41 Maximum of six, confirmed by Farajat 2012: 151–52.

Fig. 297. Dinner in the court in front of Mufleh's cave, with Kathleen, Mufleh, and Abu Shaher, 1986.

Fig. 298. Umm Sayhoun, initial 100 housing units in September 1986 [based on Bienkowski and Chlebik 1991: fig. 22].

The houses were built in semi-detached pairs of "units" (figs. 298–300). A unit or house consisted of rooms along two sides of a walled courtyard. There were two main rooms, which were each 11.2 sq. m, which was considerably smaller than their caves. Each unit also had a small kitchen, a storeroom, and a toilet. There was no provision for animals.

Dinner at Abu Shaher's New House

Abu Shaher invited Kathleen and me for dinner at his house in the new village one evening after work. The main route from the centre of Petra to reach Umm Sayhoun is along the Wadi Abu ʿOlleqa from the city centre, which passes the Turkmaniyah Tomb, before heading up the hill to the village. It is quite a long steep walk up from Petra, so I could understand why the Bdoul did not come down into Petra as much, especially the women and children.

Abu Shaher left his donkey down near the Turkmaniyah Tomb, where there was some good green pasture. We then walked up towards the houses. Before reaching the houses, we saw a few black tents which were being used for keeping the goats and sheep in at night, including Abu Shaher's, and which they were not allowed to pitch for the animals up against the

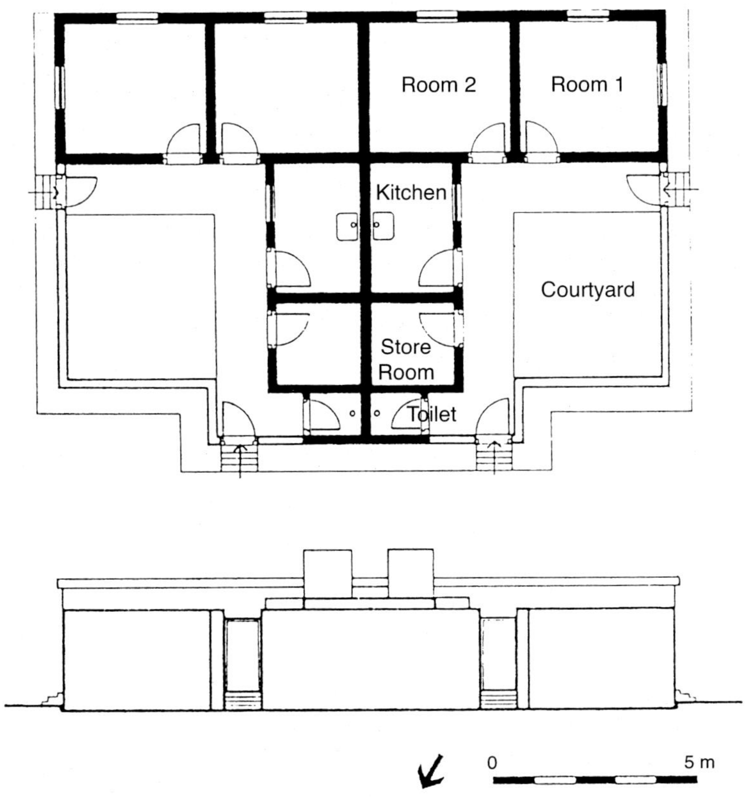

Fig. 299. Umm Sayhoun, plan of original design of two semi-detached housing units [based on Bienkowski and Chlebik 1991: fig. 24].

Fig. 300. Red brick houses at Umm Sayhoun, with breeze block enclosure walls and other additions made by the Bdoul by early 1986.

Fig. 301. Dinner at Abu Shaher's with *maqluba*, with portraits of Abu Shaher and King Hussein on the wall, 1986.

Fig. 302. *Maqluba* ready for dinner at Abu Shaher's, with his family, Amina (Shaher's wife at the time), Zahra, Umm Shaher, Abla, Fatima, Aisha, Abdallah, 1986.

Fig. 303. Shaher's room for himself and his wife, with the lion-hanging (fig. 206) from the old cave, 1986.

Fig. 304. Shaher's room, with studio portrait photographs, from the old cave walls, 1986.

houses. Frequently, houses we had driven past elsewhere where the Bedouin settled had tents and, consequently, a carpet of goat droppings. When the Umm Sayhoun houses were completed, they looked very sterile, but the Bdoul had already begun to add their own touches to the houses, with extra rooms, painted decoration, and gardens with flowers such as hollyhocks.

We arrived at Abu Shaher's house at the west end of the main street of Umm Sayhoun (fig. 298). By the light of the kerosene lamp, we could see that his lounge room was very neatly arranged, in much the same way as his cave, but in a much smaller space. It had plastic woven mats on the floor, with foam rubber mattresses, set up around three sides and covered pillows for reclining. There were some of his framed photographs from the cave on the walls. In their main room, these included the large one of King Hussein taken in about 1953 and the one of Abu Shaher in his Arab Legion *keffiyeh*, which I had made from the old copy of it in 1984 (fig. 301). There was a new hanging of Mecca on the wall opposite (fig. 302). The blue metal trunk from his main cave was in this room, which also had a small table at the side. As in Petra, a chair was used as a lamp stand for the kerosene lamp. The second room was used as the bedroom for Shaher and his wife (at the time), Amina.

Abu Shaher's married daughter Fatima was there with a small baby. As they had only one main room, we all sat

Fig. 305. Breakfast tea at Abu Shaher's, with Abu Shaher's daughter, Miriam, and Umm Shaher, 1986.

Fig. 306. Abu Shaher tending his sheep as the sun rises, 1986.

Fig. 307. Amina tending Abu Shaher's sheep, 1986.

Fig. 308. Abu Shaher explaining the game of *tāb* using a board marked in the rock on the path from Umm Sayhoun to Petra, with pebbles and sheep's droppings as game pieces, 1986.

together in it, with Umm Shaher, Amina, and his children, Zahra, Abla, Aisha, and Abdallah (fig. 302). As their main cave in Petra was not used for cooking and did not have a fireplace, the use of this room to serve a meal was little different to what they would have done in Petra, but in a compressed space.

Abu Shaher's wife, Umm Shaher, served chicken *maqluba* ("upside down") which came out of the large pot so neatly the pile kept its vertical sides, with the chicken on top of the rice (figs. 301–302). This was the first time I had been served *maqluba* by the Bdoul, rather than *mensef*. It was served with *shraak*, yoghurt, and tomato and cucumber salad. At Beidha, when Abu Shaher had looked through our theodolite telescope at a pick-up truck at Beidha, he had called it *maqluba sayara* ("upside down car").

Umm Shaher spent most of the meal chastising Abu Shaher in Arabic over the cost of the chickens and other supplies for the meal. She did not seem to realise how well we could understand Arabic. It was very embarrassing because Kathleen also realised what she was complaining about. Fortunately, we managed not to let them know. Umm Shaher was unaware that I had taken the cost of dinner for us and the family into account when I had paid Abu Shaher a "tip" on top of the agreed pay to cover the fact that he would invite us, as was his custom.[42]

Kathleen and I were given Shaher's bedroom to sleep in, which had a double bed we shared. The room was not much wider than the length of the double bed (fig. 303). The room was neatly decorated, with a hanging with a lion on it from the old cave on one wall. On another wall were framed studio portrait photographs (fig. 304). The room had bright paper decorations hanging from the ceiling, also seen on the side walls of Abu Shaher's main cave. The concrete floor was covered with a woven plastic mat, and there was a curtain on the window. Like Abu Shaher's main room, it had a table in one corner with a coffee pot and a telephone handset. I was surprised how warm the room was, considering that it was cold outside.

Abu Shaher slept down in the tent to make sure the baby goats were safe. In Petra he had also slept with them to keep an eye on them. The rest of the family slept in the main room. In the morning, Umm Shaher, and her daughter Miriam made tea and *shraak* on a fire outside, as in Petra. Abu Shaher had continued his custom of serving the breakfast tea with condensed milk (fig. 305). While we ate breakfast, Abu Shaher tended to his sheep and goats with his daughter and Amina (figs. 306–307).

The Game of *Tāb*

Kathleen and I walked back down towards Petra with Abu Shaher. Fairly soon, we came across four rows of eleven circular indentations carved in the horizontal rock surface beside the path (fig. 308). There are a few of these sets of indentations in Petra, and they have sometimes been treated by scholars as the traces of an ancient game. The Bedouin still use them, which raises the questions of who made them and when. Abu Shaher showed us how the game, *tāb*, was played using goats' droppings as one set of eleven game pieces or markers, and pebbles as the other. That afternoon, after work, when we were sitting in front of Haroun's shop, he and Abu Shaher marked four rows of ten dents in the sand to play the game (figs. 309–310). They used Pepsi lids and stones as markers. Four freshly cut springy spit-sticks (rounded on one side and flat on the other) were bounced against a hard surface to serve as the equivalent of a dice, with the score determined by which way up the sticks landed. The game was like a complex form of ludo or draughts.[43]

At the end of the last day on which we worked with Abu Shaher, we asked him what he was going to do the next day. He replied, "Live". When asked what this meant, he explained, "Wash".

42 Shoup (1985: 285–86) notes that abuse of Bdoul hospitality by tourists (as opposed to friends) became a problem, so that they had to start charging them for dinner, if the guests did not offer.

43 The game described by Marguerite van Geldermalsen (2006: 199–200, unnumbered colour plate 15) (*sieja*) is played with a square grid.

Fig. 309. Haroun and Abu Shaher ready for a game of *tāb* outside Haroun's shop, with soft drink bottle lids and stones as gaming pieces, 1986.

Fig. 310. Game of *tāb* between Haroun and Abu Shaher progresses, watched by Kathleen, 1986.

Climbing Umm el-Biyara without Ahmad

Like everyone who stayed in Petra for any length of time, Kathleen wanted to climb Umm el-Biyara, the mountain to the south of el-Habis, which Angela and I had climbed with Mufleh in 1981 (fig. 84). A guide was essential because there was still no clearly marked path and it was so steep. Ahmad, who was a Wadi Musan, not a Bdoul, kept offering to take her. He was employed by the Department of Antiquities to keep an eye on the Museum and the el-Habis caves, and do things such as fill the water tank, which he was very lax about. He had had his eye on young blond-haired Jane. This time I had brought an assistant who was a blond-haired married woman, there without her husband.

An invitation to a woman to take her alone up Umm el-Biyara was tantamount to making a pass. The chance of being disturbed up there was highly unlikely. Daoud, the cook in the British School of Archaeology in Jerusalem, who had worked for Crystal-M. Bennett when she was excavating in Petra before the 1967 Six-Day War, told me, "The women in Petra are very clever." When I asked why, he explained that one of them had said she would meet him at the top of Umm el-Biyara. He climbed the whole way up and waited, but she did not come. He considered she had had the last laugh.[44]

I had told Kathleen we would employ Abu Shaher to take her up Umm el-Biyara on her day off, if she wished to go up there. Each time Ahmad offered to take her up there on her day off, she fended him off saying she "would have to ask Judith". Near the end of her stay, the day off duly came, and off she went with Abu Shaher to climb the mountain. While they were gone, I was enjoying tea outside Haroun's shop. Ahmad was hanging around and wanted to know where they were. When I explained that Kathleen had gone up Umm el-Biyara with Abu Shaher, Ahmad relayed his acute annoyance to Haroun and all the Bdoul outside Haroun's shop. He complained about me, "She never lets the girls she brings 'do' anything." The Bdoul enjoyed his loss of face immensely, as I had trusted one of their number to be honourable.

On another occasion, one of the Wadi Musans gave Kathleen a Fanta in the Basin Restaurant, followed by the usual, "Do you drink?" line of questioning, as drinking alcohol was viewed as agreeing to go the rest of the way. He asked her if she would have dinner with him one night. She said she would have to ask me, rather than rejecting him straight off.

Torla Evans

For my final week in Petra when I needed to check a few things and take some more photographs, my helper was Torla Evans, a British professional photographer who had worked previously for other archaeological expeditions, such as the Australian one at Pella and at the British Institute in Amman. She stayed on in Petra after her time there with me in order to photograph the Bdoul. Her black-and-white photographs of the Bedouin still graced the British Institute walls over thirty years later in 2018 (e.g., fig. 311).

We met Abu Nawas's wife, Umm Gasim, down in Petra. She was headed back to Umm Sayhoun with her youngest child in a sling-crib (*muzferr*), which the women carried their babies in, hanging down their backs (fig. 165). Before we went to dinner at Marguerite and Mohammad's place, we went around to Umm Gasim's house to see her and her family. Her husband, Abu Nawas, was also at home. Umm Gasim lent me her *mudraga* with the white embroidered pattern she had been wearing earlier in the day, so that I could be photographed in it with her (fig. 312). Just as Abu Shaher's house reflected the interior of his main cave, the house of Abu Nawas's family had little more in it than the little they had possessed when living in their cave. At the same time, his children were very happy, as usual (figs. 313–315). The variations in wealth between different families seen when they lived in the caves were continued in the village.

Marguerite and Mohammad, and the Changes of al-Wahdat

Marguerite and Mohammad had moved to the village, as she had said that they would if the whole tribe moved. Their house had a beautiful view of the hills of Petra, as it stood at the far edge of the village. They did a swap with another family, so that they could have the view, in exchange for putting up a fence on the other house. Marguerite said the view mattered to her most.

I asked Marguerite about what differences the new village had made. She said the main difference was that in Petra you always knew what everyone in the tribe was doing – if they had a baby or were ill, for example, whereas now you did not. She was shocked to discover two women had had babies for a few months before she had heard about them. Also, there was less dropping in for tea with each other on the way to the shop, etc. I asked her what they did, for example, now that the young men could not see the marriageable girls taking the donkey to collect the water. She said they climbed onto the roofs of the houses to have a look at them instead. It was amazing how adaptable the Bdoul were.[45]

44 The inaccessibility of Umm el-Biyara also made it useful for other purposes. Back in 1982, Crystal-M. Bennett had related to us how on one occasion about twenty-five years earlier, the Bdoul had sent all their goats up Umm el-Biyara because the government tax collector (who taxed them by the head) was coming.

45 Another difference was that, as Marguerite van Geldermalsen (2006: 217) mentions, except for the French tourists who drowned in 1963, no tourists had lost their lives in Petra when the Bdoul lived there, whereas in the two decades after 1985 some had. When we had worked in Petra, when the Bdoul still lived there, they had monitored any strangers, which made it so safe for us to stay there with their protection. Any young men visiting Petra who were still there as dusk fell were always asked what they were doing by the Bdoul, who made sure that they left. Consequently, we had felt totally safe walking home from dinner in the dark.

Fig. 311. Uthmaiya, 1986 [Torla Evans].

Fig. 312. Trying on Umm Gasim's *mudraga*.

Fig. 313. Umm Gasim, 1986.

Fig. 314. Umm Gasim, with two of her children, 1986.

Fig. 315. Abu Nawas, with two of his sons, 1986.

The Bdoul were spread out over a bigger area when they were in Petra, but they could always see everyone come and go because of the caves being in the side of the hills. In Umm Sayhoun, with the closed courtyards for each house, they would not necessarily see other people walking from one house to another. By contrast, when they lived in the caves their outdoor living spaces all looked out onto each other, so they could see what was happening. Now, whilst inside their courtyard, they could not observe their neighbours at the same time, nor invite them in for tea as they walked past, as it was no longer possible to notice them so easily. They, equally, would need to knock on the door if they wanted to visit. Thus, interaction did not come about so casually. This was a great pity and suggested that the topography of Petra, and perhaps the small size of the tribe, had a lot to do with how caring and friendly the Bdoul tribe were, especially compared with the Wadi Musans (the Liathneh).

CHAPTER 6

Use of Space in Petra and Umm Sayhoun

Use of Space in the Caves at Petra

Before I consider how the Bdoul adapted to the Umm Sayhoun houses when they first lived in them, it is worth summarising how they organised their household space in the caves of Petra. Although there were variations between households with the time of year or family circumstances, some general observations can still be made.

Most Bdoul households had more than one cave. For their own use for living, sleeping, cooking, and eating they generally had two caves: a "main cave" for living and sleeping and a second "kitchen cave". If they had animals, they had a series of caves, with caves for stables, animal pens, and animal feed.

Main Cave

A family's main cave (usually the largest) was used for living, eating, entertaining, and sleeping.[1] A main cave could be identified by the pile of quilts piled up on a low cupboard in the daytime on one side of it (figs. 143, 209). Foam rubber mattresses were arranged around three sides for sitting on in the daytime and for dinner (fig. 143). At night time, the mattresses were moved and laid out as beds for sleeping, with quilts on top.

In some cases, the main cave had a hearth in it for cooking dinner, making tea, and for heating in winter (e.g., Hamdah's, fig. 143). If it had a hearth, a main cave had an earthen floor (e.g., fig. 143). Otherwise, the floor was made of bedrock, concrete, or polished concrete (e.g., Abu Shaher's, fig. 206). Woven plastic mats or woollen rugs were usually laid out on the floor, before the foam rubber mattresses were put down to sit on. On top of the floor mats, a plastic sheet was laid as a tablecloth for the large platter when *mensef* was served. The walls were sometimes white-washed (e.g., Abu Shaher's, fig. 206) but could also be left untouched (e.g., Hamdah's, fig. 143). Sometimes pictures or hangings decorated the walls of the caves (e.g., Abu Shaher's, fig. 206). The main cave usually also contained a locked metal trunk (fig. 244). A few families also had an iron frame bed in their main cave (e.g., Abu Shaher's, fig. 206). If there was a treadle sewing machine, it was in the main cave. Light in the evening was provided by the fire (if a cave had a hearth), a kerosene lamp or, less frequently, a Tilley lamp, with a chair used as a lamp stand. The front wall of a main cave could be built of dry stone walling (e.g., fig. 265) or of cemented stone blocks, and could have glass windows and a door fitted (e.g., fig. 169).

Kitchen Cave

Families usually had a second cave, a "kitchen cave", which normally had a hearth in the centre of it for cooking.[2] It might also have a primus (kerosene pressure) stove. This room was also used to store kitchen equipment, such as the trays for *mensef*, and large cooking pots on a wooden bench or in *loculi* (e.g., fig. 89). It often housed the 44-gallon water drum which was filled with water carried in jerry cans on donkeys from the spring (fig. 89). Other things, especially firewood, were also stored in this room.[3]

The kitchen cave was used for family dinner in winter, when not entertaining guests (which would be done in the main cave). It was also used for breakfast. The kitchen cave was usually, but not always, smaller than the main cave (e.g., Marguerite and Mohammad's, Abu Shaher's, figs. 92, 172).[4] The walls were usually not decorated. As Bedouin bread, *shraak*, needed to be cooked on a metal domed plate, a *sāj*, on a brushwood fire, this fire was usually made in the kitchen cave in winter (fig. 190). Otherwise, when the weather was warm enough, the bread was made outside, as with other cooking in summer.

The "kitchen cave" also provided more accommodation when a second room was needed for sleeping away from the main family, in order not to disturb them (e.g., by Umm Shaher when she and her baby had a cold), or to look after the baby goats at night (e.g., by Abu Shaher).

Animal Pens and Stables

Additional caves were used for the animals. These included pens for goats and sheep, if a family had them (e.g., fig. 171).

1 Bienkowski and Chlebik (1991: 151) use the term "living room" for the main cave. Sometimes their observations differ from those made here because they are not all based on the same caves and were made at different times to ours, e.g., because we were there in winter, what they call Room 4 of "Household" 2, which they describe as a "Utility Room" (fig. 5, no. 4), was used as a "kitchen cave" when we were there.

2 Bienkowski and Chlebik (1991: 154) use the term "kitchen" for these caves, but there is also some overlap with their "store/utility cave".

3 E.g., Bienkowski and Chlebik 1991: fig. 15.

4 Example of a kitchen cave larger than main cave: Tomb of the Broken Pediment (fig. 89).

Most families had black-haired goats. In a large main cave with an earthen floor, baby goats could be accommodated in one part of it at night (e.g., Hamdah's cave at Moghar an-Nasara). Caves were also used as stables for horses (e.g., Abu Nawas's, fig. 189), donkeys (e.g., Abu Shaher's), and camels (e.g., Juma's, fig. 153). Some used caves to store fodder, such as barley, and wheat and barley chaff (for which the Corinthian Tomb was used by Tuffleh's in-laws, figs. 149–150).

Outside Living Area

Each family used the area in front of their main cave and kitchen cave[5] as an additional living and activity area in the summer and for much of the winter, except when the weather forced them into their caves. Activities in this area included making tea and socialising, cooking dinner or *shraak*, washing laundry, spinning, hand-cleaning grain for grinding, and making yoghurt.

This outside living area was a continuation of the living and activity spaces of the two main caves. The side of this area furthest from the caves was not normally marked by a wall or fence, but by the edge of the bedrock in front of it.[6] The caves of a residence faced this area and looked out beyond it. They were carved at different levels up the hillside, so that homes did not look directly into one another. The division between private space, to which people could retreat when necessary (into the caves), and open space, visible in front of their caves, was similar to that of a tent.

Use of Tents

In summer, some families erected their tent in the area in front of their cave, with the open side facing the mountain for privacy (e.g., near the Tomb of the Broken Pediment, and in Wadi Farasa, figs. 221, 223).[7] Other households erected their tents a little further away from their cave, positioned on ridges to catch the summer breezes (e.g., Hamdah and Juma's, near the Palace Tomb).[8]

Some of the Bdoul only inhabited the caves in winter (e.g., at the Turkmaniyah Tomb, figs. 130–136) and moved their tents further afield in summer, usually to near their fields, such as Mohammad Abdallah's family who moved to Beidha.[9]

A tent consisted of a linear row of two or three compartments or "rooms", each entered directly from outside. The area around each tent was used as an additional activity area. Its boundary might be marked by stones, but it was not walled off. A tent was typically 3.5–4.5 m wide and the rooms in it 3–4 m long,[10] depending on whether or not a room had a set of poles in the middle of it. Thus, a room with centre poles would be 18–32 sq. m in size.

The room for men (the *shiqq*), at one end, was used for socialising.[11] The other room, the women's area in the middle, was used for food preparation, and storing bedding and other household items.[12] Even if the division of space between men and women was fluid when a family were together,[13] the division into two rooms provided an area into which women could withdraw when men who were not part of the family came to visit. A third room was used for goats and in spring to protect the baby goats (as we observed on the way to Beidha), if a family lacked a nearby cave for this.

Use of Space in Umm Sayhoun

Umm Sayhoun Houses

The houses ("units") built at Umm Sayhoun were semi-detached,[14] i.e., built in pairs. They were mirror images of each other, with a shared wall (fig. 299). Each unit (house) consisted of a courtyard with a ca. 2.4 m high wall along two sides and rooms along the other sides. Along one side of the courtyard there were two rooms of equal size (11.2 sq. m)[15] for living and sleeping. Along the side at right angles to that side, there was a small kitchen (6.4 sq. m), a storeroom (4.0 sq. m), and a toilet, but no shower. The walls were made of baked red bricks (not breeze blocks as used elsewhere in Jordan), with concrete slab floors and roofs. These surfaces were left exposed in the interiors, with the trunking for electricity visible. They had windows with bars on them. There was mains pipe running water, for which there was a water tank on the roof. The houses did not include any provision for herds, such as pens for goats or sheep, or stables for horses, or donkeys, or camels. The pairs of houses were all identical, except for the direction which they faced (fig. 298).

Adapting to the Umm Sayhoun Houses

The description of Abu Shaher and his family's home when I visited them in February 1986, nine months after the move to the new village, provides an indication of how the Bdoul initially tried to fit into the space of their new houses. These

5 Bienkowski and Chlebik (1991: 154) refer to these areas as courtyards.

6 An exception was the living area in front of Marguerite and Mohammad's cave, which had a fence to prevent their children falling off the edge.

7 Bienkowski and Chlebik 1991: 155, figs. 6–7; van Geldermalsen 2006: 169.

8 Van Geldermalsen 2006:169.

9 Van Geldermalsen 2006: 113.

10 Weir 1976: 3 (9–12 m overall); Layne 1987: 351. Bienkowski and Chlebik (1991: fig. 16) give the dimensions of a tent in household 8 as 3 m × 4.5 m for each room. See also Qublan's tent in Simms 1985: fig. 3. Banner and Köhler-Rollefson (1986: 161–62) describe the tents at Beidha as ca. 3 m wide and 9 m long, with three "compartments" (and the distance between poles) ca. 3 m long, each ca. 9 sq. m in area. For al-ʿAradah in the Jordan Valley, Layne (1987: 357) represents a tent with two compartments, each with an additional line of poles.

11 Weir 1976: 7–8.

12 Weir 1976: 17.

13 Van Geldermalsen 2006: 169. This was similar to the custom in an at-Talib tent in al-ʿAradah in the Jordan Valley: Layne 1987: 356–58.

14 Measurements from Bienkowski and Chlebik 1991: fig. 24.

15 Areas from Bienkowski and Chlebik 1991: table 4.

limitations led the Bdoul, with their characteristic initiative, to adapt to their circumstances by providing their own solutions to some of the limitations of the houses by building additions to them. Their first attempts at this were more evident by September 1986, sixteen months after the move, when Bienkowski recorded them.

These were the first indications of the methods they used to attempt to solve the problems caused by the house designs, beginning patterns of change which were to continue.

The biggest problems with the houses were a result of the small size of the rooms, their high-walled courtyard, the lack of outdoor living space, and the lack of accommodation for animals. Thus, the architecture caused changes to the Bdoul lifestyle, while the Bdoul also forced changes on the architecture to partly accommodate their way of living.[16]

Outdoor Living Space

A family's two domestic caves, their main cave and their kitchen cave, had a large area in front of them which was part of their living space, as mentioned. This area had a spacious open outlook with views across Petra. It functioned as both public and private space. It was private until you were close to it, when it became public. It was used for many activities, including socialising and cooking, except on the coldest or wettest days of the year.

By contrast, each house had been built with a small high walled courtyard off which the rooms were entered. However, unlike urban houses with courtyards, the Umm Sayhoun houses had an "outer" open space around each pair of units. The Bdoul used this "outer" area for activities, such as making the fire on which to cook *shraak* (bread). With a longer vista than from the "inner" courtyard, it was possible to have a view to the surrounding mountains, providing a feeling of spaciousness. The Bdoul had already begun to construct low boundary walls around each house along the perimeter of this "outer" space belonging to each house by the time we were there (fig. 300). Those built by September 1986 are marked on fig. 298. These low walls also protected any plants they grew from being trampled or eaten by animals.

Indoor Living Space

As mentioned, most families had two domestic main caves mainly used in winter: a "main cave" primarily used for living, entertaining, eating, sleeping, and storing bedding, and a "kitchen cave" primarily used for cooking, and storing kitchen equipment, and other utilitarian items. The main differences between these caves and the two rooms provided in the new houses were that these new rooms were much smaller (11.2 sq. m) and that a fire could not be lit in them. In the houses, cooking was thus limited to the kitchen (generally on a gas stove), except for *shraak* which was done in the open area outside, as it could only be done with a suitable wood fire. For families who had cooked dinner in their main cave, this involved more specialisation in the use of space. However, the use of space was little different for those families who did not have a hearth in their main cave. For them, use of the main cave had been limited to entertaining, eating, and sleeping, as in the new main room.

As there was a purpose-built kitchen in each house and a utility storeroom, the second room was not used as a kitchen cave equivalent. Rather, it served the same function as a third room or third cave when needed. For example, Abu Shaher had provided one of his caves for his second son Khalil and his young wife, Wath-ha, in 1984. Similarly, he used the second room in his new house as a bedroom for Shaher and his new wife. Within 16 months of their arrival in the units, some households had increased their living or sleeping space with the addition of an extra room, which was larger than the rooms provided, so that its size was more in accordance with their requirements, even if smaller than their main cave in Petra.[17] They also began to add extra rooms for additional family members, such as for a second wife or a son and his wife. This process of accretion continued so that the houses were up to three storeys high and very visible from Petra by 2001 (see fig. 334).

Seasonal Factors Affecting the Use of the Houses

Despite the site being fairly exposed, we found the Umm Sayhoun houses surprisingly warm in winter. This contrasted with a house built of breeze blocks in Wadi Musa where Angela and I had stayed one night in winter which was extremely cold, unlike our cave. The warmth of the Umm Sayhoun houses presumably resulted from their walls being made of double red baked bricks, combined with the protection against the wind from the small courtyard, the small size of the rooms, and the lack of ventilation in them.

These same features also made the Umm Sayhoun houses intolerably hot in summer. Consequently, the Bdoul began to sleep on the roofs of the houses and built stairs up to them.[18] Some members of the tribe, especially the older ones, moved out of their houses completely for the summer and lived in their tents in places such as Beidha and Stouh an-Nabi Haroun, continuing their earlier semi-nomadic sea-

16 Bienkowski and Chlebik (1991: 178) had concluded "Previous work has suggested that developments in social and economic organisation affect the use of space. The present study concluded that architecture itself affects the organisation of domestic activities through its segregation of space." In the case of the Bdoul both phenomena occurred.

17 E.g., Abu Shaher added a 21.3 sq. m room (Bienkowski and Chlebik 1991: table 4, room 7 in fig. 27). His main cave was 58.3 sq. m (Bienkowski and Chlebik 1991: table 3, room 1 in fig. 5). The *Muktar* added a 17.6 sq. m room (Bienkowski and Chlebik 1991: table 4, room 1 in fig. 26). His main cave was 37.5 sq. m (Bienkowski and Chlebik 1991: table 3, room 1 in fig. 3). Marguerite and Mohammad added a 27.0 sq. m room (Bienkowski and Chlebik 1991: table 4, room 1 in fig. 29). Their main cave was 40.8 sq. m (Bienkowski and Chlebik 1991: table 3, room 1 in fig. 9).

18 E.g., Bienkowski and Chlebik 1991: figs. 28, 33.

sonal pattern. Some also took their herds further afield. By summer 1986, the Bdoul were also erecting their tents in close proximity to their houses (marked on fig. 298).

Accommodating the Bdoul Animals

In addition to the design of the houses being unsuitable for the humans for whom they were provided, there was no provision whatsoever for their animals. This was despite the Bdoul owning sheep and herds of goats for which pens were needed, as well as donkeys, camels, and horses which required stables. The lack of this provision ignored a key aspect of the Bdoul lifestyle and of their economy. The Bdoul initially dealt with this by using their tents for their sheep and goats at the edge of Umm Sayhoun and stabling their donkeys and horses elsewhere (such as Abu Shaher leaving his donkey down near the Turkmaniyah Tomb). They also began to build pens and stables for the animals.

Despite the lack of provision, animals remained a key part of the Bdoul economy and lifestyle. Although they no longer needed their donkeys for collecting water from the spring, the Bdoul still kept donkeys, as well as horses, but for carrying tourists around the site. They subsequently also began to acquire mules and much larger donkeys for heavier tourists, as well as more camels.[19] The lack of provision for their herds in the units did not lead to the Bdoul no longer keeping them. They continued to graze goats, and more sheep.

Long-Term Consequences of the Umm Sayhoun House Design

The construction of houses with a design which was not suited to the lifestyle of their future occupants laid the foundations for the long-term problems which have developed with the village. Allowance for future population growth and its consequences also should have been considered. The small size of the houses meant that extensions both sideways and upwards were inevitable, leading to the village visually intruding on the atmosphere of Petra as an isolated site.

At the time of its construction, criticism of the new village by foreigners was a very sensitive subject with the Jordanian government. When a British archaeologist described the houses as "rabbit hutches" to Niazi Shabʿan's driver, the comment reached the Department of Antiquities in Amman and the offence caused reverberated back to the British Institute at Amman for Archaeology and History. Eighteen years later (in 2003), I would hear the Bdoul complain that the government did not understand their lifestyle or its relationship to Petra and treated them "like chickens", and that people did not understand them, but thought they "were animals".

19 In 2017, there were 400 donkeys and mules, 70 horses (the rest of the ca. 400 horses being from Wadi Musa), and 70 camels, 7,000 goats and 3,000 sheep (*World Heritage – ICOMOS – IUCN Reactive Monitoring Mission Report Petra, Jordan, 21 to 26 November 2017*: 37). For 2011, see also Farajat 2012: 155.

CHAPTER 7

Epilogue: 2003

Although I did briefly visit Petra in 2001, I was not able to visit Umm Sayhoun again until 2003. I went down to Petra for a few days at the end of that year with Shaher er-Rababeh, who was doing his doctorate at the University of Oxford on Nabataean construction techniques at Petra. It was eighteen years since the Bdoul had moved to Umm Sayhoun and seventeen years after I had finished living in a cave. By the time we had left in 1986, the main excavations had been those associated with the reconstruction work in the city centre (on the Colonnaded Street, Temenos Gate, and the Qasr el-Bint) and at the Temple of the Winged Lions. Since then, Petra had revealed its secrets as a result of further excavations adding considerable depth to our knowledge of it.

Before describing the developments in Wadi Musa observed over seventeen years, it is worth mentioning the changes in the Jordan Valley and Shaher er-Rababeh's home town in that period, as they provide some context from another part of Jordan for the changes in Wadi Musa. This picture also provides a sense of how the customs of the Bdoul, even when they lived in the caves, were not so different to those of the Bedouin populations, nomadic or semi-nomadic, elsewhere in Jordan.

Shaher er-Rababeh's Home Town, Kufr Rakib

Shaher er-Rababeh's home town of Kufr Rakib is located in the Jordan Valley east of the archaeological site of Pella. In the 1940s the nomadic and semi-nomadic populations of the Jordan Valley lived in tents and used "houses" for storage rather than accommodation in a pattern similar to the tribes in and around Wadi Musa. In 1943/44 Nelson Glueck had noted: "The Arabs living in this district (near Pella) and indeed in almost all of the valley, are still tent dwellers,"[1] observing a number of settlements, especially north of Wadi Zarqa, with "several crude mud-brick and stone houses ... which are used as storage houses rather than dwelling places".[2] In the early 1980s, some villages in the Jordan Valley still had traditional one room houses (fig. 316).

Man-made changes in the landscape of the Jordan Valley transformed the economy and way of life of its original nomadic and semi-nomadic peoples who had grazed their herds on the valley floor. The modern-day sharp contrast between the cultivated green crops on the valley floor, compared with the drier surrounding hills, results from the irrigation works which began in the Valley in 1958 and were followed, in 1966, by the 70 km East Ghor Canal.[3] These changes made agriculture the main source of income, for which people stayed in one place. The next generation had a variety of jobs as a result of increased education.[4] These developments are very similar to what happened in Wadi Musa, but there the main driver of economic and social change was the tourist industry – the Wadi Musans gave up their semi-nomadic lifestyle because of year-round employment from tourism, and with increased education, succeeding generations also took governmental and other jobs.

The first houses of the ʿAbbad Bedouin built in the late 1950s to early 1970s in the Jordan Valley, east of Deir ʿAlla, followed the design of a Bedouin tent, with two or three rooms of equal size in a row, accessed from the front wall.[5] As house plans became more complex, a further development was to have one living room for western furniture (with padded armchairs and sofas), but also a second Bedouin-style one, with mattresses on the floor, as these were considered more comfortable.[6] This development, which was observed there in the 1980s,[7] was similar to what we had experienced in Wadi Musa in Ahmad Moamaar Nawafleh's family home in 1986. The ʿAbbad in the Jordan Valley did not completely give up their semi-nomadic lifestyle. In the summer, they moved with their tents to the cooler hills, as some of the Bdoul have continued to do.[8]

Shaher's village of Kufr Rakib is 10 km east of Tabaqat Fahl, the village next to the archaeological site of Pella, still excavated by the Sydney University expedition today. Angela and I had stayed in their dig house at Christmas in 1981.

I drove with Shaher along the Jordan Valley towards Tabaqat Fahl in 2003. Most of the mudbrick houses I had observed over twenty years before (in 1981) had been replaced by houses which were larger and made of painted stuccoed breeze blocks and concrete. Many of these houses now had a second storey because, as Shaher explained, the cheapest way to build a house for your son was to add a

1 Glueck 1951: part 1, 244–45, cited in Layne 1987: 346.
2 Glueck 1951: part 1, 240, 244, 246, cited in Layne 1987: 346.

3 Layne 1987: 346–47.
4 Layne 1987: 367.
5 Layne 1987: 351–52.
6 Layne 1987: 365.
7 Layne's observations were made in 1981–83 (Layne 1987: 371 n. 14).
8 Layne 1987: 347–51.

Fig. 316. Village in Jordan Valley, with traditional one-room houses, 1982.

floor, which saved on the cost of foundations. (It would have also avoided using additional land.) Sometimes, a further storey would be added for another son. He elaborated: it was always a son on top, not a daughter.

From Tabaqat Fahl, we left the green cultivated valley, and the road climbed up the hill to drier land which was suitable only for grazing. There were herds of sheep and large brown Damascus goats. Among them there were tents made of hessian with pens of brushwood (fig. 317). Shaher explained that these families were not Bedouin (fully nomadic), but instead came from villages further east to tend their herds and thus had a semi-nomadic lifestyle.

We reached Kufr Rakib, where most of the concrete houses had been built in the previous fifteen years since ca. 1988 (fig. 318). Shaher explained that the population of the village all came from the one tribe, and that it did not have any Palestinians or other immigrants. According to Shaher, the population had expanded from ca. 800 in 1984 to 6,000 in 2003.

We went to the house of Shaher's widowed mother. Outside there was a lovely garden with pomegranate trees, grape vines, and lemon and other trees. Originally, his parents' house consisted of one room made of stuccoed stone (stone was more prone to be used than mudbrick where there was less water available, as also in Wadi Musa). Then his father added a second room. Shaher grew up with everyone sleeping in the same room. His father later built a separate room for them to study in. Eventually, he also built a house for one son. Around 1988, his father built the single storey house, in which Shaher's mother was living. It was constructed of painted concrete with two large rooms entered directly from outside. One room was for entertaining women and one for men. Stairs led to the roof.

In the main room, there was a portrait of Shaher's father, wearing a suit and *keffiyeh*, and a portrait of King Hussein on the wall. Shaher's father (like Abu Shaher in Petra) had been in King Abdallah's army when he had lived, among other places, in Nablus and Jericho. He thought of Kufr Rakib as his home country, rather than Jordan in a wider sense. His father's view was similar to that of many Palestinians of his generation whom I met, who, when asked, did not say they came from "Palestine", but rather mentioned the specific village from which they came. Shaher's father was the only one of his generation in the village who was literate.

Shaher went to both primary and secondary school in the village before he moved to Irbid to do his degree in architecture at Yarmouk University. He won a scholarship for this because of his high marks and because his father had been in the army. After university, he practised as an architect for ten years. Following his appointment to the Hashemite Uni-

Fig. 317. Bedouin tents beside the road from the Jordan Valley up to Kufr Rakib, 2003.

Fig. 318. Kufr Rakib, 2003.

versity at Zarqa, on the outskirts of Amman, he went to the University of Oxford to do a master's degree and doctorate.

Shaher's thesis, which examined Nabataean construction methods, was published as a book, *How Petra Was Built*.[9] This work was greatly helped by his knowledge of local materials and techniques because of his experience as an architect. After completing his doctorate, Shaher returned, as planned, to establish the Department of Architectural Engineering at the Hashemite University. Similarly, Dr Zeyad al-Salameen from Wadi Musa did his PhD at Manchester University, then returned to Wadi Musa to teach at the College for Tourism and Archaeology, which is part of Al-Hussein Bin Talal University (of which the main campus is in Maʿan). Shaher and Zeyad represented a new generation of Jordanians who had benefited from government schooling in their village, then gone on to do a first degree and a master's degree in Jordan, before postgraduate study overseas.

Shaher er-Rababeh's Home in Amman

Shaher's home in Amman was an apartment, on a single level, on the ground floor of a block of flats which he had designed. Most people in Amman lived in such buildings. The flat was furnished in half western-style and half Arab-style.

The western-style living room was in the centre of the flat, with lounge chairs, coffee tables, shelves, and a TV. There was a dining table and chairs between this room and the large kitchen. The corner living room was furnished in Arab style with foam rubber mattresses around three sides of it, along with another TV. The family used either of these living rooms for sitting around and chatting. They also ate dinner in either. The flat had two bedrooms. Shaher and Nawal slept in the main bedroom. The children slept in their western-style bedroom, with three single beds in it, or in the corner room on the foam rubber mattresses laid out on the floor. The terrazzo floor of the whole flat was carpeted, with rugs on top of the carpet. There were two bathrooms, one with a squat toilet, and the other with a western-style seat. The family used either.

On my first visit, we ate in the corner room, with a plastic sheet laid out on the floor for the large platter of chicken *maqluba*, which was accompanied by a bowl of broth, yoghurt, a salad of finely chopped green peppers, cucumber, and tomato, and a bowl of small bitter olives. A second large platter was piled with stuffed zucchinis and vine leaves. There were also divine small pickled eggplants (aubergines), stuffed with nuts. We had an Arab breakfast the next morning, consisting of Arab bread, boiled eggs, sliced cucumber, sliced tomato, and tea.

The next evening, Nawal served *mjeddera*, which was a large communal dish of bulgur (cracked wheat) and brown lentils, with tiny pieces of crispy fried onions on them. It could also be made with rice instead of bulgur. The *mjeddera* was accompanied by side dishes of yoghurt, stuffed tiny eggplants, fried chicken livers, a finely chopped salad, and another salad of hot peppers, carrots, and olives. Finally, we had a traditional Jordanian sweet cheese dessert of *kunafa* which was bought warm, fresh from the shop. It was made of cheese and semolina.

9 Rababeh 2005.

Changes in Wadi Musa

Tourism in Petra had increased enormously in the seventeen years from 1986 to 2003. The ca. 481,000 tourists visiting Petra by 2000 was a five-fold increase on the ca. 94,000 of 1985,[10] the year it had become a World Heritage Site. Much of this increase occurred in 1995. Following the foundation of the state of Israel in 1948, Jewish travellers were not allowed into Jordan, so that Petra had gained the status of a forbidden wonder with many of them. Consequently, in the aftermath of the signing of the peace treaty between Jordan and Israel in October 1994 (in which year there were 139,000 visitors), hundreds of Israelis came to see Petra. There were a total of 337,000 visitors in the following year (1995). The number of tourists from other countries continued to increase, even with some fluctuations caused by fear of wars and instability in adjoining countries.[11]

For me, the striking change in the standard of living in Wadi Musa, by 2003, was represented by the amazing supply of fresh fruit and vegetables, including large imported American apples (fig. 319). There was also a wide range of restaurants (fig. 320). Wadi Musa now had many hotels, ranging from five-star-standard international ones to backpacker hostels. People had also come from outside Wadi Musa to run them and work in them. At the same time, an atmosphere that saw tourists merely as a source of income had developed in the town.[12]

We had selected a hotel in Wadi Musa that was clean, but not too expensive. The first evening, we ate dinner in the hotel. It was a buffet which consisted of saffron rice, tomatoes boiled with pasta, a stew with a small amount of meat and zucchinis (courgettes), and side dishes of *hummus* and salad. The *hummus* was not garnished with olive oil. The bananas were green and the mandarins too bitter to eat. It was all cooked by the hotelier's brother and was quite expensive. To serve such obviously unappetising fare suggested some contempt for the tourists.

On the second evening, we decided to eat in a restaurant. Shaher went into the first one alone, but they insisted they would charge the foreign tourist price, even though he was

10 Statistics from Farajat 2012: 164 n. 1.

11 The number of visitors peaked at 918,000 in 2010, before the war in Syria led to the number halving (Sewell 2017) and then gradually increasing to ca. 620,000 by 2017 (Suleiman Farajat II, *Jordan Times*, 4 February 2018).

12 Shoup (1985: 286) had noted, in the early 1980s, how the Wadi Musans's traditional hostility to foreigners had made their dealings with tourists more transactional and also insulated them from some of the social consequences of contact with them.

Fig. 319. Wadi Musa, fruit-shop, 2001.

Fig. 320. Wadi Musa, Cleopetra (*sic*) Restaurant, 2001.

Fig. 321. Entrance to the Siq, 2001.

Jordanian. He walked out. In the next restaurant, the price was over three times what the hotel had charged, even if for better food. I ended up having bread and falafels, and Shaher had a chicken shawarma wrap. It was all we could afford.

After dinner, we walked up the hill to the building with three domes which housed the spring, ʿAin Musa, through which its beautifully clear water flowed. Next door to it, there was a shop where sand bottles were sold. One of the young men, who was huddled around a kerosene heater, demonstrated how the sand bottles were made. There were several bowls, each containing ground-up sand of a different colour. A small metal scoop and a metal funnel were used to pour each coloured sand into the bottle, as needed. For details like camel legs, dents were made in the horizontal layer with a metal spike against the glass. The young man demonstrated how one was made with a design of two camels with the sun, and the desert hills behind them. He poked the centre down with a metal spike to make the sand compress, then poured in more sand to fill it. Finally, he sealed the top with sugar water before adding the lid. The technique was the same as that used by Mohammad Abdallah (figs. 254–255), but the details of the patterns were different. I bought the sample. The vendor of souvenir sand bottles was in his fourth and final year studying for a degree in English literature at Al-Hussein Bin Talal University in Maʿan – a result of the increasing availability of tertiary education from the establishment of regional universities, combined with an appreciation of the opportunities it would present.

Fig. 322. Siq, with concrete paving, 2001.

Fig. 323. Siq, remains of water pipes on the paving, 2001.

Resurfacing the Siq

The first morning of our visit, Shaher and I set off into Petra walking down the Siq. Its surface was now a smooth concrete path, in contrast to the previous uneven surface of large river pebbles (fig. 321). The gravel bed had been excavated to bring it down to the level of its ancient paving, for most of its length. Where the original paving had not survived, it had been given a concrete surface, which had pink sand carefully stirred into it to make an unobtrusive colour (fig. 322). At the same time, detailed measures were taken to prevent further flooding, particularly as the floor of the Siq could no longer absorb water.

We noted the newly exposed sections of the water system on both sides of the Siq. The earlier system was a gravity flow system on the south side (fig. 322).[13] The system with pressurised pipes on the north side was constructed in the second half of the first century BC, contemporary with the Siq paving (fig. 323). The excavations exposed an amazing series of carved camels. The build-up of sand and pebbles in the Siq had been so great from past floods that these had been unknown in modern times (fig. 324). We could see that the camels were carved before the gravity flow water system on the south side of the Siq, because it was carved behind them to avoid damaging them. This means that the Siq did not have a paved surface when the camels were carved.

Further along the Siq, beyond the camels, the ground level of the repairs had not been excavated down to the level of the paving, but it was sloped so that the ground level at the exit of the Siq was level with the area in front of the Khasneh (fig. 325). We had noticed, back in 1981, that the present-day ground level was above the original one in front of the Khasneh because most of a tomb (with four dwarf columns on each side), was still buried below that level (fig. 326).

Further evidence of the ancient ground level was revealed by the recent excavation of the area directly in front of the Khasneh by the Jordanians. These excavations revealed that there was a series of facades below the Khasneh, which had been carved before it (fig. 327).[14] The tomb in the middle, in alignment with the Khasneh, was a Gable Tomb, no. 62D (fig. 328). It was carved first and had a single *loculus* in its back wall. The tomb to its left (south), no. 62E, was a Hegr Tomb, the top of which had been cut off when the Khasneh was carved (fig. 329). Both of these tombs were carved when the ground level was lower, before the Siq was paved, indicating that these tombs would have been carved before about the mid-first century BC.

13 Bellwald et al. 2003: 67–68; McKenzie 2004: 559.

14 Farajat and Nawafleh 2005.

Fig. 324. Siq, remains of carved camel and its driver, uncovered by clearance for the concrete pavement, 2001.

When the Khasneh was carved, a staircase was built leading up from the ancient ground level in front of it, passing over the Gable Tomb. Notably, this construction was designed so that there was still access to these lower tombs, indicating that the Nabataeans continued to consider them to be significant. The position of the Khasneh relative to these tombs also indicated that it too was a tomb, even if perhaps a temple tomb to a deified Nabataean queen, as suggested by the crown of the Egyptian goddess Isis on the central acroterion (fig. 73).

These two tombs are also important because they revealed that Hegr and Gable Tomb types existed before the Khasneh. Monolithic double Pylon Tombs had already been shown to have been carved before then, by the second century BC and possibly the third century BC, as indicated by evidence excavated around monolithic examples near the entrance to the Siq and at Ras Sulayman to the south of the Petra city centre.[15] Both Tombs 62D and 62E, below the Khasneh, had Nabataean capitals and pediments, which were derived from classical architecture and were simpler than those on the Khasneh. This was significant because it indicated that, contrary to what the evidence suggested when I was doing my thesis, there was a period of gradual development of such features, including Nabataean capitals, before the com-

Fig. 325. Exit from the Siq at the current level, which is above the ancient one, 2018 [Miranda Williams].

15 Mouton and Renel 2013: 160; McKenzie 2014: 311.

Fig. 326. Tombs opposite the Khasneh and beside the exit from the Siq (off to the right), originally carved when the area in front was at a lower level, 2003.

Fig. 327. Khasneh in 2003, with grill over tombs below it, which were uncovered earlier in the year.

Fig. 328. Gable Tomb 62D below the Khasneh and on the axis of the Khasneh, 2003.

Fig. 329. Hegr Tomb 62E below the Khasneh, 2003.

plexity of the ornate Khasneh was reached. I had suggested that the process had begun with the most ornate details first. But, in fact, the situation was more complex, as it was only later that a trend towards simplification occurred.

At the Khasneh, a guard in full Desert Patrol gear, in a *thaub* with lots of cartridges, was ensuring that donkeys did not go up the Siq. Donkeys and horses were no longer allowed in the Siq, but there were horse-drawn carts.[16] There were now too many tourists walking down the Siq for it to be safe to have many animals walking between them. The donkeys had frequently been led by young men or old men, i.e., those who would not easily find other employment and usually belonged to the Bdoul, whereas most of the horses had belonged to the Wadi Musans. As one of the Bdoul noted, "Every donkey has a family", so this loss of income was a problem. The donkeys were now used inside Petra, starting from beyond the Khasneh. There were also mules for taking heavier tourists up to places such as the Deir. When we arrived, the area in front of the Khasneh was very crowded, with about six coach loads of tourists.

Meeting Dakhilallah Again

We walked into Petra down the Colonnaded Street. On the left (south) beside it there was the so-called Great Temple, where we met Dakhilallah. He was directing the workmen restoring the Great Temple, which he had a free hand to do between the summer seasons of its excavation. He stopped to give us tea. He topped up the fire in the metal wheelbarrow he was using as a fireplace with more firewood to keep us warm, while we sat on plastic jerry cans (fig. 330). The tea glasses had been washed, but he still rinsed the bottom out with tea, as had been his custom. The tea was very sweet, just like it used to be.

Dakhilallah looked a lot older than when I had last seen him but was clearly in fine health (fig. 331). He was keen for me to come to his house for dinner and made pointed comments about how the Bdoul were interested in things other than money for their way of life, but that city people did not understand this.

In the area in front of his old shop, there was a huge structure under construction. It had a gabled metal roof, supported by girders and metal struts, and had sides made of breeze blocks (the completed structure is visible in fig. 363). It was being painted a reddish-pink colour. The Basin Restaurant was no longer the only restaurant to feed the large number of tourists.

16 Farajat (2012: 153) explains how in 1995 horses and donkeys were not banned on the site to stop their use in the Siq because of the Liathneh defending the horses being allowed and the Bdoul defending the donkeys and camels, so the government had taken no action against either. Numbers of horses, donkeys, and camels in 2011 given in: Farajat 2012: 155. Initially the carts were only for those unable to walk in unaided, but later became available to anyone to hire and were often driven at speed. For 2017, the *World Heritage Centre ICOMOS IUCN Reactive Monitoring Mission Report, Petra, Jordan 21 to 26 November 2017*, p. 37 notes: "Around 3000 sheep, 7000 goats, 70 camels and 400 donkeys and mules, 400 horses owned by locals graze within the park and adjacent areas…".

Fig. 330. Dakhilallah and friends in front of the Great Temple having tea and keeping warm by the fire, 2003.

Fig. 331. Dakhilallah, 2003.

Further along (north of Dakhilallah's structure), there was a less permanent structure formed by a large awning which had been walled in for a restaurant, which extended into the cave behind it (figs. 332–333). Vehicles, which were now only allowed in on the unsealed road from Umm Sayhoun, had to stop in Wadi Abu ʿOlleqa out of sight from the area at the foot of el-Habis.

Umm Sayhoun had grown, largely upwards, so that it now visibly intruded from the valley of Petra, and the muezzin's call to prayer was audible (figs. 334–335).[17] The Bdoul still referred to Umm Sayhoun as al-Wahdat, but also as Umm Sayhoun or "Bedouin village", pretty interchangeably.[18]

Shaher er-Rababeh and I met Shaher, son of Mohammad Abu Shaher, who was now the Museum guard and had some grey hair. In addition to the old Museum in the cave, there was also a museum in the same building as the Basin Restaurant. Shaher was very glad to see me, which was nice. When he was younger, my main contact had been with his father, as was more appropriate. I made us tea in the kitchen, and we had lunch of bread, cheese, cucumbers, apples, and bananas on the balcony outside the old museum.

17 Whilst some of the Bdoul, such as Dakhilallah, were devout Muslims, the presence of the mosque in the new village led to Islam becoming a more prominent part of the tribe's life.

18 Marguerite van Geldermalsen, pers. comm. 11 October 2018.

Fig. 332. Restaurant at the foot of el-Habis, north of Dakhilallah's old shop, 2003.

Fig. 333. Inside restaurant in fig. 332, 2003.

Fig. 334. Umm Sayhoun, with houses up to three storeys high prominent on the landscape beyond Moghar an-Nasara, 2003.

Fig. 335. Qasr el-Bint, looking up Wadi Abu 'Olleqa to Umm Sayhoun, 2003.

The staff from the museum in the Basin Restaurant building gave Shaher (er-Rababeh) and me a lift back to Wadi Musa to see Suleiman Farajat I, who was now the Department of Antiquities Inspector.[19] He was very suavely dressed, with a jacket and a polo-necked jumper. In his office we were served a token sip of Arab coffee, as was customary in such government offices. It was served in the usual tiny cup, but from a thermos in the shape of a coffee pot. This was followed by tea in glass mugs, rather than glasses. Mugs seemed to have become the custom, although sometimes tea glasses with gold rims from Turkey were also used. Suleiman gave us an impressive and clear presentation of the excavations near the Khasneh on his computer.

Petra Reveals More of its History

Shaher er-Rababeh's study of Nabataean construction techniques for his doctorate included a consideration of how the tombs were carved, as well as how the free-standing monuments were built, as mentioned. He was able to show how the available materials and conditions influenced the architectural designs. For example, the timber string courses in the Qasr el-Bint explained why it had remained standing despite earthquakes (fig. 336).

19 Suleiman Farajat I later did a PhD at the Polytechnic University of Valencia on "Analysis of Tourism Activities in Petra Archaeological Park" (2011).

Fig. 336. Qasr el-Bint, timber string courses in the Qasr el-Bint, 2003.

Fig. 337. Architectural fragments from the Temple of the Winged Lions, including fine limestone capitals, sandstone column drums, and rings for around the bases of columns, made of the same limestone as in fig. 338, 2001.

Fig. 338. Column base of limestone "with nail clippings", 2003.

We walked over to the Temple of the Winged Lions on the other side of the wadi, which ran beside the Colonnaded Street. This temple had various "marbles" used on it. They included rings for column bases which were made of a hard white stone which the excavator, Philip Hammond, had thought was imported marble (fig. 337). With his knowledge from constructing buildings in Amman and Irbid, Shaher recognised this stone as coming from the same beds as the best limestone in the quarries at Maʿan today. He also explained that it is described in Arabic as limestone with "nail clippings", which was an apt description of the shells visible in it when it was cut (fig. 338).

Beyond the Zibb Farʿoun column on ez-Zantur, a Swiss team had begun excavating houses in 1988.[20] Their discoveries are important, because they show that the central city area included houses and villas, as well as public buildings. The fallen columns from what Angela and I called the "pancake temple" (fig. 339) were revealed to be part of the mysterious Great Temple, which had been excavated by Martha Joukowsky's team from Brown University since 1993 (fig. 340).[21] The thin drums were necessary for such large columns because

20 Bignasca et al. 1996; Schmid 2000.

21 Excavations continued until 2008. Joukowsky 1998; 2007; 2017a.

Fig. 339. Great Temple, fallen columns with thin drums, 1986.

Fig. 340. Great Temple, viewed from the Temple of the Winged Lions, looking south, 2001.

of the weak load-bearing strength of the sandstone. When excavated, this building was found to be filled with seats of a small theatre-like structure in a second phase.

The forecourt of the Great Temple turned out to be the source of innumerable finely carved Ionic capitals with Asian elephant-head protomes (in place of volutes) which years ago had been erroneously initially restored on the Temenos Gate (fig. 341). This discovery created a new mystery: why were the Nabataeans so interested in elephants?[22] At the same time the Temple of the Winged Lions had been further excavated (visible to the right of the Qasr el-Bint, fig. 335), but unlike the Great Temple, had undergone no reconstruction.

It had long been thought that Petra declined after it became part of the Roman Empire in AD 106, with no evidence of any buildings dating later than the second century AD. The exception was the conversion of the Urn Tomb to a church in AD 446/7. However, the late antique Christian history of the site was elucidated by the excavation of the Petra Church in 1992–96,[23] which had mosaic floors. It contained a cache of carbonised papyrus, which provided valuable information about land holdings and population.[24]

The next morning, Shaher er-Rababeh and I went round to Wadi Farasa to see inside the Renaissance Tomb, which had been excavated (fig. 342). Years ago, when I had measured it in 1986, I noted it had no *loculi* in the walls, but the

22 Blagg 1990; Dimitrov 2013; Joukowsky 2017b: 134–47.

23 Fiema et al. 2001. Further information on the late antique Christian history of the Petra region was provided by the excavation of the monastic pilgrimage complex on Jabal Haroun: Fiema and Frösén 2008; Kouki and Lavento 2013; Fiema et al. 2016.

24 Frösén et al. 2002; Arjava et al. 2007; 2011; Koenen et al. 2013; Arjava et al. 2018.

Fig. 341. Elephant's head Ionic capital from the Great Temple forecourt, 2001.

Fig. 342. Renaissance Tomb, 2003.

Fig. 343. Renaissance Tomb, graves in the cleared floor, 2010.

deposit on the floor was so deep that there was no indication if the floor had any graves cut into it (fig. 217). In 2003, the ceiling was still smoke-blackened, but now the whole floor was revealed to have graves cut into it (fig. 343). They were carved to allow for two or three levels of graves to be sunk into them. Some of their covering slabs were still left (fig. 344). This excavation was directed by the Swiss archaeologist Stephan Schmid who worked for many years in the area in front of the Tomb of the Roman Soldier, revealing the foundations of its colonnaded court.

The Bdoul in Wadi Farasa

I took a lift on a donkey I hired from the Qasr el-Bint around to Wadi Farasa, with a lad called Haroun (not Dakhilallah's son). His donkey was so large that it was nearly too wide for the spread of my legs. Haroun explained how they now had to use these larger donkeys because they could carry a tourist up the steps to the Deir.

The donkeys the Bdoul used to have for their own use were much smaller. In addition to the larger donkeys, there were now also mules. The old-fashioned wooden saddles (which had no stirrups) had been suitable for carrying jerry cans of water at the same time as riding the donkey, or for carrying other loads such as firewood. As the donkeys were now solely for tourists, these wooden saddles were replaced with a pile of folded rugs and other padding (often over an old horse saddle, so the tourists could hold onto the front of it) and simple stirrups. The Bdoul had had no need of mules in the past, which also had the disadvantage of being harder to control.[25] Back in 1981/2 there were only two camels, but there were now quite a few. Camels are very expensive, so this change reflected considerably increased income, as well as having the money to invest in them in order to make more money.[26]

The souvenir stand and tea shop of Haroun's mother were located in Wadi Farasa. She served tea in glass mugs, with the sugar added separately, because many tourists didn't like it so sweet. She gave us some falafels and bread for lunch, and we bought some necklaces. Although she also had a house in Umm Sayhoun, she was living in Wadi Farasa,

25 Marguerite van Geldermalsen (2006: 114–15) describes such an example.

26 By 2011, there were 31 camels (Farajat 2012: 155).

Fig. 344. Renaissance Tomb, grave with covering slabs still in place, 2003.

because her stall was there. Haroun was also staying down there, although his wife and children were up in Umm Sayhoun. His mother felt that the Bdoul were not understood, that they needed Petra to live, noting also that firewood and outside space were needed to make *shraak* (Bedouin bread).

Dinner at Dakhilallah's New Home

On the third evening we were in Wadi Musa, Shaher er-Rababeh and I went in search of a *mudraga*. I wanted to buy one to impress his mother-in-law, as I knew the word for it. She had been impressed that I also knew words such as "baby goat" and "firewood", which not everyone in Amman now knew. We walked up the hill into Wadi Musa, beyond the tourist shops, to a dress shop for the local women, where we bought one. Wadi Musa had become sufficiently sophisticated that the dress even came with a plastic carrier bag specially made for the shop. There were many *mudragas* for sale with cross-stitch patterns on them. In the past, those with cross-stitch patterns would have been hand stitched and very expensive, but these were made in the nearby town of Udruh using a computerised machine. Some of them were so neatly embroidered that it was only possible to tell they were not hand-stitched by looking at the backside of the fabric. The new technology enabled a revival in traditional patterns and increased accessibility to them. Two years later, I wore it to Shaher's Oxford graduation.

The next day, after work, we went back to the hotel for a wash and a rest, ready for going to Dakhilallah's house for dinner. We were due there between 4:30 and 5:00 pm, which was the same as the old Bdoul time for eating, so that the meal could be prepared in daylight. I put on my new *mudraga*. On the way to Umm Sayhoun, we went to the cake shop in Wadi Musa to buy some cakes to take with us. It was a proper cake shop like in any Arab city, with huge circular trays in which sweet Arab cakes had been baked. I bought the most expensive ones, which had pistachios sprinkled on top. The shop also stocked western-style cakes, and everything was sold by weight.

Dakhilallah's house was on the main street of Umm Sayhoun (fig. 298), with a view across Petra to Jabal Haroun (fig. 345). Like all the houses, it had been extended. It was now a very large three-storey structure, neatly painted and rendered, with a corner tower decorated with crowsteps (fig. 346).

Inside, the main room was enormous. It had high foam rubber mattresses and cushions around the walls (fig. 347). There were photographs hanging on the wall, along with a very large weaving of the new king, Abdallah II (fig. 348). In the centre of the room, there was a kerosene heater with an inner set of foam rubber mattresses set up close to it for warmth, and we sat there. A dinner of chicken *mensef* was set out on a tablecloth spread in the centre (fig. 349).

Each of us was given our own pot of yoghurt and a spoon, but we each ate out of our own corner of the main dish. There were also two bowls of diced salad. We had fruit for dessert. I ate with Dakhilallah, Shaher, and Dakhilallah's son, Ismaen (fig. 347–348). Ismaen had very good English and, like Dakhilallah, had a good understanding of things. Haroun only dropped in shortly as he had to buy more supplies because it was so busy up at the Deir with so many tourists.

There was much discussion about the large construction Dakhilallah was building in front of his old shop. It was not clear whether he was going to be allowed to complete it, which was causing him much angst (fig. 350). It was a substantial permanent building (completed in fig. 363), but the agreement made with the Bdoul when they moved to Umm Sayhoun stipulated that they could have stalls but not erect "considerable" structures in Petra. This explained the use of less permanent building materials for the restaurant to the north of his structure, at the foot of el-Habis (figs. 332–333), which was made with timber supports, plywood, hessian, and corrugated iron.

When the men (and I) had finished eating, the other women ate after us, in the kitchen. I was glad I had worn my new *mudraga* (fig. 351). I was very pleased to see Dakhilallah's daughter Fatima again, as I had last seen her in 1984 up

Fig. 345. Dakhilallah's house in Umm Sayhoun, with views to Petra, 2003.

at the Deir, when she was a babe-in-arms (fig. 215). At the time, Umm Khaled and Dakhilallah were delighted because she was their first daughter after so many sons. They subsequently had two more daughters, Farah and Badriyah.[27] After dinner, Fatima and her mother reappeared so I could take Fatima's photograph. Fatima had grown up into a pretty young woman, with good English (fig. 352). She was in the last year of school and said she wanted to go to university.

Fatima made pointed comments about people not understanding the Bdoul and thinking they are "animals". Clearly the Bdoul were feeling very put upon and misunderstood. Her comment reminded me of a Bdoul woman I met down in Petra who had complained that they were treated "like chickens" by the government. For people like Dakhilallah who had for so long worked with archaeologists in Petra and had invited them into their home, these attitudes were particularly hurtful.

Although it was eighteen years since the Bdoul had moved up to the new village, apparently some people in Wadi Musa were using a version of the old argument that the Bdoul had not lived in Petra long enough to have a right to be there.[28] At the time (in 2003), the Wadi Musans already had all the hotel trade from the site, but they still wanted to deprive the Bdoul of the trade in the site itself from souvenir sales and donkey rides.[29] There was a proposal at the time to establish a tourist village in Umm Sayhoun, but I did not realise that it had included the intention to move the Bdoul from Umm Sayhoun to a location even further away from Petra. Fifteen years later (in 2018) this proposal was still being discussed.

Meeting Tuffleh Again

The next day, I noticed a young man at one of the stalls just beyond the Theatre, who looked as if he might be related to Tuffleh, as he had a slight cast (squint) in one eye. When I asked if he knew Tuffleh, he replied that she was his aunt. In the souvenir stands parallel to the Urn Tomb arches, we also met a relative of Tuffleh's who recognised us from when we had visited his tent near the Palace Tomb. He was selling plaster of Paris fakes (which he described as "fake"), as well as pottery copies, sometimes deliberately broken (which he described as "real").

On the steps leading towards the Urn Tomb, Shaher er-Rababeh asked one of the women, who had a smiling

27 Marguerite van Geldermalsen, pers. comm. 2 October 2018.

28 Farajat 2012: 155.

29 On the factors leading to the disenfranchisement of the Bdoul from decision-making processes, Shoup 1985: 281–83, 285–88, 291; Farajat 2012: 154–63. With easier access to education more Wadi Musans have also ended up in key roles, along with a greater appreciation of the advantages education can bring.

Fig. 346. Dakhilallah's house in Umm Sayhoun, with crowsteps on corner tower, 2003.

Fig. 347. Fruit dessert at Dakhilallah's, with Shaher and Ismaen, 2003.

Fig. 348. Dakhilallah and Shaher er-Rababeh, 2003.

Fig. 349. *Mensef* at Dakhilallah's house in Umm Sayhoun, with Shaher er-Rababeh, 2003.

chubby face with almond eyes, if she was Egyptian. She said she had been there twenty-two years (= since 1981). He was fascinated, because her Arabic sounded like she was a Bdoul, not Egyptian. She told us, in the end, a total of about twenty-five Egyptian girls had married into the tribe. Besides producing more boys than girls (hence the need for extra wives from Egypt), another problem which probably resulted from the inbreeding in such a small tribe was the frequency of eyes with a cast. The Egyptian women will provide a much-needed input of new genes in the long term.[30]

We continued to walk up towards the stalls leading to the Urn Tomb, run by women, when Shaher recognised Tuffleh from my description of her. She was selling souvenirs at a stand with a proper metal table like the one Mohammad Abdallah, her brother, had made twenty-two years before. She said my face had changed, but she remembered Angela and me. She also remembered playing Skippy the kangaroo and that the kangaroo's milk was in its pouch. Hamdah, her mother-in-law, had the stand beside Tuffleh and also remembered me. Tuffleh was keen to show me her little pass-

Fig. 350. Dakhilallah, 2003.

30 Van Geldermalsen 2006: 211. By 2011, twelve western women had also married into the Bdoul (Farajat 2012: 152).

Fig. 351. Dakhilallah and Judith in *mudraga*, 2003.

Fig. 352. Dakhilallah's wife, Umm Khaled, and daughter Fatima, 2003.

port-type photographs of her children, her husband, and her sister. She was very proud of her sister, Maryam, who was a teacher.[31] Tuffleh had one daughter and five sons and then, as she explained, "Stop". If Tuffleh was stopping deliberately at six children, then few other Bdoul women would now be having more than six. Shaher er-Rababeh explained that in Irbid, which was a city, people now had one boy and one girl, or two boys and two girls, but not more than four.

I thought I should buy something to help Tuffleh out. The items she had for sale included traditional handmade dolls made by Maryam. Each doll had a solid head, with twigs for legs and arms, with clothes over them. I had not seen these before in Petra. Shaher er-Rababeh later told me that they made them all the time when he was a child growing up in Kufr Rakib. They were like the dolls we had made when I was a child in Australia, with a mountain devil seed pod head and pipe cleaners for the body, which was covered by a piece of cloth. I carefully picked out a mother with old-fashioned head scarf like Hamdah, the only male, and a daughter with a tiny bit of embroidery on her skirt. They turned out to be incredibly expensive, indicating how much tourists would now pay. Tuffleh also gave me a tiny model of the Khasneh, and Hamdah gave me one with the Khasneh impressed into a vase. These were not made of plaster of Paris, but a harder material, like the modelling clay Fimo, which is baked in the oven and would have been more expensive to make.

Between the Urn Tomb and the Palace Tomb, there were further stalls run by women. It was more organised having the women with stalls, rather than just walking around. There we met a daughter of one of the Egyptian women. She spoke quite good English and also advertised her wares in Italian. She wanted to go to university to study languages. She explained that her brothers didn't like her going to high school in Wadi Musa, so they had made her take the last year of school off, telling her it was just for one year. For the young women who grew up in Umm Sayhoun, university had become something to aim for, even if not all of them achieved their dreams.

Souvenir and Pepsi Stand at the Nymphaeum

We stopped at Abu Khaled's stand at the Nymphaeum where he gave Shaher a Pepsi, much as the Nabataeans would have quenched their thirst there in antiquity. When I pointed out the group of Hungarian tourists there would not have as much money as other tourists, Shaher replied, "That is what Abu Khaled said". Accordingly, his prices for them were much lower. Even when I first worked in Petra, the Bdoul scaled their prices according to what people could afford. That evening on TV in Wadi Musa, it was announced that tourists from Hungary and Czechoslovakia had arrived. The new king, Abdallah II, had recently visited former Eastern Bloc countries to explain how all of Islam was not bad, and to encourage trade and investment. There had been some trade with Eastern Bloc countries back in the 1980s, when the blue enamel teapots came from Poland and jam from Poland and Hungary.

We took our lunch up to the old Museum to eat on the balcony. Muhammad Khadija's former driver, Awwad, was up there, looking no different, and he recognised me. I was surprised how many people had recognised me, let alone remembered me, especially when hundreds of thousands of tourists now came to Petra every year. We had lunch of bread, sardines, cheese, bananas, and cucumber, although Awwad didn't want the latter because of his teeth.

Visit to Abu Shaher

We departed from the city centre of Petra, leaving sufficient time to go to Umm Sayhoun. I wanted to drop in on Mohammad Abu Shaher, admittedly unannounced, but I very much wanted to see him. His home was on the main street of the village, west of Dakhilallah's house (fig. 298). The amount the houses had been extended varied from the three-storey high enormity of Dakhilallah's to adding a single storey, perimeter walls and painted decoration (fig. 353). Abu Shaher's house had olive trees in front, and the original house was still visible, with an extension on the side. Unlike many houses, it had not been extended vertically. After knocking on the door, his daughter appeared and was gone for some time, so that I thought he was having an afternoon nap.

Like Abu Khaled at the Nymphaeum, Abu Shaher was wearing a heavy cloak (*furwah*) lined with wool fleece and decorated with black braid. He looked little different to when I had last seen him. The older the Bdoul were when we were there twenty or so years before, the less their appearance had changed. His main room was furnished in the Bedouin style with foam rubber mattresses on the floor. We went through it to a room, like a glassed-in porch, which was in an extension visible from the outside. It had large western-style lounge chairs, a sofa, and a coffee table in it. Abu Shaher's house had a dual western / Arab arrangement, as we had seen elsewhere – in Ahmad Moamaar Nawafleh's family house in Wadi Musa, 25 years before in 1986, and in Shaher er-Rababeh's house in Amman.

Abu Shaher's daughter went to make tea. At one point, Abu Shaher went to get the photograph of himself when he was in the Arab Legion, which I had copied and framed when he still lived in his cave. He also showed us the booklet of photographs I had made of them when we were there in the 1980s, which Shaher er-Rababeh had given him from me on a previous visit. Abu Shaher also brought out his two medals from when he was in the Arab Legion, from 1946 to 1966 – at much the same time as Shaher er-Rababeh's father. Mohammad Abu Shaher had travelled round much of Palestine. One medal was the silver one from King George VI

31 Maryam went on to become the first licensed female guide from the local area in 2018, while still also working as a teacher (Marguerite van Geldermalsen, pers. comm. 11 October 2018).

Fig. 353. A house at Umm Sayhoun, with wall-paintings, 2003.

Fig. 354. Umm Sayhoun, tents used for animals replaced with built pens and stables, 2003.

with Abu Shaher's name printed around the side, which he had shown me in his cave in Petra. The other medal was from King Abdallah I and made of bronze or a similar metal.

Abu Shaher was going to Amman soon to have his cataracts done. His English seemed much the same as before, not strikingly improved, unlike that of Dakhilallah, who used English more because of his continued work with the Great Temple team. Abu Shaher now had a fax machine, however. Abu Shaher's daughter, who had missed most of the conversation while she was making tea, asked if I had been to Petra before, then said she remembered taking the donkey with me down to the spring. I was very happy to have met Abu Shaher[32] again, as well as Dakhilallah, Hamdah, and Tuffleh,[33] and to see that they were all doing well.

In the area at the edge of Umm Sayhoun, where there had been the black tents for their herds, there were now small breeze block stables and pens (fig. 354). I forgot to ask Abu Shaher if he still had goats and sheep. When I mentioned this to Shaher er-Rababeh, he replied that he was sure Abu Shaher did and Dakhilallah also. "They [the Bedouin] can't live without them." This observation later turned out to be pertinent because over thirty years after the move to al-Wahdat, the Bdoul still had herds of sheep and goats.

Shaher er-Rababeh commented that, although the people from the villages like his have many things in common with the Bedouin, the difference is that they did not move as far. I replied that I didn't think the Bdoul moved far from Petra, as many of them had lived in the caves, even if they also had used tents.

32 Abu Shaher died 27 May 2013 (Leigh-Ann Bedal, blog post, 28 May 2013).

33 Tuffleh died in 2017.

CHAPTER 8

Postscript – Developments in Petra and Weathering – Over Thirty Years Later (2018)

It seems no work of Man's creative hand,
By labour wrought as wavering fancy planned;
But from the rock as if by magic grown,
Eternal, silent, beautiful, alone!
Not virgin-white like that old Doric shrine,
Where erst Athena held her rites divine;
Not saintly-grey, like many a minster fane,
That crowns the hill and consecrates the plain;
But rose-red as if the blush of dawn,
That first beheld them were not yet withdrawn;
The hues of youth upon a brow of woe,
Which Man deemed old two thousand years ago,
Match me such marvel save in Eastern clime,
A rose-red city half as old as time.

John William Burgon, "Petra" (1845)

A Rose-Red City Half as Old as Time

When John William Burgon penned his poem "Petra" in 1845, he concluded it by describing Petra as "a city half as old as time", evoking a city lost in time and isolated from the world. That atmosphere had largely been lost by 2018, due to the enormously increased number of tourists and the extensive facilities for them (toilet blocks, souvenir shops, refreshment stands, and restaurants). More archaeological excavations and reconstruction work in the last thirty years have also meant that the landscape is increasingly no longer untouched. At the same time, because of population growth, the new Bdoul village of Umm Sayhoun can be seen from within the valley of Petra.

At the turnoff to Wadi Musa (and Petra), the old rural Jordan is still evident as the shepherd herds his flock of sheep, black haired goats, and Damascus goats across the road (fig. 355). By contrast, the main street of Wadi Musa is busy with

Fig. 355. Shepherd with his flock near the turnoff for Wadi Musa, 2018 [Steve Welsh].

Fig. 356. Wadi Musa, main street, 2018 [Steve Welsh].

Fig. 357. Wadi Musa, main street with flood abatement works, and hotels, looking towards the Crowne Plaza (former Forum Hotel), 2018 [Steve Welsh].

Fig. 358. Petra, looking south-west from the Urn Tomb, with the Theatre on the left and souvenir stands in the foreground, 2015 [Sarah Norodom].

Fig. 359. Ismaen ibn Dakhilallah, 2018 [Maria Lidova].

restaurants and other facilities for tourists (fig. 356; compare with figs. 101–102). The green surroundings of Wadi Musa have also been decreased by the construction of new buildings for the needs of the local population, such as the Petra College for Tourism and Archaeology which covers a previously green area of the hillside overlooking the approach to the entrance to Petra, while, in another part of Wadi Musa, old stone houses have been built over by a secondary school.[1]

The most striking change in Wadi Musa is the dense development of a tourist strip with multi-storey hotels built on the previously undeveloped land between the site of the former Rest House and the main shopping area of the old main street of Wadi Musa (fig. 357; compare with fig. 103). There are further hotels intermingled with the modern town. By 2011, there were 39 hotels and 27 restaurants in Wadi Musa.[2] Following Petra being voted one of the New Seven Wonders of the World in 2007, 850,000 tourists visited it in 2008. By 2011 the number had reached nearly one million – ten times the number who went there in 1985. Although that annual number subsequently decreased because of the war in Syria, the number had crept back up to ca. 620,000 by 2017.[3]

Emerging from the Siq, with its concrete floor, the effects of providing for such large numbers of tourists are also seen

1 Twaissi et al. 2016: 340.
2 Farajat 2012: 156.
3 Suleiman Farajat, *Jordan Times*, 4 February 2018.

Fig. 360. Ismaen ibn Dakhilallah, 2018 [Maria Lidova].

Fig. 361. Tuffleh's son, Khalid, 2018 [Maria Lidova].

within the site itself, as many purpose-built toilet blocks have become necessary for the high number of visitors. The way is lined with innumerable large souvenir and beverage stands. With time, these stands have become much larger. They line the route in front of the Theatre, all the way up to the Urn Tomb and the Palace Tomb (fig. 358; compare with fig. 98). The variety, quality, and quantity of the stock in these shops reflects substantially increased income, which has made it possible to invest in more expensive goods. The stands are run by the children of the Bdoul whom we knew, such as Dakhilallah's son, Ismaen, and Tuffleh's son, Khalid (figs. 359–361). The stand Dakhilallah's wife, Umm Khaled, ran in the cave opposite the Deir (fig. 362; compare with fig. 123) has been expanded with seating to accommodate serving drinks to a few coachloads of tourists at a time. It is run by their son, Mohammad, while Haroun (who used to run Dakhilallah's shop below our cave) has retired to work in his orchard in Wadi Siyyagh.[4]

The increase in the run-off from seasonal rain, because of buildings in Wadi Musa and the concreting of the Siq, has resulted in more intense flash floods. Consequently, more extensive flood abatement works have had to be constructed, incorporating wide channels with strong embankments in both Wadi Musa (fig. 357) and in Petra itself (fig. 363; compare with fig. 60 in the same location in front of the Qasr el-Bint).

Besides the innumerable large souvenir and beverage stands, the greatest change to the untouched appearance of the site results from the excavation and restoration of buildings in the city centre. The most striking of these is the Great Temple with its *in situ* theatre seats and the re-erected columns in its forecourt. Extensive excavated areas beside it have been left open to the air, revealing a large pool, houses, a bathhouse, and a small temple (fig. 364). On the other side of the wadi, there is not only the Temple of the Winged Lions facing the Great Temple, but further up the hill the Blue Chapel, with its re-erected columns (fig. 364). On the ridge of the hill of ez-Zantur, a house with wall-paintings has been re-erected (fig. 365). The most prominent archaeological feature is the Petra Church because of the white canopy covering its mosaics, which is visible from a distance (figs. 364, 366). Up at the Deir, the site has been scarred by the excavation of the circular area near it (fig. 367; compare with fig. 263). Goats' paths on the hills on either side of the Colonnaded Street have been widened into vehicular tracks by archaeologists, who have also added their dump hills to the landscape (fig. 365).

In order that vehicles servicing all of this archaeological activity, supporting the souvenir and refreshment stands, and emptying the septic tanks do not need to travel down the

4 Marguerite van Geldermalsen, pers. comm. 3 October 2018

Fig. 362. Souvenir and refreshment stand opposite the Deir, 2018 [Sean Leatherbury].

Fig. 363. Flood abatement works beside the Temenos of the Qasr el-Bint, looking west, 2018 [Sean Leatherbury].

Fig. 364. Petra, city centre, looking north-east with the Great Temple (right), the Temple of the Winged Lions (far left), the white roof of the Petra Church, 2015 [Otto Nieminen].

Fig. 365. Ez-Zantur from the High Place looking west, with reconstructed houses, 2015 [Otto Nieminen].

Fig. 366. Petra, from Umm el-Biyara looking north-east, with the Wadi Turkmaniyah access road on the left, 2010.

Fig. 367. Circular area near the Deir, after partial excavation, 2018 [Steve Welsh].

Fig. 368. Aerial view of Petra looking north, with sealed Wadi Turkmaniyah road on the left, 2017 [APAAME_20171001_REB_0689. Photographer: Rebecca Banks, courtesy APAAME].

Siq, it was necessary to construct a back-entrance road along Wadi Turkmaniyah from Umm Sayhoun (fig. 366). By 1985, this was an unsealed dirt road, with a fairly steep incline, but in 2017 it was tarred (fig. 368). The asphalt surface has made the road visually prominent, as has the scarring beside it caused by the re-grading for it, which has loosened large amounts of topsoil (fig. 369).[5] The sealing of this road makes Petra feel more connected to the outside world, not cut off from it.

The feeling of the encroachment of the outside world is completed by the visual prominence of Umm Sayhoun on the landscape (figs. 370–371). In 1985, when the Bdoul moved there, the houses were barely visible on the landscape, because they were only a single storey high (figs. 139, 266). By 2003, Umm Sayhoun had become very prominent due to the houses being extended upwards and sideways, initially for the needs of the first residents, but then to accommodate the next generation of families (fig. 334). Attempts to stop further expansion for them had created frustrations and tensions, leading to the deaths of four Bdoul in 2000.[6] The problems caused by Umm Sayhoun are the legacy of the lack of adequate allowance for population growth when the houses were built.

In the over thirty years since the Bdoul tribe moved out of Petra in 1985 to their new village of Umm Sayhoun, their lives have changed enormously. The account presented here of the Bdoul in 1981–86, in their last few years in Petra, provides a record in that specific period. An attempt is not made here to present a detailed analysis of how their life then compares with their current lives and the resultant changes, which would require a separate study. The discussion here on the use of space in Chapter 6 was limited to the adaptations they had made when they first moved into the village – both to their houses and to their lifestyle.

The Bdoul are more affluent than when they lived in the caves, and domestic work is much easier. At the same time they have benefited from easier access to education, even if there is a temptation for some children to make money from the tourist trade rather than to continue with their schooling. At the same time, the Bdoul have continued to grow cereal crops at Beidha and Stouh an-Nabi Haroun (fig. 372) and to graze goats and sheep. They now have donkeys for trans-

5 The road was built by the Petra Development and Tourism Regional Authority (PDTRA) without consultation, despite Petra being a UNESCO World Heritage Site (*World Heritage Centre ICOMOS IUCN Reactive Monitoring Mission Report, Petra, Jordan, 21 to 26 November 2017*: 29–31). There have been long-term plans for transporting tourists out of Petra on small buses.

6 Farajat 2012: 155.

Fig. 369. Access road from Umm Sayhoun along Wadi Turkmaniyah, looking south-west, 2018 [Sean Leatherbury].

Fig. 370. Umm Sayhoun from Petra, beyond Moghar an-Nasara, looking north-east, 2018 [Miranda Williams].

Fig. 371. Umm Sayhoun, with the tombs of Moghar an-Nasara in the foreground, 2018 [Steve Welsh].

Fig. 372. View from Umm el-Biyara of spring crops, 2010.

Fig. 373. Pylon tomb facades carved in the cliff face south of Tomb 825, 2015 [Marlena Whiting].

porting tourists, rather than for their own use, while they have added mules and many more camels to their flocks. The Bdoul have also retained their love of Petra and their close relationship with it. Petra is still part of their individual and tribal identity.

In 1981, when King Hussein heard of the plan to blast the Siq for tour bus access and build a road along Wadi Turkmaniyah for the buses to exit the site, after the tourists had dined at the Basin Restaurant, he vetoed the plan. He would have had the foresight to understand that part of the attraction of Petra to western tourists was its untouched nature.

From the Rock as if by Magic Grown

When John William Burgon described Petra as "from the rock as if by magic grown", in his poem "Petra", he conveyed a sense of the wonder of the rock-cut facades wrought from nature's sandstone mountains by the hand of man. Two years later, in 1847, the transitory nature of these facades was apparent to Harriette Martineau when she was in Petra. It rained in the night, and Facade 66 near the Khasneh fell down (figs. 256–257). It was the only facade with a Greek inscription, which they were one day too late recording. She explained: "Mr W. came to give us the result of his visit to the Greek inscription. ... The whole facade had fallen, – brought down, no doubt, by the rains of yesterday! When the party arrived, they found the way blocked up by masses of stone ... it is irrecoverable. That far-famed work is gone forever!"[7]

The mountains of Petra are made of sandstone, which is a sedimentary rock consisting of beds of sand grains (quartz) held together by a binder (matrix). There are two types of sandstone in Petra.[8] In the rose-red Umm Ishrin sandstone the grains of sand have a binder which includes silica, iron oxide, and calcium carbonate.[9] The creamy-yellow Disi sandstone lacks the iron, which gives the Umm Ishrin stone its wide variety of colours, ranging from reddish-brown to greyish-purple to pink. These colours occur in bands, often in undulating or alternating layers. The iron oxide and silica in the Umm Ishrin stone slow down the rate of weathering, whereas the calcium carbonate accelerates it.[10] Over a wider area, the lowest level of the stone is Umm Ishrin sandstone, with the Disi sandstone layers above. Above them, the cream stone layer is limestone, including at Umm Sayhoun.

7 Martineau 1848: vol. 3, 32.
8 Sandstone types in south-west Jordan: Migoń and Goudie 2014.
9 Paradise 2013: 371, 374.
10 Paradise 2012b: 735; 2013: 371–72; 377.

Fig. 374. Monolithic tombs at the exit of the Outer Siq: Tomb 70 (left) and Tomb 73 (far right), 2018 [Sean Leatherbury].

Fig. 375. Monolithic Tomb 73, 1984.

Fig. 376. Monolithic Tomb 73 in 2018, after the right-hand (north) half had collapsed [Sean Leatherbury].

Fig. 377. Tomb 652, 1984.

Fig. 378. Tomb 652, after the right-hand side of the facade had collapsed, 2018 [Sean Leatherbury].

The binder is more absorbent than the sand grains. Thus, when moisture penetrates the binder, the stone is weakened and begins to disaggregate. Moisture in the facades can come from: (a) groundwater wicking up the lower ca. 2–3 m of a facade; (b) rainwater soaking down inside bedrock of the mountain in which a facade is carved; and/or (c) rain directly running down the front of a facade.

As the water evaporates, it carries soluble salts (carbonates, chlorides, and sulphates) to the surface (especially calcium sulphate and sodium chloride.)[11] When these dry and crystalise on the surface they break up the binder, thereby loosening the sand grains. These then fall off because of gravity or the action of the wind. When warmed by the sun, the moist rock encourages the evaporation of the water and damage by the salts crystalising, so breaking up the stone.[12] Repeated cycles of warming and cooling and/or wetting and drying weaken the rock over a period of time. Eventually more rain or an earth tremor is enough to dislodge grains or pieces of stone. Much of the weathering causes what is called granular disintegration – releasing individual grains of sand which are easily removed by wind or water. Thus screes are rare, and so the cliffs remain steep.[13] Even large debris released by undercutting of joints often breaks down quickly.

Variations in the structure and composition of the rock also create weaknesses, along which the sandstone weathers.[14] The layers in the sandstone form its main joints and jointing which accelerate deterioration. Stonemasons take advantage of this phenomenon (which they call "cleavage planes") when they are carving the stone.

The greatest causes of weathering at Petra are damage from water (groundwater, rainwater, and humidity) and salt, as well as variations in rock composition, temperature, wind erosion, and earth tremors.[15] Whilst on any one facade, a complex combination of these factors is involved in causing weathering, a few examples will be presented here where photographs show the effects of different types of causes. Photographs taken years apart are particularly valuable in showing the timing of weathering that has occurred. My photographs taken in 1981 to 1986 have become an invaluable record from which to make such observations, as no other detailed photographic record of the principal facades was made in the early 1980s. When those photographs are compared with those from 2010 onwards, deterioration can easily be detected over a thirty-year period. Further observations can be made from nineteenth-century photographs,

11 Wedekind and Ruedrich 2006: 264; Goudie 2013: 263. On salt weathering, see also Fitzner and Heinrichs 1991: 910; Albouy et al. 1993: 910.

12 Wedekind and Ruedrich 2006: 264; Paradise 2012a: 81–82, fig. 3.1; 2013: 379–82.

13 Goudie et al. 2002; Migoń et al. 2005; Migoń and Goudie 2014.

14 Paradise 2013: 377–78.

15 Goudie 2013: 263; Paradise 2013: 371–74, 377–78. The variety of causes of weathering and the extent of the damage they have caused to the facades is strikingly depicted in: Fitzner and Heinrichs 1991: 909–10, fig. 2; Albouy et al. 1993: 379–80, fig. 3; Heinrichs 2008: figs. 19, 21–23, 26, 30, 38.

Fig. 379. Tomb 62E, 2003.

Fig. 380. Tomb 62E, 2010.

such as those taken by J. S. Smith in 1852, F. Mason Good in 1866–67, C. A. Hornstein in 1895, and R.-E. Brünnow and A. von Domaszewski in 1897 and 1898.

Catastrophic Damage along Formation Jointing

The stone of the mountains of Petra has often sheared off following the formation jointing or joints, resulting in near vertical natural mountain sides or cliff faces. The Nabataeans took advantage of these cliff faces to carve facades without having to cut away much rock in front of them, such as the row of Double Pylon Tombs at the foot of el-Khubthah on the east side of the exit from the outer Siq (fig. 373). The Double Pylon Tomb 824 near them has been carved free on three sides following the cleavage plane of the stone (fig. 373, far left). (In each of these Double Pylon Tombs, the top row of crowsteps was freestanding.)

On the west side of the Outer Siq, other Double Pylon monolithic tombs also have been carved (fig. 374). One of these tombs, Tomb 73, was still standing in 1984, but cracked along the cleavage plane (fig. 375). The orientation of this crack also underlines the extent to which the masons had taken advantage of the cleavage planes to carve it. This example also shows how the facades weather and break off along their cleavage planes. The deterioration of Tomb 73 is apparent in photographs taken over thirty years apart. By 2018, the right-hand half of Tomb 73 had fallen over and started to disintegrate (fig. 376).[16] This same process of erosion of weaknesses in the rock can be seen on Tomb 70 nearby, which will eventually split along the fault line in it, which is being widened by rainwater erosion and weathering (fig. 374). (Erosion is deterioration as a result of abrasion through movement, whereas weathering is the deterioration/recession of a material *in situ* through extrinsic or intrinsic forces, effects, or influences.)

My photographs illustrate how the right-hand side of the front of Tomb 652 at Moghar an-Nasara (in which Hamdah lived in 1986, the third tomb south of the Tomb with the Armour) has sheared off (figs. 377–378, location in fig. 371, far right). As the examples demonstrate, one of the most catastrophic forms of damage to the simpler tomb types (those crowned by crowsteps or two sets of steps) is the way the facades or parts of them shear off along the cleavage plane. This is also observed on the lower part of a tomb south of Tomb 652, and where the whole of the Pylon Tomb (which was on the far right of fig. 371, immediately south of Tomb 830) has sheared off the cliff face.

Damage to Lower Parts of Facades Due to Water Wicking Up

In the lower ca. 2–3 metres of the facade of Tomb 652, the stone has weathered much more than the surface above it (figs. 377–378). This is because the lower ca. 2–3 m of the facade is softened by the capillary action of moisture from the ground wicking up into the facade to evaporate on the surface. The weathering damage from this wetting and drying cycle is hastened by expansion and contraction due to changes in temperature from the sun's rays in the afternoon, which weakens the stone by loosening the sand grains from their binder. Paradise found that damage from heat changes was greatest on east and west facing facades, such as on Tomb 652, because these experienced the greatest heat changes.[17] He found that heat-related damage was least on north facing facades, such as the Tomb of Sextius Florentinus, as they received the least sun.

16 Another dramatic example of a tomb facade splitting apart is seen on the remains of the facade of Tomb 609 (Verezen 2017: 23, fig. 1, top left).

17 Paradise 2012a: 81–82, fig. 3.1; 2013: 371–72, 378–89, fig. 7.

Fig. 381. Palace Tomb, lower south (right-hand) side, 2010.

Damage from wicking up only occurs when a surface is exposed to the air so that the water can evaporate. As the water comes to the surface, soluble salts are transported with it which then break up the binder when they crystalise. The facade of Tomb 62E under the Khasneh was uncovered in 2003 when the tomb was excavated, and, by December that year, moisture was beginning to rise (fig. 379). By April 2010, moisture had wicked up ca. 1 m up into the facade (fig. 380). Damage due to the softening of the lower part of the facade from wicking up has occurred on all the main facades. It is particularly pronounced on the Deir (figs. 119, 262) and the Palace Tomb (figs. 155, 159).

Other Damage – Wind-Blown Sand and Case Hardening

On the lower parts of the Palace Tomb, damage from wicking up and repeated heating/cooling and wetting/drying cycles can be seen (fig. 381). The facade has also broken away along other lines of weakness. Rock composition at Petra, i.e., such flaws in the rock, is a major determinant of damage due to weathering.[18]

When the rock binder has been softened, wind-blown sand can also dislodge sand grains, especially in the lower weakened part of the facade. The Khasneh was protected from the wind-blown sand because there was no wide-open area in front of it, unlike the Deir and the "Royal Tombs" (Palace Tomb, Corinthian Tomb, Urn Tomb).[19] For much of the last 2,000 years the Khasneh also had oleander growing in front of it, holding loose sand in place. The oleander was gradually removed from in front of the Khasneh and along the Siq during the twentieth century. By the time the Bdoul were moved out of Petra, overgrazing by their flocks of goats was reducing the amount of other vegetation cover within the site.[20] Since then, the amount of vegetation cover has increased. However, photographs taken in the second half of the nineteenth century are striking for the considerably greater amount of vegetation in them, such as those of the Theatre, Palace Tomb, and the Deir (figs. 5, 6, 7). They show how the amount of grazing inside the ancient site of the Petra valley only increased once the Bdoul were spending more time there in the twentieth century, when there was more access to income from tourism and archaeological and restoration work. The markedly greater amount of vegeta-

18 Paradise (2013; 377–78) found rock composition was the most important single influence on damage due to weathering, followed by the concentration of iron, and then sunlight and moisture. Heinrichs (2008: 668) considered the greatest causes of damage as water-related.

19 Fitzner and Heinrichs 1991: 910.

20 Goats do not eat oleander (nor the leaves of the squill bulbs). The decrease in the number of oleander bushes is due to human activity.

Fig. 382. Bilingual inscription (in Nabataean and Greek), opposite the Obelisk Tomb, eroded by rainwater runoff, 2010.

Fig. 383. Urn Tomb interior, with water runoff in back left-hand corner, 2018 [Steve Welsh].

tion would have considerably reduced the amount of windblown sand and soaked up some of the groundwater.

When freshly cut, sandstone (like limestone) can form a hard oxidised crust on the surface. Depending on the minor constituents in the binder (matrix), sandstone is sometimes more durable and less friable long after exposure, so that exposure in some cases hardens the sandstone, rather than weakens it. When the hard surface is broken, the stone behind it can erode quickly, as on the frieze on the Khasneh, where the original painted surface can be seen, such as the carinations on the vase, compared with the eroded surface to the right of it (fig. 74). The weathering crust is partly biological in origin, but whatever the origin, the eventual breaching of the crust leads to the widespread formation of alveoles (honeycomb forms) and of tafones (cavernous weathering forms).[21] In its narrow chasm, the Khasneh is also more protected than other monuments from the sun and thus from changes in temperature, which has also contributed to its pristine condition[22] (except for damage from wicking up and interior moisture).

Direct Rain Damage

Rainwater running down the facades has caused extensive erosion of many of them.[23] The Nabataeans were aware of this problem, because they carved a channel above the main facades to redirect any water running down the mountainside, so that it did not run down directly over the face of the facade. In 2003, Suleiman Farajat I explained how these channels were being cleared to avoid this problem, although rainwater still runs down parts of many facades, as on Tomb 62E (fig. 379). The ability of rainwater to erode surfaces is seen from the damage to the bilingual (Greek and Nabataean) inscription opposite the Obelisk Tomb where parts of it have been completely erased (fig. 382).

Internal Moisture from the Mountain Bedrock Above

One day when it was raining, I noticed rain was dripping from the ceiling of Abu Shaher's rock-cut cave and forming a puddle on the floor. More moisture from rain penetrates the sandstone bedrock than the binder can hold. Consequently, moisture from rainwater seeps down inside the mountains so that it often comes out in the tomb chambers. In so doing, it weakens the stone, and the grains of sand are dislodged by force of gravity. In some cases, more marked water seepage is noticeable. For example, in the left hand (north-east) corner of the Urn Tomb, large water marks are visible (fig. 383). Examination of aerial photographs reveals that above this corner of the Urn Tomb, there is a cistern on el-Khubthah which might be in need of repair, by relining it with hydraulic plaster.

The ceilings and top part of the walls of the tomb chambers had previously been covered with black soot from the fires from Bdoul occupation. The Bdoul ceased to make fires in the main tombs visited by tourists from various dates since 1929 to 1965, when they were no longer allowed to occupy them. The gradual disappearance of the soot on the ceilings of these tombs provides evidence of the rate of erosion of the surface, due to moisture, a millimetre at a time. The soot on the ceilings slowly disappears as the grains of sand to which it adhered fall off as a result of the weakening by the moisture evaporating on the binder of the sand. When films like soot create skins of adhesion and harden, the process of falling off is described as "flaking" for small bits, or "spalling" for larger pieces. Flaking as a function of wetting is termed "slaking". This process is particularly evident in the Urn Tomb (fig. 383) and Triclinium 235 opposite of the Tomb of the Roman Soldier (fig. 295). The early stages of this process can also be observed in the Tomb of Sextius Florentinus (fig. 384).

Human Breath

Another source of moisture affecting the most visited tomb interiors has been found to be human breath. When there were thirty people in the Khasneh or the Urn Tomb, the level of the interior relative humidity rose noticeably, by 20 to 50 percent.[24] In the Khasneh, a detectable depth of the softened sandstone surface was dislodged by visitors rubbing against the softened stone.[25] This damage has led to the decision no longer to allow tourists to enter the Khasneh. The evidence for the loss of a thin layer of surface grains of sand is most pronounced in the chambers most frequently visited by tourists: the Khasneh, the Urn Tomb, and Triclinium 235 opposite the Tomb of the Roman Soldier.

The tombs at Beidha are carved from the paler yellow Disi sandstone which weathers and erodes differently and more easily than the reddish Umm Ishrin sandstone. This makes the facades there, such as Facade 846 at the entrance to Siq el-Barid, more susceptible to weathering, and to damage to their lower parts, if visitors rub up against them. This susceptibility also suggests that the interior of the Painted House 849 in Siq el-Barid would deteriorate markedly if large numbers of tourists were in the room at the same time, raising the level of humidity.

Conclusion

Some of the effects of human activity on the rock-cut monuments can be reduced, but ultimately the forces of nature are stronger than the hand of man. It is not simply free-standing

21 Viles and Goudie 2003; Paradise 2013: 381–83; Migoń and Goudie 2014.
22 Fitzner and Heinrichs 1991: 910.
23 Heinrichs 2008: 668, e.g. fig. 38.

24 Paradise 2012a: 84–90; 2013: 372, 385–90, figs. 8–9.
25 Paradise (2012a: 83–84; 2013: 375–78, 388–89) also recorded the damage to the surfaces of the Theatre seats from tourist traffic and other influences. In 1981–86, we had noticed a notable deterioration in the lowest rows of seats since they had been excavated.

Fig. 384. Tomb of Sextius Florentinus, interior, 2018 [Sean Leatherbury].

buildings which collapse with time, nudged by earth tremors or rain, such as the arch over the entrance to the Siq, which survived until 1895 (fig. 39), but also the rock-cut monuments. As Harriette Martineau observed after "the tomb with the Greek inscription" (Facade 66) collapsed in 1847, "This is a warning to us not to judge of what Petra was by what we see now. It is natural to suppose a sort of immutability in a rock-fastness like this: but we see here how much depends on the structure of the rock, and the influences which operate upon it. The forces of wind and water are great at Petra ... to insure the fall of works which would appear likely to greet as many generations as the everlasting hills."[26]

26 Martineau 1848: vol. 3, 32.

Glossary of Arabic Terms

This glossary defines terms as used in this book.

ʿagal	Black rope loop for a head scarf
afwan	Equivalent of "You are welcome", used in reply to "*shukran*"
alhamdulillah	"Thank God" or "Allah provides"
ard	Plough
asaba	Type of scarf
baksheesh	Gratuity or tip
barid	Cold
beit shaʿar	Traditional Bedouin tent
fellahin	Farmers
furwah	Heavy cloak
halal	Permissible under Islamic ritual
hummus	Dip made from chickpeas, tahini, lemon juice, and garlic
inshallah	"God willing"
jamīd	Dried yoghurt balls
keffiyeh	Head scarf
kunafa	Sweet cheese desert
laban	Yoghurt
labaneh	Thick, strained yoghurt
ligan	Circular dish for washing clothes
mabrouk	"Congratulations"
maqluba	"Upside down"; usually in reference to a chicken dish
mendeel	Black rope loop for a head scarf
mensef	Dish made of rice and meat (usually lamb)
mirreer	Type of head scarf
misfah	Type of scarf
mjeddera	Dish of bulgur and lentils
mudraga	Type of Bedouin dress
muktar	Mayor
muzferr	Sling-crib to carry babies
rabābah	Single-stringed musical instrument
sāj	Large domed iron plate for cooking
sayara	Car
shabriya	Type of knife
shay	Tea
shiqq	Space for men in a tent or home
shraak	Bread
shukran	"Thank you", the polite reply to which is "*afwan*"
sieja	Type of Arab board game
tāb	Type of Arab board game
taboun	Clay oven for baking bread
thaub	Full-length robe for a man
zaʿata	Mixture of herbs used to flavour Arab bread dipped in olive oil

Bibliography

Abujaber, R. S. and Cobbing, F.
2005 *Beyond the River: Ottoman Transjordan in Original Photographs*. London.

Akrawi, A. and Shekede, L.
2012 'A Unique Nabataean Wall Painting in Petra: Conservation *in situ*'. Pp. 214–19 in *Conservation and the Eastern Mediterranean*, ed. C. Rozeik et al. London.

Alberge, D.
2010 'Discovery of Ancient Cave Paintings in Petra Stuns Art Scholars', *The Guardian*, 22 August 2010. http://www.theguardian.com/science/2010/aug/22/hellenistic-wall-paintings-petra. Accessed 4 September 2018.

Albouy, M. et al.
1993 'Petra. La cité rose des sables. La pathologie des grès et leurs traitement dans la perspective d'une préservation et d'une restauration des monuments'. Pp. 376–85 in *Conservation of Stone and Other Materials*, ed. M.-J. Thiel. London.

Amiry, S. and Tamari, V.
1989 *The Palestinian Village Home*. London.

Angel, C. C.
2012 'The Bdoul of Umm Sayhoun: Culture, Geography, and Tourism'. Pp. 105–16 in *Tourism and Archaeological Heritage Management at Petra: Driver to Development or Destruction*, ed. D. Comer. New York.

Arjava, A. et al. (eds.)
2007 *The Petra Papyri III*. Amman.
2011 *The Petra Papyri IV*. Amman.
2018 *The Petra Papyri V*. Amman.

Assad, M.
2002 'For Bdouls, Four Walls Do Not Make a Home', *The Daily Star Lebanon*, 24 May 2002. https://www.dailystar.com.lb/Culture/Art/2002/May-24/98869-for-bdouls-four-walls-do-not-make-a-home.ashx. Accessed 23 June 2018.

Bachmann, W. et al.
1921 *Petra*. Berlin-Leipzig.

Baedeker, K.
1912 *Palestine and Syria, with Routes through Mesopotamia and Babylonia and the Island of Cyprus : Handbook for Travellers, with 21 Maps, 56 Plans, and a Panorama of Jerusalem*, 5th edn. Leipzig.

Banning, E. B. and Köhler-Rollefson, I.
1986 'Ethnoarchaeological Survey in the Bēḍā Area, Southern Jordan', *Zeitschrift des Deutschen Palästina-Vereins* 102: 152–70.

Bedal, L.-A.
2013 'The Loss of a Dear Friend', *Petra Garden and Pool Complex: An Archaeological Excavation in Petra, Jordan* (blog), 28 May 2013: https://petragardenexcavation.wordpress.com/2013/05/28/the-loss-of-a-dear-friend/

Bellwald, U. et al.
2003 *The Petra Siq – Nabataean Hydrology Uncovered*. Amman.

Belmonte, J. A. et al.
2013 'Light and Shadows over Petra: Astronomy and Landscape in Nabataean Lands', *Nexus Network Journal* 15: 487–501.

Belmonte, J. A. and García, A. C. G.
2017 'Petra Revisited: An Astronomical Approach to the Nabataean Cultic Calendar', *The Marriage of Astronomy and Culture (Culture and Cosmos)* 21.1–2: 131–50.

Bessac, J-C.
2007 *Le travail de la pierre à Pétra: technique et économie de la taille rupestre*. Paris.

Bienkowski, P.
1985 'New Caves for Old: Bedouin Architecture in Petra', *World Archaeology* 17.2: 149–60.
1989 'Architecture of the Petra Bedouin: A Preliminary Report', *Annual of the Department of Antiquities of Jordan* 23: 335–43.
2011 *Umm al-Biyara: Excavations by Crystal-M. Bennett in Petra 1960–1965*. Oxford.
2013 'The Iron Age in Petra and the Issue of Continuity with Nabataean Occupation'. Pp. 23–34 in *Men on the Rocks: The Formation of Nabataean Petra*, eds. M. Mouton and S. G. Schmid. Berlin.

Bienkowski, P. and Chlebik, B.
1991 'Changing Places: Architecture and Spatial Organization of the Bedul in Petra', *Levant* 23: 147–80.

Bignasca, A. et al.
1996 *Petra. Ez Zantur I. Ergebnisse der Schweizerisch-Liechtensteinischen Ausgrabungen 1988–1992*. Mainz.

Blagg, T.
1990 'Column Capitals with Elephant-Head Volutes at Petra', *Levant* 22: 131–37.

Brünnow, R. E., and von Domaszewski, A.
1904 *Die Provincia Arabia: auf Grund zweier in den Jahren 1897 und 1898 unternommenen Reisen und der Berichte früherer Reisender*, vol. 1. Strassburg.

Burckhardt, J. L.
1822 *Travels in Syria and the Holy Land*. London.
1831 *Notes on the Bedouins and Wahábys Collected During His Travels in the East*, 2 vols. London.

Canaan, T.
1930 *Studies in the Topography and Folklore of Petra*. Jerusalem.
1932 'The Palestinian Arab House: Its Architecture and Folklore', *Journal of the Palestine Oriental Society* 12.4: 223–47.
1933 'The Palestinian Arab House: Its Architecture and Folklore', *Journal of the Palestine Oriental Society* 13.1–2: 1–83.

Corbett, G. J. et al.
2016 'Archaeology in Jordan, 2014 and 2015 Seasons', *American Journal of Archaeology* 120.4: 631–72.

Counsell, A.
2007 'The Bedouin from New Zealand', *Saudi Aramco World* November/December 1985 (published online 2007 https://www.aramcoexpats.com/articles/the-bedouin-from-new-zealand/. Accessed 22 June 2018.

Crawford, S.
1930 'The Attitude of the Present Day Arab to the Shrine of "Mt. Hor" '. Pp. 285–300 in *The Sarcophagus of an Ancient Civilization, Petra, Edom, and the Edomites* by G.L. Robinson. New York.

Dalman, G.
1908 *Petra und seine Felsheiligtümer*. Leipzig.
1911 'The Khazneh at Petra', *Palestine Exploration Fund*: 95–107.

De Sandioli, S.
1983 *Itinera Hierosolymitana Crucesignatorum (saec. XII–XIII): Vol. III: Tempore recuperationis Terrae Sanctae (1187–1244*. Jerusalem.

Dimitrov, Z.
2013 'Elephant-Headed Capitals in Petra: An Analysis of Nabataean Models in Cult Architecture'. Pp. 127–35 in *Studies on the Nabataean Culture*, eds. N. I . Khairy and T. M. Weber. Amman.

Doughty, C.
1888 *Travels in Arabia Deserta*, 2 vols. Cambridge.

Farajat, S.
2012 'The Participation of Local Communities in the Tourism Industry at Petra'. Pp. 145–65 in *Tourism and Archaeological Heritage Management at Petra: Driver to Development or Destruction*, ed. D. Comer. New York.

Farajat, S. and Nawafleh, S.
2005 'Report on the al-Khazna Courtyard Excavation at Petra (2003 Season)', *Annual of the Department of Antiquities of Jordan* 49: 373–93.

Fiema, Z. T.
2002 'Petra and its Hinterland during the Byzantine Period: New Research and Interpretations'. Pp. 191–252 in *Roman and Byzantine Near East: Some New Discoveries III*. Journal of Roman Archaeology Supplementary Series 49, ed. J. Humphrey. Portsmouth, RI.
2016 'The Jabal Hārūn Site: 1000 Years of Continuity and Change'. Pp. 539–82 in *Petra – The Mountain of Aaron: The Finnish Archaeological Project II: The Nabataean Sanctuary and the Byzantine Monastery*, ed. Z. T. Fiema et al. Helsinki.

Fiema, Z. T. and Frösén, J. (eds.)
2008 *Petra – The Mountain of Aaron: The Finnish Archaeological Project in Jordan. The Church and the Chapel*. Helsinki.

Fiema, Z. T. et al.
2001 'Excavations at a Byzantine Pilgrimage Site and Monastic Center: The Finnish Jabal Haroun Project 2000', *Near Eastern Archaeology* 64.1–2: 133–34.

Fiema, Z. T. et al. (eds.)
2016 *Petra – The Mountain of Aaron: The Finnish Archaeological Project II: The Nabataean Sanctuary and the Byzantine Monastery*. Helsinki.

Finlayson, C.
2016 'Petra: ad-Deir Monument and Plateau Project'. Pp. 662–64 in G. J. Corbett et al. 'Archaeology in Jordan, 2014 and 2015 Seasons', *American Journal of Archaeology* 120.4: 631–72.

Fitzner, B. and Heinrichs, K.
1991 'Weathering Forms and Rock Characteristics of Historical Monuments Carved from Bedrocks in Petra/Jordan'. Pp. 908–11 in *Science, Technology and European Cultural Heritage: Proceedings of the European Symposium, Bologna, Italy, 13–16 June 1989*, ed. N. S. Baer et al. Brussels–Luxembourg.

Frösén, J. and Miettunen, P.
2008 'Aaron in Religious Literature, Myth and Legend'. Pp. 5–25 in *Petra – the Mountain of Aaron: The Finn-*

ish Archaeological Project in Jordan. The Church and the Chapel, ed. Z. T. Fiema and J. Frösén. Helsinki.

Forder, A.
1923 *Petra, Perea, Phoenicia*. London.

Frösén, J. et al. (eds.)
2002 *The Petra Papyri I*. Amman.

Geldermalsen, M. van
2006 *Married to a Bedouin*. London.

Glueck, N.
1951 *Explorations in Eastern Palestine*, vol. 4 (in two parts). Oxford.

Goudie, A. S.
2013 *Arid and Semi-Arid Geomorphology*. New York.

Hammond, P. C.
1965 *The Excavation of the Main Theater at Petra, 1961–1962. Final Report*. London.

Hanna, M.
2016 'As Jordan Fights to Revive Tourism, Bedouins Return to Petra's Caves,' *Middle East Eye*, 15 January 2016. http://middleeasteye.net/in-depth/features/jordan-fights-revive-dying-tourism-bedouins-return-petra-s-caves-556693977. Accessed 23 June 2018.

Healey, J. F.
1993 *The Nabataean Tomb Inscriptions of Mada'in Salih*. Oxford.

Heinrichs, K.
2008 'Diagnosis of Weathering Damage on Rock-Cut Monuments in Petra, Jordan', *Environmental Geology* 56: 643–75.

Hickey, A.
2013 'Jordan Treasure Hunters Run Ancient Artefacts,' *Huffington Post*, 30 July 2013. http://www.huffingtonpost.com/2013/07/30/jordan-treasure-hunters-ruin-artifacts_n_3676581.html. Accessed 23 June 2018.

Hittorff, J.
1862 'Pompéi et Pétra', *Revue Archéologique* 6: 1–18.

Horsfield, G. and A.
1938 'Sela-Petra, the Rock, of Edom and Nabatene', *Quarterly of the Department of Antiquities of Palestine* 7: 1–42.
1939 'Sela-Petra, the Rock, of Edom and Nabatene', *Quarterly of the Department of Antiquities of Palestine* 8: 87–115.
1942 'Sela-Petra, the Rock, of Edom and Nabatene. IV. The Finds', *Quarterly of the Department of Antiquities of Palestine* 9: 105–204.

Irby, C. L. and Mangles, J.
1883 *Travels in Egypt and Nubia, Syria and Asia Minor During the Years 1817 and 1818*. London.

Joukowsky, M. S.
1998 *Petra Great Temple. Volume I: Brown University Excavations 1993–1997*. Providence, RI.
2007 *Petra Great Temple. Volume II: Archaeological Contexts of the Remains and Excavations (Brown University Excavations in Jordan at the Petra Great Temple, 1993–2007*. Providence, RI.
2017a *Petra Great Temple. Volume III: Brown University Excavations 1993–2008, Architecture and Material Culture*. Oxford and Havertown, PA.
2017b 'The Elephant-Head Capitals of the Triple Colonnades in the Lower Temenos'. Pp. 134–47 in *Petra Great Temple. Volume III: Brown University Excavations 1993–2008, Architecture and Material Culture*, ed. M. S. Joukowsky. Oxford and Havertown, PA.

Keiser, H.
1964 *Sie kamen aus der Wüste mit den Beduinen auf den Spuren der alten Nabatäer: Ergebnisse und Entdeckungen in Petra*. Freiburg. = *Die Söhne Nabayots – Beduinen, Forscher und Abenteurer in der Felsenstadt Petra*. Freiburg, 1977.

Khammash, A.
1986 *Notes on Village Architecture in Jordan*. Lafayette, LA.

Kennedy, D.
2018 'Travellers of 1857 to Petra'. Pp. 187–207 in *Refereed Proceedings of the First Conference on the Archaeology and Tourism of the Maan Governate, 3rd–4th October*, ed. Z. M. Al-Salameen and M. B. Tarawneh. Maan.

Kinnear, J. G.
1841 *Cairo, Petra, and Damascus in 1839*. London.

Kirkbride, D.
1960 'A Short Account of the Excavations at Petra in 1955–56', *Annual of the Department of Antiquities of Jordan* 4–5: 117–22.

Koenen, L. et al. (eds.)
2013 *The Petra Papyri II*. Amman.

Kohl, H.
1910 *Kasr Firaun in Petra*. Leipzig.

Kooring, D. and Simms, S.
1996 'The Bedul Bedouin of Petra, Jordan: Traditions, Tourism, and an Uncertain Future', *Cultural Survival Quarterly Magazine* 19.4: 22–25.

Kouki, P. and Lavento, M. (eds.)
2013 *Petra – The Mountain of Aaron: The Finnish Archaeological Project in Jordan Volume III: The Archaeological Survey*. Helsinki.

Kühlenthal, M. and Fischer, H.
2000 *Petra: Die Restaurierung der Grabfassaden*. Munich.

Laborde, L.
1836 *Journey through Arabia Petraea to Mount Sinai, and the Excavated City of Petra*. London.

Layard, A. H.
1889 *Early Adventures in Persia, Susiana, and Babylonia*, vol. 1. London.

Layne, L.
1987 'Village Bedouin: Patterns of Change from Mobility to Sedentism in Jordan'. Pp. 345–73 in *Method and Theory for Activity Area Research: An Ethnoarchaeological Approach*, ed. S. Kent. New York.

Lewis, N. N.
2003 'Chronological List of Narratives of Journeys to Petra between 1812 and 1914'. Unpublished.

Lindner, M.
1986 'Archäologische Erkundungen in der Petra-Region 1982–1984'. Pp. 87–188 in *Petra, Neue Ausgrabungen und Entdeckungen*, ed. M. Lindner. Munich.

Lindsay, Lord
1838 *Letters on Egypt, Edom, and the Holy Land*, 2 vols. London.

MacMichael, W.
1819 *Journey from Moscow to Constantinople in the Years 1817, 1818*. London.

Martineau, H.
1848 *Eastern Life, Past and Present*, 3 vols. London.

McKenzie, J.
1985 'A Surveying Method for Measuring Inaccessible Mouldings: As Applied at Petra', *Levant* 17: 157–70.
1990 *The Architecture of Petra*. Oxford.
1991 'The Bedouin at Petra: The Historical Sources', *Levant* 23: 139–45.
2004 'Temples, Tombs, and Other Recent Discoveries from the Rose Red City', *Journal of Roman Archaeology* 17: 559–68.
2007 *The Architecture of Alexandria and Egypt, c. 300 BC to AD 700*. New Haven, CT–London.
2010 'Carving Petra (and Hegra)', *Journal of Roman Archaeology* 23: 751–59.
2014 'Review of L. Nehmé et al., *Atlas archéologique et épigraphique de Pétra, fascicule I, De Bāb as-Sīq au Wādi al-Farasah*', *Levant* 46.2: 309–13.

McKenzie, J. et al.
1998 'Faces in the Rock at Petra and Medain Saleh', *Palestine Exploration Quarterly*: 35–50.
2012 [2014] 'The context of the Khirbet et-Tannur Zodiac, Jordan', *ARAM* 24: 379–420.
2013 *The Nabataean Temple at Khirbet et-Tannur, Jordan*, 2 vols. Boston, MA.

Migoń, P. and Goudie, A.
2014 'Sandstone Geomorphology of South-West Jordan, Middle East', *Quaestiones Geographicae* 33.3: 123–30.

Migoń, P. et al.
2005 'The Origin and Evolution of Footslope Ramps in the Sandstone Desert Environment of South-West Jordan', *Journal of Arid Environments* 60: 303–20.

Mouton, M. and Renel, F.
2013 'The Early Petra Monolithic Funerary Blocks at Ras Sulayman and Bab as-Siq'. Pp. 135–62 in *Men on the Rocks: The Formation of Nabataean Petra*, eds. M. Mouton and S. G. Schmid. Berlin.

Murray, M. A.
1939 *Petra, the Rock City of Edom*. London.

Murray, M. A. and Ellis, J. C.
1940 *A Street in Petra*. London.

Musil, A.
1907 *Arabia Petraea*, vol. 2, part 1. Vienna.
1908 *Arabia Petraea*, vol. 2, part 2. Vienna.
1908 *Arabia Petraea*, vol. 3. Vienna.

Nehmé, L.
2012 *Atlas archéologique et épigraphique de Pétra, fascicule I, De Bāb as-Sīq au Wādi al-Farasah*. Paris.
2015 *Les tombeaux nabatéens de Hégra*, 2 vols. Paris.

Nielsen, D.
1933 'The Mountain Sanctuaries in Petra and its Environs III', *Journal of the Palestine Oriental Society* 13.4: 185–208.

Ohannessian-Charpin, A.
1986 'L'utilisation actuelle par les bedouins des grottes archéologiques de Petra', *Annual of the Department of Antiquities of Jordan* 30: 385–95.
1995 'Strategic Myths: Petra's B'doul', *Middle East Report* 196: 24–25.

'Organised Tours to Petra – Hilda Waldron and the Lunn Tour of 1908', *East of Jordan*, 3 August 2016. http://eastofjordan.wordpress.com/tag/jordan/. Accessed 26 June 2018.

Paolini, A. et al.
2012 *Risk Management at Heritage Sites: A Case Study of the Petra World Heritage Site*. Amman.

Palmer, E. H.
1871 'The Desert of the Tíh and the Country of Moab', *Palestine Exploration Quarterly*: 3–80.

Paradise, T.

2012a 'Architecture and Deterioration in Petra: Issues, Trends, and Warnings'. Pp. 79–104 in *Tourism and Archaeological Heritage Management at Petra: Driver to Development or Destruction*, ed. D. Comer. New York.

2012b 'Petra: Solar Influence on Sandstone'. Pp. 734–36 in D. R. Keller, 'Archaeology in Jordan', *American Journal of Archaeology* 116.4: 693–750.

2013 'Natural and Anthropogenic Influences on Sandstone Weathering: Lessons Learned from Petra, Jordan'. Pp. 371–426 in *Des déserts et des hommes: Wādi Ramm (Jordanie): Histoire économique, religieuse, sociale, et environnementale*, ed. S. Farès. Nancy.

2014 'Petra: Nabataean Stone Dressing and Lithology'. Pp. 659–60 in G. J. Corbett et al., 'Archaeology in Jordan, 2012 and 2013 Seasons', *American Journal of Archaeology* 118.4: 627–76.

2016a 'The Bedouins of Petra, Jordan: A Geographer's Life with the Bdoul', *The Arab World Geographer* 19.3–4: 209–224.

2016b 'Petra: Earth-sun Relationships and Architecture in Petra'. P. 659 in G. J. Corbett et al. 'Archaeology in Jordan, 2014 and 2015 Seasons', *American Journal of Archaeology* 120.4: 631–72.

Paradise, T. and Angel, C.

2015 'Nabataean Architecture and the Sun', *ESRI ArcUser* Winter: 16–19.

Parr, P. J.

1957 'Recent Discoveries at Petra', *Palestine Exploration Quarterly*: 5–16.

1960 'Excavations at Petra 1958–59', *Palestine Exploration Quarterly*: 124–35.

1965 'Chronique archéologique: Pétra', *Revue Biblique* 72: 253–57.

1967–68 'Recent Discoveries in the Sanctuary of the Qasr Bint Far'un at Petra: Account of the Recent Excavations', *Annual of the Department of Antiquities of Jordan* 12–13: 5–19 (= *Syria* 45 [1968]: 1–24).

1970 'A Sequence of Pottery from Petra'. Pp. 348–81 in *Essays in Honour of Nelson Glueck*. New York.

1980 'Vierzig Jahre Ausgrabungen in Petra (1929 bis 1969)'. Pp. 139–49 in *Petra und das Königreich der Nabatäer*, ed. M. Lindner. Munich.

Peake, F. G.

1958 *A History of Jordan and its Tribes*. Coral Gables, FL.

'Petra Witnessed Increase in Number of Visitors in January', *The Jordan Times*, 4 February 2018. http://www.jordantimes.com/news/local/petra-witnessed-increase-number-visitors-january%E2%80%99. Accessed 18 August 2018.

Pringle, D.

2005 'The Castles of Ayla (al-'Aqaba) in the Crusader, Ayyubid and Mamluk Periods'. Pp. 333–53 in *Egypt and Syria in the Fatimid, Ayyubid, and Mamluk Eras IV*, ed. U. Vermeulen and J. van Steenbergen. Leuven.

1998 *The Churches of the Crusader Kingdom of Jerusalem*, Vol. II. Cambridge.

'Protecting Petra: UCT Team Maps 'Wonder of the World,' *University of Cape Town News*, 12 November 2012. http://www.news.uct.ac.za/article/-2012-11-12-protecting-petra-uct-team-maps-wonder-of-the-world. Accessed 4 July 2018.

Rababeh, S.

2005 *How Petra was Built: An Analysis of the Construction Techniques of the Nabataean Free-standing Buildings and Rock-cut Monuments in Petra, Jordan*. Oxford.

Roberts, D.

1855 *The Holy Land*, vol. 3. London.

Robinson, E.

1841 *Biblical Researches in Palestine, Mount Sinai, and Arabia Petraea*, vol. 2. London.

Runciman, S.

1952 *A History of the Crusades. Volume II: The Kingdom of Jerusalem and the Frankish East, 1100–1187*. New York.

Russell, K. W.

1993 'Ethnohistory of the Bedul Bedouin of Petra', *Annual of the Department of Antiquities of Jordan* 37: 15–35.

Schmid, S. G.

2000 *Petra. Ez Zantur II. Teil 1: Die Feinkeramik der Nabatäer. Typologie, Chronologie und kulturhistorische Hintergründe*. Mainz.

Schmid, S. G. et al.

2012 'The Palaces of the Nabataean Kings at Petra'. Pp. 73–98 in *The Nabataeans in Focus: Current Archaeological Research at Petra: Papers from the Special Session of the Seminar for Arabian Studies Held on 29 July*, ed. L. Nehmé and L. Wadeson. Oxford.

Sewell, A.

2017 'Meet the Man Living in a Lost City Carved in Stone', *National Geographic*, 20 November 2017. http://www.nationalgeographic.com/travel/destinations/asia/jordan/petra-unesco-world-heritage-bedouin/. Accessed 5 July 2018.

Shaer, M.

2000 'Plaster and Colour on the Rock-Cut Tomb Facades of Petra'. Pp. 133–48 in *Petra. The Restoration of the Rockcut Tomb Facades*, ed. M. Kühlenthal and H. Fischer. Munich.

Shoup, J.
1985 'The Impact of Tourism on the Bedouin of Petra', *Middle East Journal* 39.2: 277–91.

Simms, S. R.
1988 'The Archaeological Structure of a Bedouin Camp', *Journal of Archaeological Science* 15: 197–211.

Sinibaldi, M.
2016 'Settlement in the Petra Region during the Crusader Period: A Summary of the Historical and Archaeological Evidence'. Pp. 81–102 in *Crusader Landscapes in the Medieval Levant. The Archaeology and History of the Latin East*, eds. M. Sinibaldi et al. Cardiff.
2018 'Did Petra's Inhabitants Really Abandon the City?' *British Academy Blog*, 6 March 2018. http://www.britac.ac.uk/blog/did-petras-inhabitants-really-abandon-city. Accessed 15 August 2018.

Stanley, A. P.
1856 *Sinai and Palestine in Connection with their History*. London.

State of Conservation Report: Petra World Heritage Site.
2017

Stephens, J. L.
1839 *Incidents of Travel in Egypt, Arabia Petraea, and the Holy Land by an American*. New York.

Tholbecq, L.
2016 'Petra: Wadi Sabra'. Pp. 666–67 in G. J. Corbett et al. 'Archaeology in Jordan, 2014 and 2015 Seasons', *American Journal of Archaeology* 120.4: 631–72.

Twaissi, S. A. et al.
2016 'The Architectural Aspects of the Traditional Villages in Petra Region Some Anthropological Notes', *Mediterranean Journal of Social Sciences* 7.4: 336–52.

Vella, C. et al.
2015 'Looting and Vandalism Around a World Heritage Site: Documenting Modern Damage to Archaeological Heritage in Petra's Hinterland', *Journal of Field Archaeology* 40.2: 221–35.

Verezen, V. A. M.
2017 'The Crumbling Wonder: A Damage- and Risk-Assessment of Sandstone Monuments and Natural Features in the Petra Archaeological Park (Jordan)', *International Journal of Student Research in Archaeology*: 20–34.

Viles, H. A. and Goudie, A. S.
2004 'Biofilms and Case Hardening on Sandstones from al-Quwayra, Jordan', *Earth Surface Processes and Landforms* 29: 1473–85.

Wedekind, W. and Ruedrich, J.
2006 'Salt-Weathering, Conservation Techniques and Strategies to Protect the Rock Cut Façades in Petra/Jordan'. Pp. 261–68 in *Heritage, Weathering and Conservation*, vol. I, ed. R. Fort et al. London.

Weir, S.
1976 *The Bedouin*. London.

Wilson, J.
1847 *Lands of the Bible: Visited and Described*, 2 vols. Edinburgh.

World Heritage – ICOMOS – IUCN Reactive Monitoring Mission Report Petra, Jordan, 21 to 26 November 2017.
2017

Zayadine, F. et al.
2003 *Le Qasr al-Bint de Pétra: l'architecture, le décor, la chronologie, et les dieux*. Paris.

Indexes

A. NAMES OF INDIVIDUALS AND PEOPLES (INCLUDING THOSE FROM MYTHS, LEGENDS, AND HISTORY)

B. GEOGRAPHICAL LOCATIONS, INCLUDING MONUMENTS AND INSTITUTIONS AT PETRA AND ELSEWHERE (ANCIENT AND MODERN)

C. GENERAL INDEX